BEHAVIOR MODIFICATION PROCEDURES
for School Personnel

BETH SULZER, *Southern Illinois University*
G. ROY MAYER, *California State College*

THE DRYDEN PRESS INC. HINSDALE, ILLINOIS

FOREWORD

This book is about the laws of behavior. That may not seem a remarkable subject for study. After all, we have assumed for a long time that we inhabit an orderly universe. Acting on that assumption, we have produced some science, and we have used that science to change our lives—for the better, we think. Thus, science has become an accepted part of our existence, and we freely suppose that new problems will be overcome by scientific research just as past ones have. Therefore, why not a science of our own behavior?

Indeed, that is what is discussed in the chapters that follow. Behavioral science is almost certainly a seriously incomplete science, but it is far enough along to codify into laws and principles. These laws and principles tell us that behavior falls into certain regular patterns and, thus, is understandable and predictable. In those respects, behavior is much like everything else we study—it is all understandable and predictable according to pattern. However, some science has remained beyond our control. The movements of the planets, for example, are readily understood as an exercise in the physics of moving bodies; the formulas explaining their balanced motion and a timetable predicting their travels through space are readily available in precise forms. Nevertheless, it has not been within our ability to change those motions. Although we know how the planets move and why they move that way, we are powerless to change them. Some knowledge is different, however. Our understanding of physiology and of microorganisms has made available to us not only an explanation of many illnesses and much about death; it has also told us that we can control some of the causes of illness and death. As a result, we now practice sanitation and immunization and thereby routinely avoid disease, plagues, and poxes that once killed man in wholesale lots. Thus, all science is understandable and predictable; some of it, in addition, is manageable to our own ends. Which kind is the science of behavior?

This book shows that behavior is a phenomenon not only understandable and predictable, but also controllable. Certainly the causes of behavior are multiple, complex, and only partly appreciated. However, some of those causes lie within the immediate environment of the behavior; they lie in the immediate stimulus consequences and stimulus antecedents of each behavior. True, some of those stimuli are intrinsic to the structure of the organism and are not readily changed. But many other causal stimuli are simple events in the surrounding physical and social environment. *Those* events are readily changed, right now, by methods well within our capabilities. Indeed, many of those events are produced by *us:* our patterns of attention, approval, or disapproval of the acts of others, for example. To paraphrase a hero of our folk mythology, Pogo, "We have met the causes of our behavior, and they is us." We can manipulate those causes and thereby can change some behavior.

I began this foreword by saying that this book is about the laws of behavior. That was an innocent enough statement, but it must now be sharpened: This book provides a *technology of behavior control.* That is, it provides the methods that make it practical to change people's behavior. No special apparatus or instrumentation are needed nor are a large staff of specialists; only the ability to translate the written word into action and the fairly ordinary skill of interacting pleasantly with others. Not all the behavior of everyone will come within the range of this ability to change—but much of it will. The science is not difficult to learn, and its technology is not difficult to implement.

So, if behavioral technology has come, has freedom left? Rephrase the question, and it may take on a clearer meaning—and a very human answer. If a behavioral technology was always *possible,* what could freedom ever have been? That is, if behavior had causes, manageable causes, then in what sense were we, the behavers, free?

We might have considered ourselves free if no one was systematically managing those manageable causes. But, as Pogo has hinted, and Sulzer and Mayer will prove, many of the causes of our own behavior are the behaviors of the rest of us. It is how people attend to us, approve of us, disapprove of us, love us, and so on, which frequently controls our behavior. Those causes simply will not be left alone unless we live alone.

If the causes of our behavior are there to be managed, and certainly will be managed, then we might still consider ourselves free as long as we remain ignorant of those causes and how they are being managed in our own case. At least, we will feel free. One hundred years ago, that ignorance was the essential freedom available. No thorough and systematic explanation of the causation of behavior, other than by magical mechanisms, had been stated. A political craftsman such as Machiavelli could offer only some incomplete rules of thumb (satirically in *The Prince* and seriously in *The Discourses on Livy*) based on a partial appreciation of punishment. Today, by contrast, the technology of behavior is based on principle and is a good deal more thorough. The knowledge exists, is codified, is available, and is presented here. When such knowledge exists, it is used. Thus, freedom through ignorance, comfortable as it may have been by contrast to today's sophistication, is no longer practical. Any one of us may remain ignorant of the causes of our behavior, but some of those causes are being managed by some of our fellows. In the old days, neither we nor they understood the process. Today all may understand and use it; even if *we* decide not to know, some of *them* inevitably will decide to know as clearly as possible and act as systematically as possible. They may, for instance, want to sell us something . . .

That suggests a somewhat different, more functional meaning of freedom. If you understand behavioral control, you may detect its application to you and defend yourself against that application, if you do not like the probable outcome—or if you do like the probable outcome, you can lend yourself completely to the application. Fortunately, behavior is generally not a pushbutton phenomenon. It usually does not come instantly under the control of environmental stimuli; it is gradually shaped through repeated, consistent experiences. Thus, we may recognize the processes beginning to control some of our behavior before they have gone very far and take steps accordingly. We may remove ourselves from the undesired environmental contingencies that otherwise eventually would change us; we may ourselves change the behaviors of those trying (deliberately or inadvertently) to change ours; or we may expose ourselves more thoroughly than before to the change and help it proceed faster. That is, we can if we know about behavior technology.

It is easy to recommend taking steps to defend against or help along a behavior-changing process being applied to yourself. But what if the "steps" are not within your behavioral capabilities? Suppose that poverty is steadily shaping you to a bad outcome. Understanding the principles of behavior, you might see few likely alternatives other than crime, drugs, alcohol, or behavioral vegetation. None of these patterns is a good one, in your opinion, yet you can see that your environment is constantly applying forces to your behaviors which push them to one or another of these results. It is useless to say, "leave that environment," if the behaviors necessary for a way out are missing. The path out of the poverty environment may often require high school level skill in the language patterns and styles of the affluent middle class of the society. If those skills are absent, appreciation of how the environment shapes behavior is of small use, and no freedom from the usual outcome is likely. Yet those missing skills are merely behaviors themselves. An application of behavioral technology to that case might take control of your behavior, sufficient to guarantee that you acquire the necessary new behaviors. That control of academic and language behaviors could function to allow an escape from the usual consequences of the poverty environment. In short, behavioral control could maximize freedom. More precisely, a certain form of behavioral control would free you from another form of behavioral control. The appropriate judgment here is whether the one form of control is preferable to the other, not whether behavior should be controlled.

Thus, freedom in this sense requires not only an appreciation of behavioral laws and technology; it also requires the range of behavioral skills that make self-defence and self-development possible. It may seem a paradox, but it is not: the deliberate development of many diverse skills in a person, through deliberate control of learning behaviors in school and elsewhere, in fact may maximize that person's freedom. It is capability that means freedom, in this sense; and capability is a collection of skills. Skills are exactly the targets of behavioral technology. Thus, freedom through behavioral technology.

The same point can be stated differently: control of behavior, when used to diversify the individual's repertoire of skills and abilities, is its own self-destruct mechanism. If the individual's abilities are indeed maximized, then that new behavior produces contact with a much greater range of environment than previously was available. Inevitably, that greater range of environmental experience will mean an increased input of behavior-controlling events. In the language of behavior modification that means, more reinforcers, many alternative schedules, more discriminative stimuli, and new behavior-developing contingencies. In simple English, the possibilities of *choice* increase. These choices represent sources of behavioral control different from and competitive with the deliberate program that initiated this exposure. Thus, the initial program, if properly conducted, deliberately develops those behaviors that will undermine its own power to continue control—or any *single* source's power to control. That surely is one meaning of freedom.

The key phrase in that pie-in-the-sky promise is, "if properly conducted." Deliberate behavior control over an individual, especially a child, need not be aimed at expanding a repertoire in the interests of freedom. It depends entirely on which behaviors are developed by the program and which are not. A "proper" selection for these purposes is one that will in fact maximize the child's control over the environments of the future. To some extent, we know what those behaviors are; to some extent, we can guess what they are, and to a very considerable extent, we do not know what they are. In part, this is because we have not often looked at man in terms of the laws of behavior. More curiosity from that point of view will solve some of these problems. Such curiosity can lead to a reexamination of old values and to some much needed research. For example, this book discusses behavioral techniques used to decrease out-of-seat behaviors by students in classrooms. Teachers do not like disruptive, noisy, or violent classrooms; and out-of-seat responses are components of such problems. And, while it is reasonably obvious why teachers do not like violent classrooms, it may not be so obvious why they do not like noisy ones. They often say it is because they cannot teach and children cannot learn in such classrooms. If it is a fact that learning proceeds better in quiet classrooms within which children remain seated than in noisy classrooms with a good deal of movement, then a behavioral technology that lends itself to decreasing out-of-seat behaviors is lending itself to a more effective classroom. And that, in turn, may teach the skills that expand repertoires and thereby maximize freedom. However, if it is not a fact that in-seat classrooms teach better than out-of-seat classrooms, then a behavioral technology that lends itself to decreasing out-of-seat behavior will have been serving only the teacher who prefers in-seat to out-of-seat children; and we should ask why it is acting as her special agent. And if it is a fact that out-of-seat classrooms teach better than in-seat classrooms, then a behavioral technology that lends itself to suppressing out-of-seat behavior is in fact involved in an anti-repertoire-expanding application. If we value freedom, in the meanings it can have coexisting with a behavioral technology, then this application should not occur.

Thus, the "proper conduct" of behavioral technology in such instances depends on facts not yet established, such as whether in-seat classrooms teach differently than out-of-seat classrooms, under any conditions, for any types of children. There are many such instances of incomplete or insufficient facts. You are about to learn behavioral technology; you will therefore need those facts, or you may prove to be something of a threat. Find them out.

But first, read the book.

DONALD M. BAER
*Professor of Human Development
and Psychology
University of Kansas*

PREFACE

This book applies many of the operant learning principles that govern human behavior to the modification of behavior in the school setting. It is a pragmatic text that has been written primarily for elementary and secondary school educators, such as teachers, administrators, school psychologists, counselors, social workers, and others concerned with the development of children. Other individuals, such as parents, college professors, clinicians—those concerned with effective teaching—will also find the book useful, though they may have to provide illustrations from their own experience. After completing the text, the reader should be able to assist students, educators, parents, and others to handle school-related behavioral problems more effectively as well as to more successfully prevent the occurrence of new problem behaviors.

The book is divided into six main sections. The first chapter is an introductory chapter. It provides the reader with a basic overview and a model for a behavior modification program. Part I discusses the use of various procedures designed to increase the occurrence of existing behaviors; Part II, the application of procedures designed to teach new behaviors; Part III, methods for maintaining behaviors; Part IV, methods for reducing behaviors. Part V, on carrying out and evaluating the program, has been written primarily for those who will be engaged in educational consulting research activities.

Preceding each chapter, specific student learning objectives are listed. The completion of those objectives should be used by the student as his criterion for mastery of the chapter. Each chapter also contains a number of practical exercises that have been field tested by over a hundred students. Students have one general reaction performing the exercises: they report that the activities contribute immeasurably to their acquisition of the various concepts in the book. Although the exercises are designed as optional activities, the reader will probably find that performing them contributes toward his learning. It is assumed that not every reader will be registered in a formal course, workshop, or seminar and that he may not have access to classrooms for observational purposes. For this reason other observational facilities, such as the playground, the beach, the supermarket, the library, or similar public places where groups of children and adults gather, are suggested as alternatives. For instructors of more formally organized groups, the following are some ways in which the exercises might be used: (1) assign them as homework or use as a discussion topic; (2) allow them to be used as optional activities for bonus points toward a grade; (3) use them as activities for a laboratory section of a course; (4) assign various exercises to small groups and have a spokesman from each group present the material to the whole class; (5) use them as examination questions; (6) simulate episodes in class by means of role playing, microteaching, vidio tapes and films so that all the students can work on a common situation.

A note of caution: Many of the procedures described in this text are based on extrapolations from laboratory research. Some of them have not yet been tested in the schools. Therefore the book should be regarded not as a difinitive work but as a flexible guidebook to be used for the time being, while increasingly more precise laws of school-related behavior are discovered. The authors do, however, believe that currently available data justify the existence of this text and that the procedures described herein will make a distinct contribution toward increased educational effectiveness. Yet they wish to state that new findings will come along that will suggest alterations and refinements in the procedures. We hope that those who use this book will be sensitive to this issue and attempt to keep abreast of new findings in the field.

November 1971

BETH SULZER
Carbondale, Illinois
G. ROY MAYER
Los Angeles, California

ACKNOWLEDGEMENTS

The authors wish to express their thanks to the large number of individuals who have assisted them in the development and preparation of this text: their students and colleagues. We are particularly indebted to Robert Benoit, Gerald Kranzler, Donald Beggs, J. Murray Lee, and Nathan H. Azrin for their encouragement and helpful suggestions; to Sharon Hunt, Andy Loving, Lawrence Payne, Barbara Zimmerman, Andrew Wheeler, Tom Mawhinney, and the many other graduate students who field-tested exercises and read and made suggestions for the improvement of the text; to Georgia Randolph Marcum, who worked many long, hard hours not only typing the major portion of the manuscript but also keeping the Sulzer household intact during many difficult months; to Joanna Gutilla and to the secretarial staff of the Guidance and Educational Psychology Department at Southern Illinois University who also assisted with sundry typing and clerical activities.

We also wish to thank the Graduate School at S.I.U. for underwriting the costs of the manuscript preparation.

To our families: Barbara, Kevin, and Debbie Mayer and David, Richard, and Lenore Sulzer, we wish to express our sincere appreciation. They have sacrificed many a weekend activity while we were engaged in writing this book. We thank our parents as well; and above all, our deepest gratitude goes to Edward Stanton Sulzer, to whom this book is dedicated.

CONTENTS

1 AN INTRODUCTION TO STUDENT BEHAVIOR CHANGE

Objectives

By the end of this chapter you should be able to

1. Describe the purpose of the book.
2. Describe the basic approach the book will take.
3. Tell which individuals may be involved in a program of behavior change.
4. Discuss some of the ethical issues faced by persons involved in designing programs in behavior change.
5. List some of the directions that programs in school behavior change might take.
6. Outline the steps included in the model for behavior change.
7. List the major points included in each step.
8. Define and illustrate the following terms:
   a. behavior modification
   b. behavioral specialist
   c. operational definition
   d. behavioral contract
   e. criteria
   f. contingencies
   g. independent variable
   h. adaptation
   i. operant level
   j. functional relationship
   k. dependent behavior
   l. behavioral goal

The field of education is in a state of turmoil. Student rebellion, teacher strikes, and financial shortages plague the system. There are as many theoretical explanations of the causes as there are disruptive events. It is, however, safe to say that one of the major contributing factors to the current state of discontent is frustration: teachers' frustration with students; students' and parents' frustration with school programs. Teachers are frustrated because many of their students fail to reach an acceptable level of achievement. This is often a function of the fact that the students fail to "pay attention" or to follow directions or else they do things that are incompatible with learning or that interfere with their classmates' learning. The frustration of the student and parent may be a result of the student's failure to "accomplish" and his subsequent failure to receive society's rewards for scholastic accomplishment. He may be responding to overpunitiveness on the part of school personnel or floundering because of insufficient controls.

If teachers, school administrators, school psychologists and social workers, guidance counselors, and other school personnel were better prepared to handle behavioral problems and to avoid the compounding of such problems, the situation might be more satisfying to teachers, students, and the public. Above all, school personnel need to discover techniques for improving student learning. The basic purpose of this text is directed to those ends. It is intended to provide a set of procedural guidelines that the school practitioner may use to improve his own classroom management skills, to become more adept at providing conditions which facilitate student learning, and to help students to become more motivated.

Due to the influence of B. F. Skinner, recent years have witnessed a burgeoning of basic behavioral laboratory research as well as applied research in settings such as schools, clinics, and institutions. Both types of research have been striving to identify those factors which control behavior. It is the results of those investigations which have yielded behavioral principles which hold great promise for practitioners in applied settings like schools (Krumboltz & Thoreson, 1969; Bandura, 1969; Tharp & Wetzel, 1969; Ullman & Krasner, 1965; Krasner & Ullman, 1965; Ulrich, Stachnik, & Mabry, 1966; Ayllon & Azrin, 1968; Meacham & Weisen, 1969; Sloane & MacAulay, 1968). When the methods of behavioral science and its experimental findings are systematically applied with the intent of altering behavior, the technique is called *behavior modification.* The principles and procedures to be presented here are based upon experimental findings. They deal with *increasing, extending, restricting, teaching, maintaining,* and *reducing* behaviors. In many cases, there are adequate data on humans to back up an assertion or suggestion. In others, only data from the animal laboratory are available. For example, painful stimuli have been rarely used in experimentation with humans. Because the application of behavioral analysis to the field of education is relatively new, the material presented in this text should be thought of as a set of working hypotheses rather than as a set of standard methods for behavior change.

The fundamental approach in this text is behavioral. The basic assumption is that what students *do* is of primary importance. If the student is functioning as he should, accomplishing his own goals, and satisfying his parents and the academic community, fine! If not, then it becomes necessary to institute a program of behavior change.

DECIDING TO CHANGE BEHAVIOR

Behavioral change is implicit in any school program. Students come to school expecting to learn; and learning implies changes not only in quantity of information or verbal material acquired but also in skill performances, such as writing, computing, and using tools. The student also experiences more subtle changes in interpersonal relations, "listening" and "attending," following directions, and other complex behavioral sequences. Parents send their children to school with the justifiable expectation that their behavior will change. Teachers work under the assumption that changes will take place in their students' behavior, changes involving both academic development and emotional and social growth. Programming for behavioral change is, then, hardly a novel phenomenon. The decision, is not *whether* behavior should be changed, but *who* will change it, *what* the goals will be, and *which* specific program of behavior change will be used.

INDIVIDUALS INVOLVED

The decision to institute a program of behavior change may come from a variety of sources. Most frequently the classroom teacher will identify a problem; but often parents, the student himself, or other school personnel voice concern about specific student, or even their own, behaviors. Teachers usually attempt to solve a behavioral problem on their own. But when the problem persists, other persons are often consulted: the student; the parents; the principal; and perhaps a special consultant, such as a school psychologist, counselor, visiting teacher, social worker, or child development specialist. Often such contacts result in a concerted effort by all concerned toward a mutually agreed upon solution. In this text a consultant who has special training qualifying him to assist children directly and advise the school about developing programs in behavioral change is called a *behavioral specialist.*

3

THE PROGRAM IN BEHAVIOR CHANGE

Once a problem has been identified and the decision has been made to solve it, the planning of a program in behavior change can begin. To facilitate such planning, we offer a model with a series of steps. This model, based on one offered by Ellen Reese (1966), can be used to provide one, but certainly not the *only,* structure from which such a program for change can evolve. The model, diagrammed in Figure 1.1, covers such basic issues as selecting the *goals, criteria, behavioral procedures,* and *contingencies; providing a favorable environment;* methods for *carrying out the procedures, evaluating* the program's effectiveness, and *communicating* the results.

SPECIFYING BEHAVIORAL GOALS

The first step in a program of behavior change is to specify goals, or *target* or *terminal behaviors* by describing exactly what the individual is expected to be able to do at the end of the program. Any school-related goal is a potential candidate for a behavior modification program, as long as it can be behaviorally stated. For a student, these goals may relate to academic performance, such as increasing the number of problems, experiments, or projects he completes, pages he reads, pages he writes according to specified criteria, or unusual or novel solutions he discovers. The goals may also include classroom behaviors that are not strictly academic: remaining seated, following directions, participating in discussions and group activities, contributing to group projects, making noise, rebeling, being compliant, working independently, acting in leadership roles, and so on. They may include goals for personnel as well: being able to apply specific behavioral procedures, contribute to group discussions and staff activities, hand in reports, complete assignments, smile more frequently, and various other behaviors. In addition to being able to state the goal behaviorally, the aspect of practicality should be considered. Some goals are practical; others are not. A goal is practical only if it can be achieved. Therefore, those involved in behavior modification prefer to work with a series of easily achievable goals, rather than a single long-term goal. Limitations in personnel, material, and other environmental factors can also render a goal impractical. (Those factors are discussed in more detail in Chapter 14.) Since a great many behavioral goals are amenable to behavioral manipulation, ethical considerations become extremely important and must play a significant role in the selection of the behavioral goal.

The behavioral approach   Behavioral analysis restricts itself to the consideration of responses that are directly observable and measurable.

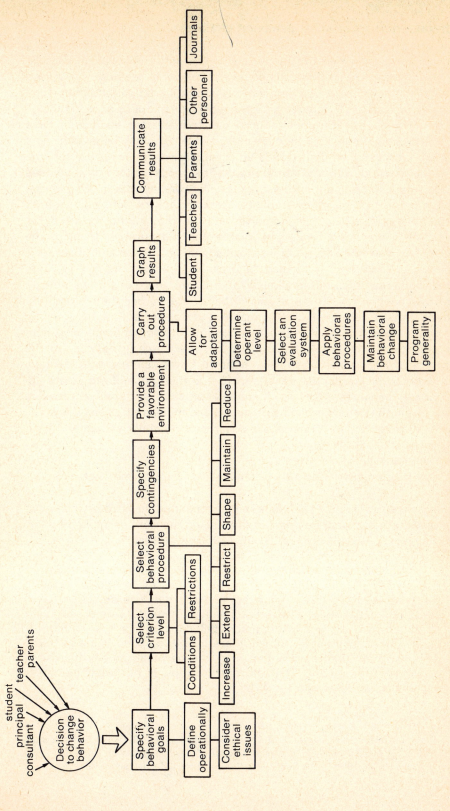

FIGURE 1.1 The program in behavior change

Behavioral goals are often stated in such general terms as: (1) increasing or maintaining the rate of completing homework, reading, or writing assignments; (2) the development of classroom participation skills, such as contributing to a discussion; (3) the reduction of out-of-seat, shouting, or hitting behaviors. Before a program can be instituted, such goals have to be broken down into sets of measurable terminal behaviors. The *number* of times a student stands up or sits down, the *length* of time he remains in or out of his seat, the *number* of words written or sentences read aloud can be quantified, as can the *frequency* of his making verbal statements or biting other students. Descriptions of behavior such as "approving," "anxious," "aggressive," or "hostile" cannot be used because they are not directly observable and measurable. Instead, the behavioral specialist must define these adjectives in terms of observable behaviors. A student is termed "aggressive" because he frowns; hits other students; says things like, "Wait 'til I get you"; or throws objects at other people. It is these observed behaviors, rather than broad, abstract concepts, with which this material is concerned.

When a broad concept is broken down into its set of component acts or operations, the concept is said to be *operationally defined.* In the preceding paragraph, "aggressive behavior" was operationally defined. If the behavior is operationally defined, it is then possible to select appropriate measures such as frequency or time so that progressive changes in the behavior can be observed and measured. (Behavior modification measurement systems are described in detail in Chapter 15.)

Exercise 1.1

Operationally define either "anxious" or "approving" behavior.

In goal specification, the issue is what the student *is to do,* not what he will *say* about what he *does.* In discussing the field of applied behavioral analysis Baer, Wolf, and Risley (1968) note that:

> . . . it usually studies what subjects can be brought to do rather than what they can be brought to say; unless of course, a verbal response is the behavior of interest. Accordingly a subject's description of his own non-verbal behavior usually would not be accepted as a measure of his actual behavior unless it were independently substantiated. Hence, there is little applied value in the demonstration that an impotent man can be made to say that he no longer is impotent. The relevant question is not what he can say, but what he can do [p. 93].[1]

---

[1] Reprinted by permission from D. M. Baer, M. M. Wolf, and T. R. Risley, Some current dimensions of applied behavior analysis. *Journal of Applied Behavior Analysis,* 1968, **1,** 91–97. Copyright 1968 by the Society for the Experimental Analysis of Behavior, Inc.

Ethical issues Behavior modification is an approach that is concerned with *how* to change behavior, not *which* behaviors should be changed. Behavior modifiers, like everyone else, have differing ideas about what constitutes desirable behavior in an educational setting. Some think all children should sit quietly and follow directions without question. Others think that the ideal student is one who freely questions and interacts with his fellow students. However, behavior modifiers have no more right to make personal decisions about what they want to achieve in a behavior modification program than any other citizen. The decision regarding the goal of the program is the responsibility of others. The state board of education and the local boards, composed of community representatives, decide on educational policy: what is to be taught in the schools. Educators, psychologists, guidance counselors, and behavior modifiers are supposed to have the technical skills to carry out a program designed to achieve these goals, and they are infringing on the rights of the citizenry when they select the goals unilaterally.

Although there often is a general agreement about the selection of behavioral goals among the key persons concerned, sometimes complete accord is not reached. When there is such a difference, it presents an ethical issue. Who has the right to determine a behavioral goal for a particular individual? The student himself? His teacher? His parents? The behavioral specialist? When the goal involves academic performance, the school has typically assumed the right to structure the program. In other areas, however, the responsibility for selecting behavioral goals is not so clear. Suppose, for instance, a teacher decides that a student, Doug, is too quiet, and she would like him to become "freer": to be more outgoing, play more vigorously. Suppose, however, his parents say that Doug is rambunctious at home and the last thing they want or need is more noise. How can a decision be made? Ethical considerations suggest that some mutual agreement among the concerned parties be reached before a program is instituted. Compromises might be made. For instance, the program to help Doug become "freer" might be accepted with the limitation that those behaviors be encouraged only under clearly defined conditions that least resemble the home setting. If no accord can be reached, it is probably best not to pursue the goal, since the individuals involved would be working at cross purposes, to the possible detriment of the student.

Behavioral contracts One way of avoiding ethical problems is to draw up a behavioral contract. The use of such contracts has been suggested by several authors (Keirsey, 1965; Krumboltz, 1966; Sulzer, 1962) as a means of specifying terminal behavior and the roles played by all individuals concerned with the program. The contract is drawn up so that it explicitly states the terminal behavior and the consequences to be applied to specific behaviors and the stipulations mutually acceptable to the student, teacher, parents, and behavioral specialist. For example, it has been mutually agreed that Mike must stop speaking out in class without permission. A contract is drawn up that specifies that terminal behavior. The consequences to be applied to specific behaviors are stipulated: his teacher is to send him out of the room for five minutes if he does speak out, his parents are to praise him if he brings a note from the teacher stating that he has not called out that day, and so on. The contract is written so that it is clear and satisfactory to all parties who sign it.

A second example of the behavioral contract will further clarify its function. Jimmy, a nine-year-old boy, fails to complete any of his school assignments. In a series of interviews with a behavioral specialist, Jimmy and the specialist decide that from now on Jimmy will complete his *math* assignments. They select the completion of math assignments as the terminal goal because they consider it to be achievable and one that the natural environment will tend to sustain when the program is completed. To augment this decision, the behavioral specialist draws up a contract stating that Jimmy will now complete his math assignments each day. It is signed by Jimmy, his teacher, his parents, and the behavioral specialist.

SELECTING A CRITERION LEVEL

The second step in instituting a program of behavior change, once the behavioral goal has been selected, is to state a set of *criteria* by which to determine that the terminal goal has been reached. For example, there is a youngster in a particular class who consistently fails to complete more than 20 percent of his arithmetic assignments. The teacher has evidence that this student is capable of doing the problems because he has done similar ones in the past. The teacher states that the child's terminal behavior should be that he "completes his arithmetic assignments." Does this mean that he must complete every single problem on every single assignment? Suppose the teacher considers his completion of 90 percent of the problems for ten consecutive arithmetic assignments a demonstration of success. The teacher then states the criterion as: 90 percent of the problems in ten consecutive assignments should be completed. If the teacher is interested in obtaining an accurate performance as well, she might add the criterion that an 80 percent accuracy level is required for achievement of the terminal goal.

When determining criteria for some behavioral goals, it is very important to consider the *conditions*[2] under which the behavior is to be ulti-

---

[2] See R. F. Mager, *Preparing instructional objectives* (San Francisco: Fearon Publishers, 1961), for a similar treatment of instructional goals.

mately executed. In Mike's case, for example, it was agreed that he was not to speak out without permission during lectures, films, library period, and the like. But it would be perfectly all right for him to speak out without permission during informal class discussions, lunch, and recess. Of equal importance are the *restrictions* that should be placed on the performance of the terminal goal. You will recall that in Jimmy's case, it was agreed that he was to complete his math assignments. However, it was further stipulated that he was not expected to when doing math would interfere with his reading assignment.

Clearly specifying the criteria for judging the success of the behavioral goal and indicating what, if any, conditions and restrictions are to be placed on the execution of the goal behavior should help the teacher or behavioral specialist decide on the directions that should be taken in planning the program.

Exercise 1.2

Select a terminal goal for eliminating "aggressive" behavior. Specify an appropriate measure for determining change. State a criterion by which the success of reaching the terminal goal can be evaluated and indicate what conditions and restrictions will be placed on the performance of the terminal goal.

SELECTING A BEHAVIORAL PROCEDURE

After forming an idea of where one wants to go and how to determine when he has arrived, the next step is to select an appropriate behavioral procedure. Behavior change takes many directions; the change that one may wish to accomplish often falls into one of several categories. These categories include *increasing,* or strengthening, a weak behavior; *extending,* or *generalizing,* a behavior to a new setting; *restricting* a behavior to specific settings; forming, or *shaping,* a new behavior; *maintaining* a behavior that shows signs of weakening over time; and *reducing* or *eliminating,* a behavior. (Parts I through IV will discuss each of these categories in detail.) If a student fails to *complete* his work, he is already engaging in a behavior; and, obviously, the strength of that behavior is too weak to satisfy the teacher. Instead of completing only part of the assignment, the teacher wants the student to complete the whole assignment. A procedure designed to *increase* the work output may bring about the desired results. The child who frequently moves around the classroom probably sits at his desk at least some of the time. Here again, a strengthening procedure might be appropriate. That same student may actually sit very still on some occasions, for instance, while waiting to be sent to lunch period, during a film showing, or perhaps while waiting to be selected to participate in a specific group activity. In this case, a procedure designed to *extend,* or *generalize,* sitting still to other situations, such as during lectures by the teacher or group discussions, may be in order. A response which is considered rude by the teacher may be perfectly acceptable to a group of peers. A student's friends may not mind when he shakes his fist or sticks out his tongue or uses expressions like "cool it, man" or "shut up." On the other hand, his teacher would probably consider these behaviors rude when directed at her. In this instance, the teacher might turn to a procedure designed to *restrict* such responses to peer interaction situations. The kindergarten teacher may want to teach her students the new behavior of hand raising as a request for being allowed to speak. She may also want to *maintain* that behavior over time once it has been learned. Principles for teaching and maintaining behavior are appropriate in that instance. Fighting in school is a behavior that most teachers would want to eliminate, substantially reduce, or, at least restrict, to the boxing ring. One of the procedures for *reducing* or *eliminating* behaviors might achieve the objective.

Chapters 2 through 12 discuss how to use each procedure effectively, its temporal characteristics, the durability of the change, and other factors involved with each. By examining that material it should be possible to select an appropriate course of action. Chapter 13 is devoted to further assisting the reader with the selection of procedure(s). It does so by summarizing the major characteristics of each procedure.

SPECIFYING THE CONTINGENCIES[3]

The next step in the program of behavior change is to select the *contingencies* to be utilized in the program. *Contingencies are the relationships between a given response and its environmental consequences.* Contingencies may occur "naturally"; they may be a part of a planned program. When someone dives into a pool of water, he gets wet. That is a natural contingency. The stimulus event *(S)* of getting wet is naturally contingent upon the response *(R)* of diving into the pool.

$$R \longrightarrow S$$
diving   wet

Teachers use contingencies all the time as they conduct their school programs. When Sally gives the right answer, her teacher smiles and says, "Good." In this example, smiling and saying good are being applied *contingently* because they are related to, or dependent upon, Sally's giving the correct answer. Contingencies may have the effect of strength-

[3] Some behavioral analysts prefer the term "dependency" to the term "contingency."

ening, maintaining, weakening, or eliminating a behavior. Contingencies that serve to strengthen behaviors can also be used to teach new behaviors. (These contingencies will be discussed at length throughout Chapters 2 through 12.)

Exercise 1.3

Watch a mother with her child. List at least three contingencies that the mother uses following some of the child's behaviors. (*Note:* It is not necessary for the mother to appear to be aware of her use of contingencies.)

Exercise 1.4

Watch a mother with her child. List at least three contingencies used by the child following some of the mother's behaviors.

PROVIDING A FAVORABLE ENVIRONMENT

Having selected the appropriate contingencies for the planned procedure, the next step is to find an *environment* that is suitable for the program of behavior change; an environment where the desired behavior is most likely to occur and where incompatible behaviors are least likely to occur. If the terminal goal is to increase out-of-school study time, it is probably best accomplished in a quiet room that is free of distractions. If the terminal goal is to teach a child to say please and thank you, at least one person other than the child will be necessary. If the target goal is to teach a student to pay attention to the teacher during lectures, it is best to seat him away from the friend with whom he carries on frequent conversations. The environment must be arranged so that it is *possible to control the contingencies.*

Suppose a teacher has a young adolescent in his class who makes frequent wisecracks that disrupt the class. The teacher may have decided that the best way to handle the situation was to use the contingency of removing his attention from the boy following all such remarks. This plan would probably be quite effective if the teacher and the boy were always alone together in the room. This, of course, is not usually the case. There are others in a classroom, and enough of them will laugh or smile at the boy's wisecracks so that he has reason to maintain his behavior. For the teacher to just remove his attention is likely to be insufficient. It would be necessary to control the responses of the other students in the class as well, before the behavior would begin to diminish. This may or may not be possible. The alternative would be to alter the contingencies or to change the behavior within a different setting and then arrange the situation so that the newly reduced behavior would *generalize* to the class situation.

Exercise 1.5

a. Suggest an appropriate setting in which to

1. teach a kindergarten child to play cooperatively with other children

2. teach a high school student to work on his history assignment

3. teach a child to whisper in the library

4. teach a junior high school student to participate in group discussion

b. Briefly discuss your reasons for selecting each environment.

CARRYING OUT THE PROCEDURE

Allowing for adaptation   How do people behave when they enter a room filled with unfamiliar faces? What does a child do when he first enters a new class in the middle of a school year? When a new kitten or puppy is brought home, is its behavior at the onset typical of its later behavior? Probably not. The man entering into an unfamiliar group often remains quiet for a while and only gradually begins to approach others. After a time he begins to settle into the situation and behave in a manner more typical of his usual behavior. The child entering the class in mid-year responds in a similar manner. A kitten or puppy will cower in a corner for a while and then begin to sniff about, seeming to explore the environment. Is it appropriate to begin collecting behavioral data as soon as a person or animal enters a new environment? Obviously not, since the initial behavior is not a typical behavior. This suggests a major consideration: The individual should be allowed to *adapt* to the new environment before anything else is done. Suppose a teacher has decided that a good plan for increasing a particular student's participation in group discussion is first to get him together with a group of two other students in a small room. The two other participants and this student are only slightly acquainted. The room is totally unfamiliar to all three. Assuming that some measure of verbal interaction had been determined, would it be a good idea to start measuring the behavior the first day? Probably not. It would be better to give all three students a chance to become acquainted first and to get used to the room. Data collection could begin after a day or two.

Programs in classroom behavior change are often carried on in the natural setting. When a behavioral specialist is called in to observe and record data, the major adaptation requirement is to have the student(s) or subject(s) become accustomed to the presence of the observer who is to record the data. This can usually be accomplished within a few days. Adaptation is facilitated by having the observer sit in an inconspicuous spot, making every attempt *not* to interact with the students. The reason for this should become clear in the discussion on social reinforcement in Chapter 2.

Exercise 1.6

a. When you go into a classroom to observe, spend a while observing how the students and teacher respond to your presence. List the adaptation responses. Do these behaviors subside after a while? How long does it take?

b. Go back to the same classroom a second time. List the same adaptation behaviors you noted in Exercise 1.6a. How long does it take until those behaviors subside this second time?

Determining the operant level   Once the individual settles into the altered environment, measurement of the *dependent behavior,* that is, the behavior that is to be changed by the program, can begin. Various methods for measuring behavior are discussed in detail in Chapter 15. Measurements are first made to show how the behavior is typically being emitted in that particular setting. Behavioral measures must be taken under the conditions that are to be held constant throughout the program. These preliminary measures supply a standard that will be called interchangeably in this text either *baseline, operant level,* or *base rate.*

For example, a teacher decides to try to increase the number of times a student stands in line without pushing. Before trying a modification procedure, he needs to know what percentage of the time the student typically lines up without pushing. Suppose he found that his student lined up without touching any other children about 20 percent of the time during a six-day period. Figure 1.2 is a graph of the baseline data as it would appear diagrammed.

It is important to measure the operant level prior to the start of the program. First, it is necessary to demonstrate that the behavior occurs at a fairly stable level; that is, the distribution of the measures varies within a well delineated range. Second, changes that occur in the behavior during the program as a result of the procedures can be measured against the operant level. In the illustration above, the percentage of times the student lined up without pushing ranges between 10 to 40

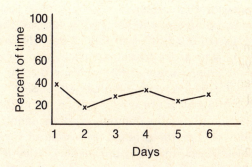

FIGURE 1.2   Percentage of time *S* lines up without pushing

percent. The following example also demonstrates the importance of repeated behavioral measurements. Suppose a teacher is concerned about a student who is frequently out of his seat without permission. Before selecting and using a procedure to increase his in-seat behavior, the teacher must determine how often (or how long) the student is out of his seat; that is, the operant level. The first day the behavior is measured a new colorful work book is distributed to the class, and the student remains in his seat for much of the session. But, on the next three or four days, he is out of his seat frequently. Usually a relatively stable rate for no less than three sessions gives an adequate standard against which to measure any change that might occur under a given procedure. One or two sessions are subject to too much error.

There is an additional advantage to the collection of operant level data. It allows the observer to objectively measure the occurrence of a behavior that may have seemed worse than it actually was. For example, it might be that a large student was seated near the teacher. And, while he did not leave his seat any more often than the other students, it was more obvious to the teacher when he did.

Exercise 1.7
a. Select and observe a very simple behavior of your pet, yourself, a student, a friend, or a relative. Count the number of times the behavior was emitted during a specified period of time each day for several days.

b. Plot your data from exercise 1.7a on a graph. The horizontal line, or *abscissa,* should be labeled "Days." The vertical line, *ordinate,* should be labeled with numbers to show the frequency with which the specific behavior was emitted (see Fig. 1.2).

c. Answer these questions about your data.

    1. Are the measurements about the same from one day to the next?

    2. Do you think another observer would have obtained the identical measurements that you did?

Selecting an evaluation system   The individual conducting the program must devise a plan that will assure himself and the others involved of the effectiveness of his particular procedures. He will need to analyze the behavioral data in order to demonstrate that a relationship exists between *the dependent variable,* the behavior that he plans to change (lining up without pushing, remaining seated, and so on), and *the independent variable,* the procedure which will be instituted (reinforcement, punishment, and so on). Such a demonstration is called *the experimental analysis of behavior.* For the student who was observed to frequently leave his seat without permission, the teacher selected as the terminal goal that the student was to "stay in his seat, unless given permission to leave, over 80 percent of the time for three days in a row." Baseline observations showed that the student "stayed seated" less than 70 percent of the intervals scored. A procedure was begun in which the teacher *reinforced,* that is, praised and otherwise attended positively to the student when he remained in his seat. The desired behavioral change occurred, but was it possible to conclude that the reinforcing procedure was solely responsible? Not without a proper *control.* The student's behavior could have changed because he "matured," because the building that had been under construction across the street had been completed and he stopped going to the window to watch, or any number of other reasons. In order to demonstrate a *functional relationship* between the dependent behavior (in this case, remaining seated) and the independent variable (in this case, positive teacher attention) some further manipulation has to be planned. One of the commonest methods for demonstrating the existence of a functional relationship is to *reverse* the behavior change procedure for a few days during the program. In the program described above, the student began to remain in his seat for increasing lengths of time. He was, in fact, spending about 90 percent of the time in his seat. A *probe,* consisting of several days without reinforcement for the desired behavior, was planned. During the probe there was a substantial drop in the student's in-seat behavior, further supporting the idea that the reinforcement procedure was directly related to the initial increase in his in-seat behavior. When the reinforcement contingencies (positive teacher attention) were subsequently reinstated, the desired behavior recovered. It was then possible to have even greater confidence in the efficiency of the procedure. Figure 1.3 shows how that data looked plotted on a graph.

The increase in in-seat behavior is shown in Figure 1.3 by the rise in the percentage of intervals scored. Under *reversal* (probe), a drop in sitting occurs. With the reinstatement of reinforcement, sitting again increases. The data demonstrate that there is a functional relationship between "sitting" and the reinforcing contingency. Reversal of the contingencies is but one of several experimental designs for demonstrating functional relationships. Chapter 15 includes a detailed discussion of various experimental designs appropriate for educational settings.

Appling behavioral procedures   After the behavioral contract has been made, the criterion level and appropriate procedures have been selected, and the contingencies specified, the behavior modification procedure can start. Several different behavioral techniques are discussed in Parts I through IV and, in fact, form the major thrust of this text. Those procedures will be summarized in Part V. It is important to recognize here that once a behavior modification procedure has been carried out, the goal behavior must be maintained.

Maintaining the behavioral change   The fact that a behavior has been changed does not mean that the change will persist. Many people study foreign languages and musical instruments, yet few become experts. In

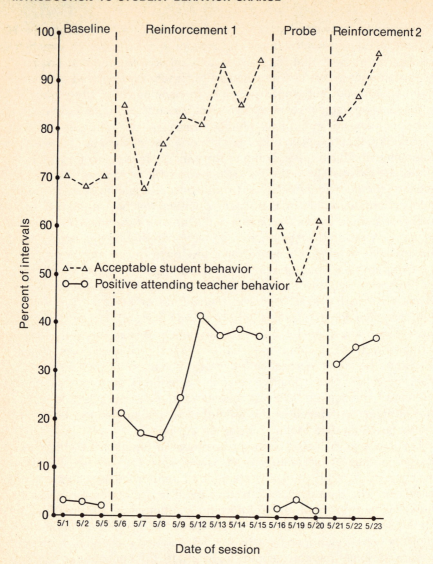

FIGURE 1.3   **Acceptable student in-seat behavior as a function of positive attending teacher behavior**

Based on a study reported by Engelhardt, Sulzer, and Alterkruse (1970).

much the same way, the worst trouble maker in the class occasionally behaves like an angel. Why do these ideal behaviors not persist? Many factors contribute to such backsliding. From a pragmatic point of view, however, the failure of a behavior to maintain over time is due in part to an elimination or weakening of the contingencies acting upon the behavior. It is, therefore, important to consider this issue in advance of beginning the behavior modification program. It is crucial that some structuring of the environment take place which is designed to keep the newly altered behavior going. For example, the number of times the contingency is applied to the behavior can be gradually and progressively reduced. Such procedures will be discussed in detail in Part III.

Programming generality   Jimmy has successfully completed a program in which he has reached his criterion performance of completing math assignments. A plan for maintaining that performance has also been selected. Does this necessarily imply that Jimmy will automatically begin to complete his assignments in spelling, reading, and social studies? Perhaps. The *generality* is not accomplished automatically, though frequently it is a by-product of a specific program.

> That generality is not automatically accomplished whenever behavior is changed also needs occasional emphasis, especially in the evaluation of applied behavior analysis. It is sometimes assumed that application has failed when generalization does not take place in any widespread form. Such a conclusion has no generality itself. A procedure which is effective in changing behavior in one setting may perhaps be easily repeated in other settings, and thus accomplish the generalization sought . . . In general, *generalization should be programmed, rather than expected or lamented.* [Baer et al., pp. 96–97, 1968]. [Italics added.]

If generality of a newly modified behavior is desired, provision must be made to assure that the generalization occurs. In Chapter 3 there is a section devoted to the programming of generalization.

GRAPHING AND COMMUNICATING THE RESULTS

It is not the intention of the authors to turn all the school behavioral specialists and teachers who may utilize some of these procedures into full-time researchers. How necessary, therefore, is it to provide for this next step of handling and communicating results?

Graphing data   There are various factors to consider in deciding how the results should be handled, who should see them, and how they should be communicated. These factors include both scientific and ethical considerations. From a scientific point of view, it is essential that a continual record of results be maintained. This can best be accomplished by either plotting each measurement on a graph or recording it on a table. (Chapter 15 describes various techniques for measuring behavior in the schools.) To reiterate, data recording is essential because the data demonstrate how effectively a procedure is working. A graph allows for visual evaluation of the effectiveness of the procedure. If, after a sufficient period of time, change has not taken the desired direction, the data will indicate the need for an evaluation of the program. Perhaps an entirely different approach is called for. On the other hand, the record may suggest that, while the procedure is working, the change is occurring very slowly, indicating the need for some changes in procedure.

A second factor in favor of the continual plotting of data is the effect this form of information has on the individuals responsible for the program in behavior change (that is, the teacher or behavioral specialist or both). That this is no small consideration should become increasingly apparent as the potency of reinforcement in strengthening and maintaining behavior continues to be stressed throughout this text. If a student's behavior is to be changed, those responsible for the program must also carefully maintain their own behavior. They must continually make the effort to structure the situation designed to bring about the change. When the teacher and behavioral specialist see their plan beginning to take effect, as they do when keeping records, they are encouraged to maintain their efforts. They are themselves, in essence, reinforced. Consider the case of a student who is very disruptive in class. A procedure is introduced by which the student is reinforced for appropriate classroom behavior. Now suppose that this student begins to make gradual progress, say, going from an operant level of 10 percent desirable classroom behavior to 20 percent desirable classroom behavior. The teacher or behavioral specialist would probably not realize that this small, gradual improvement had been achieved without the data graphically plotted. After all, when a student is being disruptive for 80 percent of his school day he is still being pretty much of a monster. All concerned could logically presume that the program was not working well and, perhaps, be tempted to give it up. On the other hand, once presented with a slow but definitely rising curve, they would be more apt to persist with the procedure.

Communicating results   Once the behavior modification program is completed and a desired change accomplished, with whom should the results be shared? This is an ethical issue. Certainly if an effective method for working with a particular student is discovered, it seems obvious that at least he and his present and future teachers should be made aware of both the results and the procedures for achieving them. Under some circumstances, it might be beneficial to share the material with the student's parents. When one goes beyond the school or immediate family to report results, other issues should be considered. If the student is identified, parental permission should be obtained before the reports are distributed. Sometimes a new procedure is discovered that could be effectively used by other professionals in related fields. In that case, characteristics that could identify the particular student should be removed and the material submitted to various media such as professional journals and conventions for professional workers.

SUMMARY

The rationale for an approach to student behavior change has been presented. It was contended that behavioral principles derived from scientific data are now available that may have direct application to the amelioration of classroom behavioral problems. Methods for defining student problems in behavioral terms were also presented.

A model for behavior change was introduced in order to provide a frame of reference for the subsequent material in this text. This model included specifying behavioral goals, the selection of a criterion level and the contingencies, providing a favorable environment, carrying out the procedure, and provisions for handling and communicating the results. If the reader, as he considers the subsequent material, will refer back to this model, he should find that the various procedures will fit together into a meaningful and functional whole. It should provide him with potential methods for achieving behavioral change in the school setting.

REFERENCES

Ayllon, T., & Azrin, N. H. *The token economy.* New York: Appleton-Century-Crofts, 1968.

Baer, D. M., Wolf, M. M., & Risley, T. R. Some current dimensions of applied behavior analysis. *Journal of Applied Behavior Analysis,* 1968, **1,** 91–97.

Bandura, A. *Principles of behavior modification.* New York: Holt, Rinehart and Winston, 1969.

Englehardt, L., Sulzer, B., & Altekruse, M. The counselor as a consultant in eliminating out-of-seat behavior. *Elementary School Guidance and Counseling,* 1971, **5,** 196–204.

Keirsey, D. W. Transactional casework: A technology for inducing behavior change. Paper presented at the annual convention of the California Association of School Psychologists and Psychometrists, San Francisco, 1965.

Krasner, L., & Ullmann, L. P. (Eds.) *Research in behavior modification.* New York: Holt, Rinehart and Winston, 1965.

Krumboltz, J. D. *Revolution in counseling: Implications of behavioral science.* Boston: Houghton-Mifflin, 1966.

Krumboltz, J. D., & Thoreson, C. E. *Behavioral counseling.* New York: Holt, Rinehart and Winston, 1969.

Meacham, M. L., & Wiesen, A. E. *Changing classroom behavior: A manual for precision teaching.* Scranton: International Textbook, 1969.

Reese, E. P. The analysis of human operant behavior. In J. Vernon (Ed.), *Introduction to general psychology: a self-selection textbook.* Dubuque, Iowa: Brown, 1966.

Sloane, H. N., & MacAulay, B. D. (Eds.) *Operant procedures in remedial speech and language training.* Boston: Houghton-Mifflin, 1968.

Sulzer, E. Reinforcement and the therapeutic contract. *Journal of Counseling Psychology,* 1962, **9,** 271–276.

Tharp, R. G., & Wetzel, R. J. *Behavioral modification in the natural environment.* New York: Academic Press, 1969.

Ullmann, L. P., & Krasner, L. (Eds.) *Case studies in behavior modification.* New York: Holt, Rinehart and Winston, 1965.

Ulrich, R., Stachnik, T., & Mabry, J. *Control of human behavior.* Glenview, Ill.: Scott, Foresmen, 1966.

PART I

INCREASING
THE OCCURRENCE
OF EXISTING BEHAVIORS

Part I will deal with the techniques for increasing behaviors that are already part of the individual's repertoire, that is, behaviors that the individual has been observed to emit in the past.

Chapter 2 will be concerned with increasing behaviors by means of positive reinforcement. Chapter 3 will cover negative reinforcement, and it will also discuss several other methods for facilitating the emission of the desired behavior.

Reinforcement is an integral part of all the procedures described in later chapters. The reader may profitably refer back to Part I as he progresses to later sections.

2 REINFORCEMENT

Objectives

Using examples not described in this chapter, you should be able to

1. Define and offer school illustrations for each of the following terms:
  a. positive reinforcement
  b. reinforcer
  c. stimulus
  d. primary reinforcer
  e. conditioned reinforcer
  f. generalized reinforcer
  g. social reinforcer
  h. token reinforcer
  i. Premack principle
  j. deprivation
  k. satiation
  l. reinforcement schedules

2. Describe two different methods which can be used to identify reinforcers.

3. Describe how to develop reinforces. Give an educational illustration.

4. List the major variables that influence the effectiveness of a reinforcement procedure. Describe the optimal conditions for each variable that has been identified as an influence on the effectiveness of a reinforcement procedure.

Many of the problems encountered by teachers in the daily management of their classes could be resolved if the emission[1] of desirable student behaviors was increased. Kindergarten and primary school teachers strengthen the behaviors of their students as they train them to participate in school procedures. Children enter school with a broad array of behaviors. For instance, most kindergarten and first grade students use speaking vocabularies containing thousands of words, will sit quietly for a time, will look at materials being shown by the teacher, and can handle many materials such as blocks and crayons. As a result of strengthening these behaviors over time, the pupil's vocabulary is increased and he can sit and work for increasingly longer periods of time, pay attention to a greater degree, and handle his materials more efficiently.

Often, a teacher's report will contain comments about a student who chats with his friends continuously, never sits down, or does not finish his assignments. This may often be translated to mean that the student spends considerable time chatting and being out of his seat and that he rarely finishes his work. The student is, however, spending at least occasional moments sitting quietly and working. And even if he does not complete his work, he does sometimes finish a portion of an assignment. Terminal goal behaviors for this student might include: (1) increasing the time he is quiet to x percent of the school day; (2) increasing the time he is in his seat to x percent of the school day; (3) increasing the units of work he completes to x percent. Positive reinforcement is a procedure for strengthening low frequency behaviors of this type, and it will be emphasized in this chapter.

POSITIVE REINFORCEMENT

Reinforcement is a procedure through which behaviors are increased or maintained, and it is defined solely by its effect upon behavior. If a behavior decreases in frequency, it is not being reinforced. There are two distinct reinforcement operations that increase and maintain behavior: *positive reinforcement* and *negative reinforcement.* (Negative reinforcement is discussed in Chapter 3.)

---

[1] "Emission" is a technical term used in behavioral analysis. The verb, "to emit," is used specifically with a certain category of behavior called "operant behavior." Operant behaviors are modified by their consequences. Operant behaviors correspond closely to the behavior colloquially referred to as voluntary (Catania, 1968). The term "emit" will be used throughout this text since almost every school related behavior discussed here is an operant behavior.

POSITIVE REINFORCEMENT DEFINED

The contingent presentation of a stimulus that increases or maintains a response is called *positive reinforcement.* The contingent stimulus, the *positive reinforcer,* may be an object or an event. For example a child asks for milk, "Milk, please" (the response, R), and he is given milk (the positive reinforcer, S^+); a boy throws a basketball (the response, R), and it falls through the hoop (the reinforcer, S^+). These two reinforcing events are diagramed below:

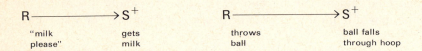

| $R \longrightarrow S^+$ | | $R \longrightarrow S^+$ | |
| "milk please" | gets milk | throws ball | ball falls through hoop |

SELECTING A REINFORCER

Educators who are concerned with increasing low rate behaviors such as task completion, participation in group activities, use of polite language, and countless others, need to find effective reinforcers. This section discusses different types of reinforcers and offers some guidelines for their selection.

Primary reinforcers   When the reinforcing stimulus has the effect of *maintaining or perpetuating life,* it is often referred to as a *primary reinforcer.* Food, water, sex, warmth, and similar stimuli are examples of primary reinforcers. A human infant quickly learns to turn his mouth to the side on which his cheek is touched when food is the consequence. On the other hand, if food is delivered when he turns his head *away* from the touch, he will rapidly learn to turn his mouth away (Siqueland & Lipsett, 1966). Primary reinforcement can be an extremely potent type of reinforcing stimulus, especially when the individual has been deprived of those reinforcers for a long time. The presentation of primary reinforcement will, with rare exception, strengthen or maintain the behavior that it follows. The hungry performing seal continues his performance as long as he receives an occasional fish. If a child receives a cookie when, and only when, he says "Please" when asking for it, the frequency of saying please will increase.

Primary reinforcement has been used by practitioners to teach language, physical, and social skills to children with severe behavioral deficits. Wolf, Risley, and Mees (1964) gave a severely disturbed (autistic) boy small bits of food to train speech acquisition and teach him to wear his glasses. Meyerson, Kerr, and Michael (1967) were able to teach a nine-year-old retarded girl to walk by reinforcing her with edible items. Risley (1968) used candy reinforcers to teach preschoolers to imitate the behaviors of their teachers, and Azrin and Lindsley (1956) reinforced children's cooperative responses with candy. Even more complex social behaviors, such as the use of syntactical sentence structure (Wheeler & Sulzer, 1970) have been facilitated with the use of edible reinforcers.

Primary reinforcement and the school "Should primary reinforcement be used in the school setting?" is a philosophical issue, not a scientific one. Initially, many people recoil from the thought of "paying" or "bribing" children to behave properly. But let us look at the behavior of most adults. No matter how much a person is dedicated to his profession, how long would he continue at his job in the absence of a contingent paycheck, which could later be exchanged for many primary reinforcers? Probably not indefinitely. "Then," one might ask, "why not limit reinforcement to the traditional reinforcers such as grades and praise, which educators have always used with relatively good effects?" The answer to this question is a simple one: traditional reinforcers do not work well for some youngsters; for others, they fail completely. The readers of this text are probably particularly interested in seeking alternative solutions for students who are not responding appropriately to traditional reinforcers.

Related to the issue of primary reinforcement in the classroom is the often repeated question, "But what about the other children? Is it fair to give something to one youngster and not to the next?" This, again, is a decision that must be made by those conducting the procedure. Often it is possible to deliver the same reinforcers to the other children noncontingently but simultaneously or to deliver them at the end of the day or experimental period.

When it is determined that a behavioral change in a specific student can be achieved most readily with primary reinforcement, it is still possible (and even desirable) to plan ahead and program the development of more usual traditional reinforcers, such as grades and praise. The process through which this is accomplished is called *conditioned reinforcement* and will be discussed in the next section.

Here we will turn to the question "Can primary reinforcers be used in the classroom?" The answer, here, a scientific one, is "Of course!" They are being used by teachers all the time. Children are given snacks, milk breaks, and lunch. They are allowed into a warm building when the weather is cold and to get drinks of water. Teachers often distribute primary reinforcers on a contingent basis, though they may not be aware of doing so. When a teacher waits until her class lines up quietly for lunch before allowing them to eat, the behavior of lining up quietly is contingently reinforced by the primary reinforcer, food. Teachers will occasionally plan a party, replete with edibles, contingent upon the students' achieving a specific goal. But, on the whole, the primary reinforcers normally available in the classroom are delivered on a noncontingent basis. How can these reinforcers be utilized more effectively? Perhaps an illustration will help: There is a student in a class who consistently turns in very sloppy papers. Because the student usually drinks his milk enthusiastically, the teacher decides to try using the morning milk break as a reinforcing contingency for improvement in neatness. She first requires that the student write one line neatly before he receives his morning milk. It is essential that the response requirement initially stipulated be easily achieved by the youngster. Otherwise the reinforcer may not be forthcoming and reinforcement may fail to occur. It is possible that the teacher might make a poor prediction and that one neat line is too much of a requirement for the student. The teacher would then have to alter the requirement to a level that the student could achieve. It is usually a good rule of thumb to start a response requirement at or below the level at which the student is currently functioning. The requirement can then be gradually increased, and the teacher runs little risk of having to withhold the reinforcer (an event which would be disturbing to many teachers).

Exercise 2.1
a. Observe a class for a full day. Make a list of the primary reinforcers that are available in the setting.
b. Select one student to observe closely. What evidence, if any, is there that one of the primary reinforcers that you noted in 2.1a would be reinforcing for him?
c. Devise a plan for utilizing that reinforcer in order that the student might achieve a simple behavioral change.

Conditioned reinforcers   As effective as primary reinforcement might be in achieving behavioral change, it is neither practical nor desirable to utilize only reinforcers like food, water, and warmth in the classroom. Would it not be ludicrous to have a college professor walking around his classes dispensing candy to his students each time one gave a proper response? Students eventually go out into the adult world, and there they will be expected to work not for sides of beef and chocolate cakes but for accomplishments, praise, points, tokens, or money. The demands of society would not be fulfilled if students were not trained to work for those "conditioned reinforcers." Besides, conditioned reinforcers can be delivered much more easily, and they often cost nothing.

What, then, is a conditioned reinforcer, and how does it acquire its reinforcing properties? A *conditioned reinforcer* is a stimulus, an object, or an event that initially was neutral but, *through frequent pairings with primary or strong conditioned reinforcers has assumed reinforcing properties.* By itself, it serves to increase or maintain the behavior of a specific individual. Conditioned reinforcers are developed as the individual interacts with his environment. Therefore, their strength varies from individual to individual, depending upon his past experiences. Early in the lives of most children, an adult smiles and says, "Good baby" while feeding him or making him comfortable. When the child does something nice, frequently he is praised or cuddled and, often enough, fed. Over time, events such as smiles, praise, affection, attention, and so forth, begin to signal all the good things in life. When these events by themselves and in the absence of the primary reinforcers begin to strengthen behavior, they have become conditioned reinforcers.

A conditioned reinforcer may also be an object. It is easy to understand how pennies, trading stamps, or box tops become conditioned reinforcers. These objects are frequently paired with the good things in life. But what happens if the objects or events that usually become conditioned reinforcers for most of us fail to be paired with primary reinforcers or other effective conditioned reinforcers? Trading stamps would have no effect on the behavior of someone who has no way to redeem them. Some children grow up without experiencing typical combinations of primary and conditioned reinforcers, such as food and verbal praise. This explains why some students apparently do "not respond" to praise, affection, smiling, or good grades.

In the event that typical conditioned reinforcers are not effective with a particular student, it may be necessary to first turn to primary reinforcement or unusual conditioned reinforcers. Those reinforcers can then be paired with the more usual school reinforcers, and over time the latter should take on reinforcing properties on their own. For example, a young child enters first grade. The teacher finds that the child fails to follow many of the routine class directions. Praising him when he occasionally engages in desired behavior appears to have little or no effect. The teacher notices, however, that hugs and pats seem to be very effective. Most teachers will agree that it is fine to hug and pat a six year old, but such treatment is not appropriate for a student who is, say, eleven or twelve. What should the teacher do with the older student? If this illustration seems familiar, it is because many teachers handle situations like this one in a most appropriate manner. They link praise, smiles, and, perhaps, good grades with the delivery of affection. Over time, the conditioned reinforcers often do begin to take hold, and physical expressions of affection can be gradually reduced.

Another example from one of the author's clinical cases may serve to clarify how a child may be trained to respond to the conditioned reinforcers found in the natural environment. A five-year-old girl was brought into the clinic. She hardly spoke a word that made sense in the context of a given situation, and she would only rarely look at or respond to gestures or verbal directions given by the clinician. On the rare occasion when the child did something that was an approximation to a desirable behavior, the behavioral specialist would say "Good" or smile. This appeared to have little effect. It was then decided that a more effective reinforcer, food, would be used to teach the child how to use appropriate language and to follow directions. Lunch was brought to the clinic, and the child was given small bites of food for any approximations to functional speech or to following directions. This was a very effective method. Before long the youngster was saying many words and responding appropriately to a wide variety of directions. At the time, the child was not attending school, but her parents and the behavioral specialist agreed that she should be prepared to go to school as soon as possible. Since all concerned knew that it would be impractical for the child's teacher to follow her around with lunch and a spoon, a program for developing conditioned reinforcers was carried out. From then on, each time food was given, it was linked with either phrases, such as "good," "fine," "yes," or "you're doing so well," or actions, such as a smile, hug, or nod. As time progressed and she learned some behaviors well, it was possible to omit food reinforcement for those behaviors. The child soon was engaging in the desired behaviors even when she was told only a word like "yes." At the end of a year of this type of treatment, the little girl entered a special education class. She has since completed her third year in that class and has been progressively learning with only the conditioned reinforcers used by the teacher.

Generalized reinforcers Many of the conditioned reinforcers that have been discussed, such as praise, affection, and money, are paired in many situations with a wide variety of primary and other strong conditioned reinforcers. When reinforcers of this type develop the property of *serving as reinforcers for a wide range of behaviors,* they are labeled *generalized reinforcers.* Again, the strength of a generalized reinforcer for an individual depends upon his own experiences, that is, his learning history. Shells or shrunken heads have strong reinforcing properties for members of certain primitive tribes because they have been paired with other material goods or prestige. For a member of our society, those items are usually pretty weak reinforcers. On the other hand, a thousand dollar bill would probably do little to alter the behavior of a member of the primitive society. Praise, affection, or even money will fail to reinforce people if those individuals have failed to learn the connection between those stimuli and the good things in life. If a student fails to respond according to expectations when he is praised or given a high grade, it may be that those are not strong generalized reinforcers for him.

There is a strong argument for making an effort to develop generalized reinforcers for all students. The argument is based on the fact that a well developed generalized reinforcer is only minimally dependent on fluctuating conditions, that is, on *deprivation,* or how long it has been since the reinforcer was last delivered, and on *satiation,* or too much of the reinforcer having been delivered at one time. For most adults, a dollar, a smile, or praise from a respected person is reinforcing, irrespective of the number of dollars, smiles, or praises in the immediate past. If all students in a class can be reinforced by praise, approval, and good grades, the teacher's task is much easier. She will not have to worry about giving too much praise or about how long a period has passed since she last praised a student. She can be fairly certain that the student will be reinforced by such generalized reinforcers. The procedure for developing a generalized reinforcer is the same as that for developing any other conditioned reinforcers. The important point is to structure the situation so that the stimulus is paired with other effective reinforcers under *many* circumstances. If the teacher wishes to have a student respond to praise, she might pair praise with the delivery of reinforcers known to be effective for a particular student, such as milk, recess, pats on the head, and so on. For instance, "You did a fine job of putting your materials away, Suzy, you may have your milk now." Or as she pats Suzy, she says, "I was so happy to see how hard you worked on your writing today. Good for you." It would be a good idea to have other significant persons in the child's life, such as parents, friends, and other relatives, use the same procedure.

Exercise 2.2

Train an animal to respond to a conditioned reinforcer: Present a specific audible sound just prior to presenting him small bits of food: Do this for several days. Be sure the animal has not eaten for several hours prior to the training sessions. Then try to train the animal to perform a simple trick, such as approaching you on command, by presenting the sound (without the food) as he approaches.

Exercise 2.3

Observe a classroom to see what conditioned and generalized reinforcers the teacher uses. Make a list of them. Are they used contingent upon student accomplishment? Ask the teacher what she does when a student accomplishes something. Based on her description, judge whether or not she appears to be "aware" of all of the reinforcing contingencies she uses? Is it necessary for the teacher to be aware of her reinforcing procedures for them to be effective?

CONDITIONED AND GENERALIZED REINFORCERS IN THE SCHOOL

Within the last few years, a good deal of research has been conducted in the area of school-related behavior change by means of reinforcement. In general, it has been found that, through a careful programming of reinforcing contingencies, it is possible to teach children a wide variety of behaviors. Included among those are some that have been extremely difficult to teach by conventional means. In the following sections a few types of reinforcement procedures are presented that may be effectively used to teach such difficult behaviors in the classroom.

Social reinforcers A social reinforcer is a conditioned reinforcer. Social reinforcers are presented by other individuals within a social context. Examples of common social reinforcers include such things as "attention" (that is, looking at, answering, nodding, and so on), smiling, and verbal statements. The literature abounds with studies demonstrating that various social reinforcers can be used to increase the occurrence of children's behaviors. For example, Johnston, Kelly, Harris & Wolf (1966) used social reinforcement to modify a preschool boy's playground equipment behavior. The boy not only started using the equipment more but so did other children on the playground. Allen, Hart, Buell, Harris & Wolf (1964) report a study of a child whose play activity was characterized by withdrawal from her peers, accompanied by a demand for teacher attention. Appropriate play was strengthened by giving her teacher attention consequent upon the child's interaction with another child. No attention was given when she played by herself or when she attempted interaction with an adult.

Several investigators (Allen, Henke, Harris, Baer & Reynolds, 1967; Kennedy & Thompson, 1967) have increased student attending behavior. For example, Kennedy & Thompson (1967) used reinforcement during counseling. The child was rewarded with candy, accompanied by verbal praise and smiles, when he maintained eye contact with the counselor for at least a minute. The student's attending behavior was reported to increase in counseling and, also, in the classroom.

Reinforcement, in the form of praise or social approval, has also been indicated to enhance students' self-esteem or self-reference statements, assessed by paper and pencil tests. For instance Ludwig and Maehr (1967) found that when approval kinds of statements were made regarding students' performance in a physical education class, the students' self-reference statements changed in a positive direction. The following list will provide the reader with a varied array of such kinds of statements. It contains a number of social reinforcers that have been used in actual behavior modification work.

Some Typical Social Reinforcers that Can Be Delivered
Immediately to Children and Adults

Children	Young adults and adults
Nod	Nod
Smile	Smile
Pat on shoulder, head, knee	Laugh (with, not at)
Wink	Wink
Signal or gesture to signify approval	Signal or gesture approval
Touch cheek	Orient glance directly towards his face
Fulfill requests	Give assistance when requested
Tickle	Comment positively on appearance
Give assistance	Pat on the back
Say	Ask individual to discuss something before group
yes	Ask individual about items of interest to him
good	Ask him to demonstrate something
fine	**Say**
very good	very good
very fine	o.k.
excellent	beautiful
marvelous	good for you
at-a-boy	_____ is excellent
good boy (girl)	yeah
right	right
that's right	I agree
correct	good idea
wonderful	fine
I like the way you do that	what a clever idea
I'm pleased with (proud of) you	you really are creative, innovative, and so on
that's good	see how you're improving
wow	that looks better than last time
oh boy	keep up the good work
very nice	you've apparently got the idea
good work	little by little we're getting there
great going	see how _____ has improved
good for you	
that's the way	
much better	
o.k.	
you're doing better	
that's perfect	

Children	Young adults and adults
that's another one you got right	mmmm
you're doing very well	you're really becoming an
look how well he (she) did	expert at this
watch what he (she) did. Do it	do you see what an effective
again	job _____ has done?
	you are very patient
	I admire your persistence,
	courage, idealism,
	enthusiasm, dedication,
	and so on

TOKEN REINFORCEMENT

Token reinforcement is another special case of conditioned reinforcement. A token is an object that can be exchanged at a later time for another reinforcing item or activity. Many token reinforcement systems are being used in schools today. For example, a teacher uses a token system when she gives points for school achievement which will raise the student's final grade. She is also using a token system when she gives gold stars that can be turned in later for a prize or a special privilege. But such token systems have often been used in a haphazard fashion. Through the use of appropriate behavioral methodology, the system can accomplish effective and efficient behavioral change. Therefore, the value of token systems in education and how they can be effectively used will be elaborated.

Token reinforcement systems have been used in a variety of settings and applied to a variety of behaviors with positive results. Formal token systems were first used in mental hospitals (Ayllon & Azrin, 1965). Tokens were given to patients for appropriate behaviors in the ward, such as mopping the floors, making their beds, and keeping themselves neat. These tokens were exchanged for privileges such as food, candy, trips to town, walks, and movies. The procedure was effective in maintaining desirable ward behaviors. This procedure has also been used with autistic children (Ferster & DeMyer, 1962) with similar results.

Similar studies have been done with such populations as mental retardates (Bijou, 1965; Orlando, Schoelkopf & Tobias, 1967); delinquents (Cohen, 1967); "problem" children in public schools (Wolf, Giles, & Hall, 1966; Orme & Purnell, 1968); and with children in regular classroom settings (Bushell, Wrobel & Michaelis, 1968; Karraker, 1968). The system has been used with these kinds of populations primarily to strengthen academic or school-related behaviors such as reading, writing, arithmetic problem solving, doing assignments and tasks at the proper time, asking questions, being quiet, and attending to lessons presented and tasks assigned.

Tokens that can be used in a school setting include check marks in a book, stars, point systems, small colored chips, or similar items that can be easily dispensed and can acquire conditioned reinforcing properties. The token is given immediately following the emission of a desired behavior, and a specified number of tokens can then be exchanged for a *back-up reinforcer*. A back-up reinforcer refers to an object or event that has already demonstrated its reinforcing effect on an individual. The child may choose an item from an assortment in a store, the place where all the back-up reinforcers are displayed, or, he may be allowed to take part in a preferred activity. Back-up reinforcers used in this manner are not influenced by momentary states of deprivation or satiation. If a store includes a wide variety of items, it is more likely that there will be an item that will be reinforcing for each child at a particular time. If the tokens are to be effective, it is essential to have items that are reinforcing to the children. Examples of back-up reinforcers that are frequently used are: candy, soda, tiny toys, personal grooming items, books, or any item that seems appropriate for the children with whom one is working. The delivery of the tokens can easily be paired with ordinary conditioned reinforcers such as grades, approval, attention, and so on. Eventually, such conditioned reinforcers should replace the tokens as the contingent reinforcers. The following list contains the forty-two back-up reinforcers used by Campbell and Sulzer (1971) in a token program designed to increase reading and spelling performance by an intermediate level, educable mentally handicapped class of children.

1. Extra swim period
2. Ten minutes for a game at milk break
3. Fifteen minutes in library
4. Film on Friday
5. Field trip (available once every two weeks)
6. Feed fish for a week
7. Choose story
8. Ride elevator
9. Turn filmstrip projector
10. Turn off lights
11. Five minutes writing on chalkboard
12. Crafts activity
13. Put blinds up or down
14. Leader in line
15. Get milk at break
16. Pass out milk at break
17. Pass out straws at break
18. Distribute milk at noon
19. Carry library books upstairs
20. Carry library books downstairs
21. Run errands by the day
22. Pull down screen
23. Erase and wash chalkboard
24. Clean erasers
25. Captain of team at recess
26. First up to bat at recess

27. Lead the pledge
28. Take care of calendar by the week
29. Sit at teacher's desk for reading
30. Sit at teacher's desk for spelling
31. File Peabody cards
32. Pass out paper
33. Pass out scissors
34. Buy extra straws
35. First in line for drink at recess
36. Help collect displays, and so on, for units
37. Time in science laboratory
38. Help custodian
39. Answer telephone by day
40. Make phone call
41. An extra cookie at break
42. Help secretary get milk for other classrooms

This next list contains some short reinforcing activities that these authors have found to be effective with young children (three to twelve years old). These can be delivered immediately or can serve as back-ups for tokens. The child should be limited to spending only a few minutes at any of these activities.

Blow up a balloon; let it go
Jump down from high place into arms of adult
Play with typewriter
Watch train go around track
Run other equipment, such as string pull toys, light switch
Listen to own voice on tape recorder
Build up, knock down blocks
Push adult around in swivel chair
Pull other person in wagon
Look out window
Play short game: ticktacktoe, easy puzzles, connect the dots
Blow bubbles: soap, gum
Read one comic book
Write on blackboard: white or colored chalk
Paint with water on blackboard
Pour water through funnel, from one container to another, and so on

Cut with scissors
Model with clay, putty
Throw ball, bean bag
Climb ladder
Turn on flash light
Sit on adult's lap
Look at projected slide
Listen to short recording
Watch short film, view master, filmstrip
Walk around in high heels
Wear funny hats
Carry purse, briefcase
Roll wheeled toy down incline
Pop balloon, paper bag, milk carton
String beads
Play with magnet
Operate jack-in-the-box
Play with squirt gun
Solve codes and other puzzles
Sing a song
Listen to a song
Perform before a group: sing a song; tell a poem or riddle; do a dance, stunt, or trick

Blow out match	**Be**
Comb and brush own or adult's hair	hugged
	tickled
Look in mirror	kissed
Play instrument: drum, whistle, triangle, piano, and so on	patted
	swung around
Use playground equipment: slide, swings, jungle gym, merry-go-round, see-saw	turned around in swivel chair
	pushed on swing, merry-go-round
Draw and color pictures	pulled in a wagon

The type of token used, the behavior which must occur to earn the tokens, the method for presenting the tokens, the items used as back-up reinforcers, the arrangement of these items, their cost, and the time for exchange are all important variables in the effectiveness of the token system. Because no two classrooms or situations are the same, the token system must be tailored to the situation. The reader may wish to refer to the discussion in Orlando et al. (1967) of classroom applications of token reinforcement for additional information. They give a detailed report on the use of a token system in classrooms for retarded children, and they include an account of how the system fits into the classroom situation and details on exchanging tokens and the management of the store.

Advantages and disadvantages of token reinforcement   The token system has several advantages. Tokens take on the properties of a generalized reinforcer. This eliminates many of the problems which are associated with temporary satiation and deprivation. The extent to which the tokens are reinforcing is dependent on the back-up items available. Tokens may be given at any time with little difficulty. Delivery of tokens can be combined with individual attention and praise at the time that the student engages in an appropriate behavior. Another advantage is that a token system can include all the students in a class without much difficulty.

But token systems have also been criticized. Some people feel that the child will tend to maintain the newly acquired behavior only as long as the tokens are contingently employed. While this is a risk, careful programming can avoid such a regression. And some evidence to the contrary has been found. In a study by Orme and Purnell (1968), students' altered behavior was transferred to another classroom in which no tokens were given. This was also found by Bushell et al. (1968) when special events were made contingent on a behavior that had been strengthened with tokens. Although tokens were no longer given, the behavior continued. O'Leary and Becker (1966) also found that reinforcement could be delayed up to four days without the loss of the strengthened behaviors.

A possible disadvantage is cost. This technique for improving behavior requires back-up reinforcers. Because of the price of these items it may be difficult to employ the system in some school settings. However, as Bushell et al. (1968) point out, "there are many school activities (recess, early dismissal, extracurricular events) which might be employed to develop and maintain higher levels of study behavior [p. 61]." The following discussion of the Premack principle will suggest some freely available alternative back-up reinforcers.

PREMACK PRINCIPLE

Premack (1959) suggested another possible reinforcer, subsequently labeled the "Premack principle." On the basis of a series of laboratory studies with both animals and humans, Premack was able to demonstrate that behaviors which a person engages in may actually be used to reinforce low frequency behaviors. This phenomenon occurs when access to the high frequency behavior is made contingent upon performance of low frequency behavior. If a child plays with a doll a great deal but does not do her spelling exercises, the teacher can make access to the doll contingent on completion of an exercise. This principle has been used with impressive effectiveness by Ayllon and Azrin (1965) with a population of hospitalized, long-term psychiatric patients. In order to engage in high frequency behaviors, such as leaving the ward, interacting socially with the staff, playing games, and making commissary purchases, the patients must have begun to perform socially useful work behaviors. Similarly, a group of nursery school children had been observed to spend considerable time running and screaming, as reported in a study by Homme, diBaca, Devine, Steinhorst, & Rickert (1963). By making running and screaming contingent upon sitting quietly, the frequency of sitting quietly increased.

For educators, the most appealing aspect of a reinforcement procedure in which the Premack principle is employed is probably the fact that potential reinforcers are already present in every classroom setting. There are always some behaviors in which students engage (even if they are sitting and "doing nothing") with greater frequency than others. All that remains is to reorganize the classroom program in such a way that access to those high frequency behaviors is made available to the student directly following his performance of the low frequency behavior that the teacher wishes to strengthen. Many students, for example, will work for extra minutes of recess.

At this point the reader may say that this procedure is not new, which is certainly the case. Parents, teachers, and behavioral specialists do make frequent use of the Premack principle. When a mother says, "You must clean up your room" (low frequency behavior), "then you may go out and play" (high frequency behavior); or a teacher schedules a ball game (high frequency behavior) contingent upon the class's completion of an assignment (low frequency behavior); or a behavioral specialist says, "After we resolve this particular difficulty, we can discuss your other concerns," they are employing the Premack principle. Premack's contribution was the fact that he studied this phenomenon empirically with careful measurement and quantification. The principle gives an objective base for a commonly practiced procedure. This is important because it carries with it the requirement that there be some *objective verification* of the fact that certain behaviors for a specific individual are indeed high or low frequency behaviors. The reinforcing activity must be selected on the basis of formal observation (that is, how often or for how long a period of time does the student spend engaged in the activity) rather than what he "seems" to enjoy doing, what the teacher or others *think* all children like to do, or even what the *student* himself reports he likes to do. Though the three latter criteria for selecting a reinforcing activity might well be synonymous with the "real" high frequency behavior, often enough they are not. Try the following exercises and see what happens.

Exercise 2.4

a. List in descending order the five things you spend the most time doing other than eating, sleeping, and working the number of hours your job requires.
b. Keep a daily record for at least a week of how much time you actually spend engaging in the activities you listed in 2.4a. List the time spent with each in descending order.
c. Compare 2.4a and 2.4b.

Exercise 2.5

Observe a specific student in a preschool or kindergarten free-play group. List the activities in which he engages, and measure the amount of time he spends in each. Without telling the teacher the results, ask her what school activities the student likes best. Ask the student the same question. Compare the results.

If you have performed Exercises 2.4 and 2.5, you should now have an array of effective reinforcing activities for yourself and for the student you observed. Suppose you found that you spend your largest block of time watching television. You could then make television watching contingent upon the performance of some lower frequency behavior, say writing a letter.

The teacher of the class you observed for Exercise 2.5 could use her student's high frequency behavior to reinforce some desired behavior that he does not emit too often. If, for instance, a student spent a great deal of time playing alone with clay but rarely played cooperative games with other children, the teacher, wanting to encourage the latter activity, might allow the student the clay only after he had played with the other children for at least a short period of time.

At times, it may be difficult to immediately dispense high frequency activities to students in a classroom. There are circumstances during which certain activities are inappropriate. Shooting a ball into a basket would be clearly inappropriate while the rest of the class is engaged in a quiet activity, such as taking a spelling test. One solution is to use tokens that can be exchanged at a later time for access to the high frequency behavior.

USING REINFORCEMENT EFFECTIVELY

By now the reader should be familiar with a wide array of reinforcers that lend themselves to classroom use: primary reinforcers (food), conditioned reinforcers (praise, attention), tokens, and access to high frequency behavior. The selection of appropriate reinforcing contingencies, however, is only part of the process. Once those contingencies have been selected, several factors need to be considered so that their effective use can be maximized. Among these factors are delay of presentation, amount or quantity of reinforcement, quality or type of reinforcer, novelty, reinforcer sampling, and scheduling.

DELAY OF REINFORCEMENT

A basic principle of behavior is that *immediate* reinforcement is more effective than delayed reinforcement (Skinner, 1938). One of the main reasons for this is discussed by Reynolds (1968):

> . . . Delayed reinforcement is not as effective as immediate reinforcement, partially because it allows the organism to emit additional behavior between the response we wish to reinforce and the actual occurrence of the reinforcer; thus, the intervening behavior is also reinforced, with the result that what is reinforced is the response followed by some other behavior rather than just the response alone [p. 29].

A teacher may decide to give a student an A on his report card because he has improved in his classroom behavior. She may fail to reinforce him in any other way for this improvement, deciding that the A alone will be rewarding enough. Now suppose that the student is misbehaving at the time that the report cards are delivered. The A might well reinforce that misbehavior. The teacher, then, must indicate to the child which of his behaviors is being reinforced. Immediate reinforcement would have helped the student make such a discrimination.

The desirability of immediate reinforcement presents a problem to many teachers who are interested in managing their classes more effectively. When a strong reinforcer is used in a large classroom setting, it is often difficult to reinforce the behavior of individual children. A teacher may decide to take her students on a field trip as a reinforcement for their having completed all of their assignments for a week. Naturally it would be impossible to deliver the trip to each student immediately contingent upon his completion of the assignment. Fortunately, there is an alternative, and that alternative, again, lies in the use of conditioned reinforcement. As individual students complete segments of their requirement, the teacher can say, "Good, I see you are getting your work finished. This way you'll be able to go on the trip Friday." If that type of reinforcer is not effective, she might try a token system. She could give a token immediately to each student as he completes each subsection of his work and require each student to have a set number of tokens to go on the trip.

There is another factor that may serve to encourage the teacher who feels it is impossible to immediately reinforce the many students in her class. The fact is, people can learn to tolerate, gradually, longer and longer reinforcement delays. Probably every one of our readers has experienced long delays in the receipt of his pay check or of a grade; yet the behavior of working or studying does not disintegrate. How do people learn to tolerate long delays of reinforcement? Through experiencing *gradually* longer and longer delays.

Most students, too, learn to accept delays in reinforcement. If this has not occurred with a particular student, he can be taught to tolerate those delays if they are programmed into the routine gradually. When a student persists in pestering a teacher to look at his work or constantly asks her to praise his accomplishments, he probably has not learned this type of tolerance for delayed reinforcement. The teacher might then set up a program to help the youngster to bridge the time gap. For a while she might try to check his work when he requests it. Eventually she could put the student off and take a look in a moment or two. After many instances with a brief delay, she could gradually lengthen the delay interval. (This type of procedure closely approximates a *shaping* procedure, which will be discussed in Chapter 4.)

Exercise 2.6

Observe a specific student in a class. Try to find three occasions during which reinforcement was delivered immediately and three occasions when it was delayed. How did the student react to the immediate and to the delayed reinforcement? What conclusions can you draw from your observations?

Exercise 2.7

Visit a class of students at the preschool or primary level.

a. Give one illustration of the way in which the teacher used conditioned reinforcement to bridge the gap in a delayed reinforcement situation.

b. Describe an episode in which the teacher apparently tried to assist a student to accept a delay in reinforcement.

AMOUNT OF REINFORCEMENT

The decision about *how much* reinforcement to deliver depends on a number of factors: the type of reinforcer used (primary or conditioned), the deprivation conditions, and empirical data. If a primary reinforcer is selected, deprivation (the length of time the student has been deprived of the reinforcer), plays an important part. If the student has not eaten for several hours, a small amount of food may be reinforcing. Too much will satiate him quickly, and food will temporarily lose its reinforcing effectiveness. In a procedure referred to earlier, very small bites of food were given to the children who were learning to speak. If too much food were given all at once, the children would gradually stop working.

With conditioned reinforcers, deprivation and satiation play a smaller role. A smile or saying "good boy" may be effective even though the child has received several such reinforcers in the recent past. However, school personnel need to be aware that it is possible for a student to become satiated by conditioned reinforcers. Sulzer, Mayer, and Cody (1968) have illustrated the possibility of such an occurrence with the following example:

> . . . suppose praise from the teacher is reinforcing to Jim. Jim does not successfully complete his math assignments but does well on all of his other subjects. The counselor observes that Jim's teacher gives him lavish praise for the well done subject matter. The counselor might conclude that Jim is satiated. He would then suggest to the teacher that she stop, or reduce, the amount of praise she gives Jim for his performances on subject matter other than math, and that the praise given to math assignments be contingent on their successful completion. Hopefully, Jim would do better in math in order to receive the teacher's praise [p. 45].

Conditioned reinforcers may also be too mild (a slight nod or a weak smile) or too strong (vigorous nodding or an ear-to-ear grin). People who socially overreinforce are referred to as "gushy" or "saccharine," and the social reinforcers that they deliver lose much of their value.

As previously mentioned, generalized reinforcers are the least affected by satiation conditions. No matter how much money an individual has, he will usually be reinforced by receiving more. The same is true of tokens as long as they can be exchanged for items or activities that are reinforcing to the individual. By now it should be apparent that there is no simple formula for determining what quantity of reinforcement to deliver. The final judgment must be made on the basis of empirical data.

Exercise 2.8

What quantity of reinforcement increases or maintains a desired behavior over time? Try to get your pet to stay at your side by reinforcing him with pieces of food. What is the minimum amount that he will accept in order to remain? How many pieces of food did he eat before he stopped eating and walked away (satiation)?

QUALITY OR TYPE OF REINFORCER

Many different types of reinforcers have already been described. In order to select an appropriate reinforcer, it is a good idea to try it out first on a behavior other than the terminal goal behavior. If a student works hard at his spelling for teacher approval, it is likely he will also work hard at arithmetic for the same reinforcer. On the other hand, if praise has only a minor effect on the student's spelling performance and spelling is an activity he enjoys, it is less likely that praise will be effective with a nonpreferred activity, and it would be better to seek out alternatives.

Exercise 2.9

Watch a student in one of the classes that you have been observing. Identify a reinforcer that appears to be effective for that student. Support your finding with evidence. (You should be able to show that the reinforcer increases or maintains a specific behavior).

It has already been mentioned that primary reinforcers vary in effectiveness according to deprivation and satiation conditions. In selecting a reinforcer it is a good idea to keep this in mind. Often one does not have sufficient control of the environment to maintain deprivation or avoid satiation conditions. In such cases, it is better to select a strong conditioned or generalized reinforcer, which is not as vulnerable to those fluctuations.

NOVELTY

"Other things being equal, organisms will often prefer to put themselves in novel situations (Millenson, 1967, p. 397)." This conclusion was based on the results of a number of studies that indicated that an organism would work for the opportunity to experience novel stimuli. Teachers often learn to make use of this phenomenon. When they, for instance, say something like, "As soon as you finish your assignment, I have a surprise for you," they note that the students tend to work more efficiently. Elementary school teachers often program their class activities so that there is variation from one to the next: first reading, then gym, math problems, art, and so on. In so doing, they are utilizing the reinforcing effects of novelty.

Exercise 2.10

Observe a class for a day.
a. Note the instances in which novelty acts as a reinforcer.
b. List the order of class activities. Suggest an alternative program, using the same activities but also arranging to maximize novel situations.

REINFORCER SAMPLING

Novel reinforcers do generally tend to be very effective, sometimes an individual reacts emotionally to new, potentially reinforcing situations. And such responses may interfere with the reinforcing capabilities of the stimulus. People may be "scared stiff" the first time they get up on water skiis or ride a roller coaster or perform before an audience. Yet we all are acquainted with persons for whom these events have become very reinforcing. Those individuals have undoubtedly adapted to the situation; the event is no longer so frightening because they have had an opportunity to experience it sufficiently often.

Sometimes the individual has not had experience with an object or an event and therefore its reinforcing properties are unknown to him. Holz, Azrin, and Ayllon (1963) found that when mental hospital patients were persuaded to try reinforcers, such as candy, they would subsequently work to acquire those reinforcers. We have observed that children were much more apt to "purchase" the privilege of watching a film if they were exposed to a portion of the film than if they were not shown anything. For these reasons Ayllon and Azrin, in their book *The Token Economy* (1968), suggest a reinforcer sampling rule: "Before using an event or stimulus as a reinforcer, require sampling of the reinforcer in the situation in which it is to be used [p. 91]."

Many teachers make it a practice to first display a new text, start a fascinating story, teach a new game, organize new projects, and otherwise expose their students to novel events or objects. Once the students begin to apparently enjoy the experience, the teacher then requires the performance of another task that will allow access to the now effective reinforcer: "As soon as we finish our spelling test, we will use the remainder of the period to play the new game we played yesterday."

Exercise 2.11

Tell how you might use the reinforcer sampling rule to increase the reinforcing effectiveness of:

a. a game

b. an arts and crafts project

c. a science experiment

d. any other (you specify)

Exercise 2.12

Cite an example of reinforcer sampling used by a teacher in one of your classroom observations.

SCHEDULING

Scheduling of reinforcement refers to the ". . . rule followed by the environment . . . in determining which among the many occurrences of a response will be reinforced [Reynolds, 1968, p. 60]." If a student is called on *every* time he raises his hand, his hand raising is being continuously reinforced. Hand raising for that student is on a *continuous reinforcement schedule* (CRF). More than likely, however, a student is only occasionally called upon when he raises his hand. In that case, hand raising is on an *intermittent reinforcement schedule.*

There are many different schedules of reinforcement, and each has different properties or effects. Different schedules may be suited to procedures designed to shape, increase, maintain, or decrease behavior. It is primarily with the issue of increasing behavior that the present discussion is concerned. The effects of scheduling on other behavioral aspects will be considered in detail in Part III.

When the teacher desires to increase behavior, a very rich or continuous schedule of reinforcement will most effectively serve the purpose. This means, for example, that if a teacher is trying to teach her students a new classroom routine, the more often she reinforces her students, the better. The teacher may want to teach her students how to hold a class election. As part of the procedure, she may want to increase those behaviors required by parliamentary procedure, for instance, awaiting recognition from the chair before speaking. Each time the students show restraint (that is, wait to be recognized) she might praise them. When the behavior is pretty well established through continuous reinforcement, the frequency of reinforcement could be reduced. The fact that reinforcement frequency can be reduced once a behavior is fairly well learned is fortunate. It is physically impossible for a teacher to reinforce every occurrence of every desired behavior. Indeed, as we shall find later on, continuous reinforcement is not a desirable method for maintaining well-learned behaviors. It serves the purposes of behavior management best when, and only when, a behavior is to be increased.

SUMMARY

Many of the problems that face school personnel in the management of student behaviors can be handled by using procedures designed to increase the occurrence of already existing behaviors. One very useful strengthening procedure is reinforcement. In this chapter several types of reinforcers were described, including primary, conditioned, and generalized reinforcers. Illustrations of reinforcement procedures were presented. These included social reinforcement, token reinforcement, and the use of the Premack principle. It was also suggested that reinforcement could be used more effectively by presenting it as quickly and as often as possible following the desired behavior.

REFERENCES

Allen, K. E., Hart, B. M., Buell, J. S., Harris, F. R., & Wolf, M. M. Effects of social reinforcement on isolate behavior of a nursery school child. *Child Development,* 1964, **35,** 511–518.

Allen, K. E., Henke, L. B., Harris, F. R., Baer, D. M., & Reynolds, N. J. Control of hyperactivity by social reinforcement of attending behavior. *Journal of Educational Psychology,* 1967, **58,** 231–237.

Ayllon, T., & Azrin, N. H. The measurement and reinforcement of behavior of psychotics. *Journal of the Experimental Analysis of Behavior,* 1965, **8,** 357–383.

Ayllon, T., & Azrin, N. H. *The token economy.* New York: Appleton-Century-Crofts, 1968.

Azrin, N. H., & Lindsley, O. R. The reinforcement of cooperation between children. *Journal of Abnormal and Social Psychology,* 1956, **52,** 100–102.

Bijou, S. W. Application of experimental analysis of behavior principles in teaching academic tool subjects to retarded children. Paper presented at Kansas Symposium, Lawrence, Kansas, 1965, U.S. Public Health Service, NIMH, MH-01366 and MH-02232.

Bushell, D., Wrobel, P., & Michaelis, M. Applying "group" contingencies to the classroom study behavior of pre-school children. *Journal of Applied Behavior Analysis,* 1968, **1,** 55–61.

Campbell, A., & Sulzer, B. Naturally available reinforcers as motivators towards reading and spelling achievement by educable mentally handicapped students. Paper presented at the American Educational Research Association meeting, New York, February 1971.

Catania, A. C. *Contemporary research in operant behavior.* Glenview, Ill.: Scott, Foresman, 1968.

Cohen, H. L. Motivationally orientated designs for an ecology of learning. Paper presented at the American Educational Research Association Symposium on Application of Reinforcement Principles to Education, New York, February, 1967.

Ferster, C. B., & DeMeyer, M. A method for the experimental analysis of the behavior of autistic children. *American Journal of Orthopsychiatry,* 1962, **32,** 89–98.

Holz, W. C., Azrin, N. H., & Ayllon, T. Elimination of behavior of mental patients by response produce extinction. *Journal of the Experimental Analysis of Behavior,* 1963, **6,** 407–412.

Homme, L. E., diBaca, P. C., Devine, J. V., Steinhorst, R., & Rickert, E. J. Use of the Premack principle in controlling the behavior of nursery school children. *Journal of the Experimental Analysis of Behavior,* 1963, **6,** 544.

Johnston, M. K., Kelley, C. S., Harris, F. R., & Wolf, M. M. An application of reinforcement principles to development of motor skills of a young child. *Child Development,* 1966, **37,** 379–387.

Karraker, R. J. Token reinforcement systems in regular public school classrooms. Paper presented at the American Educational Research Association annual meeting, Chicago, February 1968.

Kennedy, D. A., & Thompson, I. Use of reinforcement technique with a first grade boy. *The Personnel and Guidance Journal,* 1967, **46,** 366–370.

Ludwig, P. J., & Maehr, M. L. Changes in self concepts in stated behavioral preferences. *Child Development,* 1967, **38,** 453–469.

Meyerson, L., Kerr, N., & Michael, J. L. Behavior modification in rehabilitation. In S. W. Bijou & D. M. Baer (Eds.), *Child Development Readings in Experimental Analysis.* New York: Appleton-Century- Crofts, 1967.

Millenson, J. R. *Principles of behavior analysis.* New York: Macmillan, 1967.

O'Leary, K. D., & Becker, W. C. Behavior modification of an adjustment class: A token reinforcement program. *Exceptional Children,* 1967, **33,** 637–642.

Orlando, R., Schoelkopf, A., & Tobias, L. Tokens as reinforcers—Classroom applications by teachers of the retarded. *IMRID Papers and Reports,* Vol. IV, No. 14. Nashville: George Peabody College, Institute on Mental Retardation and Intellectual Development, 1967.

Orme, M. E. J., & Purnell, R. F. Behavior modification and transfer in an out-of-control classroom. Paper presented at the American Educational Research Association meeting, Chicago, February 1968.

Premack, D. Toward empirical behavior laws: I. Positive reinforcement. *Psychological Review,* 1959, **66,** 219–233.

Reynolds, G. S. *A primer of operant conditioning.* Glenview, Ill.: Scott, Foresman, 1968.

Risley, T. Learning and lollipops. *Psychology Today,* 1968, **1,** 28–31, 62–65.

Siqueland, E. R., & Lipsitt, L. P. Conditioned head-turning in human newborns. *Journal of Experimental Child Psychology,* 1966, **3,** 356–376.

Skinner, B. F. *The behavior of organisms.* New York: Appleton-Century-Crofts, 1938.

Sulzer, B., Mayer, G. R., & Cody, J. J. Assisting teachers with managing classroom behavioral problems. *Elementary School Guidance and Counseling,* 1968, **3,** 40–48.

Wheeler, A., & Sulzer, B. Operant training and generalization of a verbal response form in a speech deficient child. *Journal of Applied Behavioral Analysis,* 1970, **3,** 139–147.

Wolf, M. M., Giles, D. K., & Hall, V. R. Experiments with token reinforcement in a remedial classroom. *Behavior Research and Therapy,* 1968, **6,** 305–312.

Wolf, M. M., Risley, T. R., & Mees, H. L. Application of operant conditioning procedures to the behavior problems of an autistic child. *Behavior Research and Therapy,* 1964, **1,** 305–312.

3 NEGATIVE REINFORCEMENT AND OTHER PROCEDURES FOR INCREASING BEHAVIOR

Objectives

Using examples not described in this chapter, you should be able to

1. Define and offer school illustrations for each of the following terms:
   a. negative reinforcement
   b. aversive stimulus
   c. interfering conditions
   d. generalization
   e. imitation
   f. occasion
   g. stimulus change
   h. discriminative stimulus
2. List the major variables that facilitate imitative behavior and describe them in behavioral terms; give school examples of how each variable might be applied to facilitate imitation.
3. Select illustrative stimuli and tell how you would go about developing them as discriminative stimuli that reliably occasion school related behaviors.
4. Select specific student behaviors and describe how you would increase the occurrence of each by combining several behavioral procedures.

Positive reinforcement, one procedure for increasing the occurrence of a behavior that already exists in an individual's repertoire, has been discussed in Chapter 2. We will now look at some alternative procedures that will accomplish the same end: negative reinforcement, a different type of response contingent procedure, and several other procedures involving alterations in other environmental conditions—the reduction or removal of conditions that interfere with desirable classroom behaviors, generalization, stimulus change, and providing a model.

NEGATIVE REINFORCEMENT

NEGATIVE REINFORCEMENT DEFINED

Reinforcement is a procedure that *serves to maintain or increase a behavior.* This is true whether the process is labeled "positive" or "negative." Positive reinforcement as it was presented in Chapter 2 is the *presentation* of a stimulus that has the function of increasing or maintaining the dependent behavior. If a child says, "Milk, please" and receives milk, the milk is a *positive reinforcer* if the child's rate of saying please increases. With *negative reinforcement,* the increase is a function of the *removal* of a stimulus. Therefore, *a behavior or response has been negatively reinforced if it increases or maintains due to the contingent removal or reduction of a stimulus.* If the removal of a stimulus has the effect of increasing or maintaining a behavior, that stimulus is referred to as an *aversive stimulus.* Like positive reinforcement, negative reinforcement is defined solely by its effect upon behavior.

There are many everyday situations in which negative reinforcement occurs in our lives. We are reinforced when we move out of the heat of the noonday sun; close a window to shut off a draft; respond to a child to stop his crying; take off our shoes when they pinch our feet, and kindle a fire to escape the cold. Negative reinforcement is a universal phenomenon.

A classroom example should help to further illustrate what is meant by negative reinforcement. Suppose the teacher constantly scolds Jim. These stimuli are aversive to him. If Jim leaves class for a drink of water or stays at home, that terminates the aversive stimuli and negatively reinforces his behavior. Whether or not this is the desired behavior, his leaving class and staying home will increase in frequency. If Jim continues to be negatively reinforced for escaping the classroom, he may become a school dropout. On the other hand, Jim may discover that if he yells back at his teacher when she scolds him, she will stop scolding. Under such conditions, Jim's yelling behavior towards the teacher would increase because it was negatively reinforced, (that is, yelling removes or stops the aversive scolding). Here is an illustration of the negative reinforcement operation:

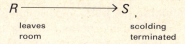

$$R \longrightarrow S \; ,$$

leaves room

scolding terminated

Negative reinforcement compared with other procedures In the language of the layman, the term "negative reinforcement" is often confused with other procedures. But, as we shall see in subsequent chapters, behavioral analysis gives each procedure its own specific operational definition. It would probably be helpful for the reader to be alerted to the differences in those various operations. For instance, negative reinforcement involves the *removal* of an aversive stimulus; the *punishment* procedure (Chapter 10) consists of the *presentation* of an aversive stimulus. The timeout and response cost procedures (Chapter 9) consist of the *removal* of a positive stimulus contingent upon a response. The following diagram should help the reader to make this distinction. For the time being, however, he should concentrate upon clarifying the negative reinforcement operation and distinguishing it from any other operation.

	Positive stimulus	Aversive stimulus
Contingent presentation	positive reinforcement	punishment
Contingent removal	timeout and response cost	negative reinforcement

NEGATIVE REINFORCEMENT IN THE SCHOOL

If negative reinforcement is an effective method for increasing a behavior, should it be used in the classroom? Let us again look at the procedure. To use negative reinforcement, an *aversive* stimulus must be present. Then it is possible to reinforce a behavior by removing the aversive stimulus contingent upon the emission of the behavior. However, as will be seen in more detail in Chapter 10, undesirable side effects are likely to occur with the use of aversive stimuli (Azrin & Holz, 1966). In addition to their role in the reinforcement process, aversive stimuli often produce responses that allow the individual to escape the environment in which the stimuli occur, such as when Jim stays away from school. Beside escape and avoidance, another undesirable side effect of using aversive stimuli is aggression. A common reaction when someone is physically hurt, ridiculed, or teased is anger, sometimes to the point of overt aggression. This disrupts social relationships and also may produce competing responses that interfere with classroom learning. A youngster who is clenching his fists, experiencing physical responses (such as perspiration and increased pulse rate), or actually fighting will not be in the best shape to profit from the teacher's instruction at that moment.

Some circumstances may, however, justify the use of negative reinforcement. For example, there are many people who will refuse to do something even though the attempt might result in financial gain, increased prestige, or other forms of strong positive reinforcement. Yet they might make the effort if it would stop the ridicule by their friends. A fifty cent piece may not entice a man to plunge into a cold ocean, get up on a pair of skiis, ride a horse, stand on the rim of a cliff, or walk into the depths of a cave, while the ridicule by his friends may be sufficiently aversive to make him want to terminate it and therefore take the "plunge." There are times when some very strong reinforcing contingencies are needed to assist a student over a hurdle, to try something new, or to make an extra effort to continue to make progress. Occasionally available positive reinforcers may not be sufficient to motivate the student to do something that is very difficult for him, and negative reinforcement may be the only answer.

In general, then, negative reinforcement is a less desirable means of strengthening a weak behavior, not because it does not work, but because its use may have undesirable side effects. Negative reinforcement should be saved for situations where no reasonable positive alternatives are available.

Exercise 3.1

Try to find an episode in your class observations in which negative reinforcement has been used. What was the aversive stimulus? How did you know that the termination of the stimulus was reinforcing? Did you notice any reactions on the part of the student or others in the class that might suggest that the reinforcement was accompanied by any undesirable side effects?

OTHER PROCEDURES FOR INCREASING BEHAVIOR

Positive and negative reinforcement are procedures that serve to strengthen, or increase, the likelihood that a behavior will be emitted in the future. The operation in both cases is performed following the emission of the behavior. There are several procedures, however, that involve environmental changes *prior to* the emission of the behavior. Such changes can be used by school personnel for purposes of increasing the likelihood that a particular response will occur. Those to be discussed here include first, removing interfering conditions; then, generalization training; stimulus change; and, finally, providing a model.

REMOVING INTERFERING CONDITIONS

Situations occasionally occur that prevent or interfere with desired behavior. Sometimes the desired behavior fails to occur even though the behavior is present in the individual's repertoire and the environment has reinforcers ready for it. Teachers often encounter a situation like this: A question is asked of the students in the class. The teacher is fairly certain that a particular student is able to respond to the question correctly (he has answered similar questions in the past). Yet the student fails to volunteer the response. Were the teacher able to discover the conditions that interfered with the student's responding and remove them, the student might be more likely to respond. There are many possible interfering conditions in this situation. The response has been punished in the past; the situation suggests that the response will be followed by the delivery of aversive stimuli; the stimulus conditions, such as a jet plane flying by, produce incompatible responses, such as looking out the window.

It is possible, for instance, that the student was ridiculed by his friends for being a know-it-all. The task for the teacher would be to get rid of the ridiculing, which is an aversive stimulus for the student. It is also possible that, though the student himself has never been ridiculed for giving a correct response, he has observed others being ridiculed for that behavior. The stimulus situation might then suggest that he, too, will be putting himself in jeopardy by offering the correct answer. Again, a procedure designed to eliminate the ridiculing behavior would be appropriate. On the other hand, the student may fail to respond to the question because he is engaging in behaviors that are incompatible with giving the answer. For instance, something might be going on which serves to distract him: another student asking him a question or signaling, people entering the room, something happening outside the window. In that case, an obvious approach would be to remove the distracting stimuli. Chapters 8–12 (Part IV) will emphasize procedures designed to reduce or eliminate undesirable behaviors, including those that interfere with desirable classroom behavior.

Exercise 3.2

During one of your classroom observations, try to identify a student behavior that you believe is not being emitted due to interfering conditions. Support your belief that the behavior is present in the repertoire of the student by offering some data as evidence. Try to isolate the conditions that are interfering with the response.

GENERALIZATION TRAINING

Generalization defined   Generalization is a process through which *a behavior learned or strengthened in one stimulus situation tends to occur in other stimulus situations.* When a child stops what he is doing at the word "no" in a new situation, he may be generalizing a response he learned at home. A two year old who calls all quadrupeds "doggies" is also generalizing. Similarly, adults may attempt to kill harmless or even beneficial spiders and snakes because they are generalizing from the harmful species.

Generalization is a process that teachers and behavioral specialists assume will occur, though this does not always happen. Indeed, effective education requires that behaviors learned in the classroom generalize to numerous situations in and out of the classroom. The student is expected to apply the skills acquired in reading lessons to handling materials in social studies and science as well as to reading menus, application forms, novels, and rest room door signs.

A basic, but not always valid, assumption implicit in the school counseling and guidance process is that behavior learned in the guidance office will generalize or transfer to the classroom and other settings. One study (Kennedy & Thompson, 1967), for example, reported that increased attending behavior learned in counseling by a first grade child did generalize to classroom subject matter. The time he spent attending during arithmetic lessons increased by 14 percent even though contingencies were not manipulated during arithmetic class.

Generalization can lead to appropriate or inappropriate behaviors. The child who learned to "attend" in the guidance office appropriately generalized this behavior to the classroom. Teachers who have used positive reinforcement effectively with one student and then apply it to others are generalizing appropriately too. However, the child who calls all quadrupeds "doggies" or a geometry student who calls all rectangles "squares" is generalizing inappropriately, and it will be necessary for them to learn to discriminate among different quadrupeds or rectangles. If, through generalization, the likelihood that a particular response will occur is increased, school personnel might profit by learning how to train generalizations effectively.

Effective generalization training *Emphasize common elements.* Situations arise in which the teacher or behavioral specialist wants a student to generalize a behavior from one situation to another; that is, given the conditions (stimuli) similar to those under which the student *first* acquired a response, he will be likely to emit the same acquired response. When it is possible to identify the circumstances (stimuli) under which he first emitted the response, it is naturally, easier to teach him to generalize. Once those stimuli have been identified, many of them can be introduced into the new situation. The two situations will then share many common elements.

Teachers who are effective make frequent use of methods for facilitating generalization training, though they may not be aware of doing so. This occurs when they teach academic subjects as well as social and other behaviors. This type of teaching goes on all the time. For example, when a teacher says:

You know the word *ball*.
Now we are going to learn the word *fall*.
Notice the *a-l-l* at the end of the word *ball*.
It says *all*.
The word *fall* also ends in *all,* and it is pronounced *f-all*.
Now, how do you pronounce *t-a-l-l?*

She is selecting the common elements among the words "ball," "fall," and "tall." The common elements are emphasized, and that tends to facilitate learning.

Here is another illustration of the use of generalization training in the schools. The first time a teacher takes her young students into a library she wants to emphasize the need to be especially quiet. She might lower her own voice to a whisper and says:

You know how quiet you have to be when you go to a religious service or are in a movie theater? You have to be quiet because everyone wants to listen without being disturbed. People in the library want to read without being disturbed, so try to be quiet, like you are when you go to services or to the movies.

The teacher is emphasizing the common elements among religious services, movie performances, and the library. By lowering her voice she is adding another stimulus element common to the other places already familiar to the children.

A teacher may want a student, Jim, to be friendly with his classmate Mike; to talk to and smile at him. She observes that Jim is already friendly with Ron. She notes several similar characteristics between Ron and Mike. Deciding to use generalization training in an attempt to achieve the goal, she points out to Jim the characteristics that are similar between Ron and Mike. She hopes that Jim might then be more likely to start responding to Mike as he does to Ron.

Such episodes show how teachers and behavioral specialists can facilitate the generalization of student behaviors by emphasizing the existing similarities of two situations. In the counseling illustration given above (Kennedy & Thompson, 1967), the behavioral specialist might have indicated to his client that he was now "attending" better to the counselor in that setting, therefore, he should be able to do the same with other adults in the classroom. It would seem, however, that such generalization to the classroom from a counseling setting would be even more likely to occur if *group* counseling, rather than *individual* counseling, were used as a transition. A group counseling situation bears a greater resemblance to the child's classroom than the individual counseling setting does.

Exercise 3.3

Design a simple instructional program to teach a spelling word or a word in a foreign language or the rules of a game by using generalization training. Be sure to have at least two elements common to both the material already learned and the new material.

Exercise 3.4

A new teacher is preparing her class for a trip. Give an example of how she might use generalization training.

Exercise 3.5

A speech teacher taught a student to pronounce *r*'s correctly in the corrective speech session. The student continued to pronounce *r*'s as *w*'s in his class. Can you account for the failure of the proper pronunciation to generalize to the classroom. Suggest some methods to facilitate the generalization.

Exercise 3.6

A student learned to stop speaking angrily to his guidance counselor, but continued to speak angrily to his classroom teacher. Can you account for the failure of the change to generalize? Suggest some methods for facilitating that generalization.

STIMULUS CHANGE

Stimulus change defined All behaviors occur in the presence of complex set of stimuli. The student engaging in specific school behaviors does so in the presence of the physical surroundings of the room, of his teacher and the things she does and says, and of his peers and what they do and say. All of these objects and events are stimuli that *may* have an effect upon the subsequent behavior of the student. When reinforcement takes place in the presence of a set of such stimuli, the stimuli themselves, over time, may tend to *occasion* the behavior. These stimuli do not necessarily *elicit* responses in the sense that a bright light *elicits* a pupilary contraction. They merely indicate to the individual that the occasion is right for reinforcement, making him more likely to respond. They function, in a sense, as promises: "All the students who complete their work books by the end of the month will receive A's," is a verbal stimulus that informs the student that completing the workbook will be reinforced.

Behavioral analysts have adopted the term "occasion" to describe the effect these stimuli have on the response. Therefore "occasion" will be used in this fashion throughout the remainder of the text. When a stimulus takes on this "occasioning" function, it is referred to as a *discriminative stimulus* (Holland & Skinner, 1961): the individual has *discriminated* that under certain specific circumstances, it is likely that engaging in a certain behavior will be followed by reinforcement. S^D is a commonly used symbol for discriminative stimulus that we will occasionally use hereafter in place of that term.

A *smiling* teacher says, "All right, children, line up," possibly providing as S^D (discriminative stimulus) for the students to respond by casually grouping themselves near the door. These students have learned in the past that the two stimuli—the smile and the statement—are paired with reinforcement, they are allowed to leave the room. On the other hand, the same statement paired with a frown may occasion a different response from the students, such as lining up in a precise line, because they have learned that this combination of stimuli—the frown and the statement—has been followed by reinforcement only when they behaved in that manner. By observing that a specific behavior usually occurs in the presence of a set of discriminative stimuli, it becomes possible to rapidly increase the occurrence of the behavior by presenting such S^D's. *When an S^D is presented in order to set the occasion for a particular behavior, the operation is called* **stimulus change.**

Stimulus change in the classroom   Stimulus change is the procedure used by teachers and behavioral specialists when they alter verbal directions, change the *decor* or arrangements of the room, move a student into a different class, or provide different instructional materials. For instance, Dan is observed to perform poorly on exams that are written on the blackboard when he is seated near the rear of the room. However, when nearer the blackboard, he performs well on the exams. Perhaps he had difficulty seeing the board from the back of the room or, perhaps, there are too many distractions for him in that location. In any event, changing the stimulus, the room location, by having Dan sit near the front of the room would lead to an increase in his exam performance. It would, of course, also be advisable for him to have his eyes checked by a specialist. Obviously, a major drawback of such a procedure is that the permanence of the behavioral change is relative to the duration of the altered stimulus conditions. Place Dan near the rear of the room again and his performance on such exams would likely decline.

Using stimulus change effectively   Because of the fact that various stimuli become discriminative stimuli as a function of the learning history of each individual, the selection of stimuli appropriate to the procedure may need to be selected individually. Take a situation in which many students begin to work at the signal "time to work," but several students fail to do so. Perhaps getting to work at the signal has not yielded those students sufficient opportunity for reinforcement in the past. The task of the teacher or behavioral specialist would then be to observe each of those children to determine which set of stimuli do tend to occasion the desired behavior. For one student this may be a loud command, for another it may be a softly spoken personal request, while for a third it may be isolation in an area in which distractions are minimized. Efficient use of a stimulus change procedure, therefore, requires objective observation of the individual so that appropriate S^D's may be selected.

Developing discriminative stimuli   Sometimes a teacher may be unwilling to use S^D's known to effectively occasion the desired behaviors for a particular student. Though a sharp command may cause a student to start working, the teacher may decide that she does not want to shout at that student every time she wants him to begin his work. She may decide that it would be worth making an effort to have the student start working in response to the same signal she uses for the other students. How can she do this? Going back to our definition of discriminative stimuli, it will be recalled that S^D's develop from stimuli that have been present during a series of reinforced responses. The task of the teacher is to provide the student with activities for which he will probably receive reinforcement. She can plan instructional assignments that the student had appeared to enjoy in the past. By pairing the signal "time to work" with the opportunity for the student to respond and be reinforced often enough, the signal should begin to take on discriminative properties. The teacher could then begin gradually to bring in short portions of the regular class assignment. As long as the student continues to receive sufficient reinforcement, the S^D should remain effective. Even though, the work may be harder for the student and he may not be as successful with his assignment, the teacher can supplement the intrinsic reinforcement of success with comments such as "Good," "I see you're trying hard," or "Even with this harder work, you're doing well." The development of an S^D is diagrammed below:

$$\begin{bmatrix} S_{\text{"time to work"}} \\ R_{\text{works}} \longrightarrow S^+_{\text{praise}} \end{bmatrix} \xrightarrow{\text{over time}} \begin{bmatrix} S^D_{\substack{\text{"time to} \\ \text{work"}}} \longrightarrow R_{\text{works}} \end{bmatrix}$$

(in the presence of "time to work," the student works and the teacher praises him)

(the instruction develops into an S^D)

Combining stimulus change with other procedures   Stimulus change used by itself can facilitate only a temporary increase in existing behavior. But, combining it with other procedures may yield long lasting effects. In the previous section it was suggested that stimulus change could be combined with a reinforcement procedure in the development of S^D. With a slightly different method, it is possible to combine stimulus change with reinforcement so that the temporarily occasioned weak behavior may be strengthened. First the weak behavior can be occasioned by changing the stimulus conditions. Once the behavior is emitted, it is then possible to strengthen it by presenting contingent reinforcement. Returning to the illustration used above, suppose the teacher occasioned the behavior of starting to work by speaking sharply to a student. Once the student started to work, she then reinforced this behavior by saying, "Good. I like the way you started to work so quickly." This method, used over many trials, should gradually strengthen the work behavior, and it will be possible to gradually drop out the discriminative stimulus of the sharp tone of voice.

To summarize, stimulus change is a procedure in which an S^D occasions a fairly rapid response. In so doing, it may increase the frequency with which an existing behavior is emitted. Though the increase only occurs while the altered stimulus conditions remain in effect, it may provide an opportunity to utilize other, more durable strengthening procedures.

Exercise 3.7
List five illustrations of stimulus change used by the teacher you have been observing.

Exercise 3.8
Note an occasion when the teacher gives a direction to her class. Do all the students respond in the same way to the verbal stimulus? Was the direction a discriminative stimulus for all of the students? Support your conclusion.

Exercise 3.9
Try to watch a class or a coaching session in which the students are being instructed to respond to a particular signal. Describe the procedure used by the teacher or coach to train the students to respond to the signal.

PROVIDING A MODEL

Children learn to imitate (match or duplicate) the behaviors of adults and other children early in life. The first time a child responds to a person's smile with a smile or the wave of a hand with a wave of his hand, he is usually given profuse reinforcement. He is hugged, praised, and cooed at. As he continues to imitate words, gestures, songs, and expressions, reinforcement is received from the environment. As time progresses, most children learn to imitate very effectively. Sometimes, of course, they learn to imitate undesirable behaviors, such as the series of four-letter words Dad utters when he hits his thumb with a hammer.

Because people learn early in life to imitate effectively, providing a model becomes a powerful means not only for increasing the occurrence of behaviors already within the repertoire of the individual but also for establishing new behaviors and reducing undesirable ones (Bandura & Walters, 1963; Bandura, 1968). In this section, the emphasis will be on imitation as a means of increasing the likelihood that a specific response will occur. The role of imitation in teaching new behaviors and in reducing undesirable ones, will be discussed in Chapters 4 and 11, respectively.

Exposure to the behavior of a model can occasion an individual's previously learned behaviors in much the same way that other S^D's do. But in the case of imitation, the responses match or resemble those exhibited by the model. The following illustrations should help to clarify how this may occur: An individual who has "forgotten" the idioms and accents of his birthplace, finds upon returning home that his original speech and pronunciation patterns quickly come back to him. Simply hearing the language is sufficient, while it would probably take a stranger a much longer time to acquire the same speech patterns. Teachers often find that when their students return from a vacation, they appear to have forgotten much of what they previously learned. However, a set of imitative prompts (for example, "Let's review the 8 table: 8, 16 . . .") quickly returns the students to their prior level of performance. Observing others emit the previously learned behaviors is a cue for their own emission of such behaviors.

Using modeling effectively Since providing a behavioral model helps to set the occasion for the emission of some previously learned behaviors, it would be advantageous to consider a few variables that can facilitate this procedure. Reinforcement factors, the characteristics of the model, and combined use with other procedures all contribute to the effectiveness of imitation.

Reinforcement of imitative behavior Imitative behavior, as has been previously indicated, is greatly influenced by reinforcement. When imitative behavior is not reinforced, imitation will not occur (DeRath, 1964; Kanareff & Lanzetta, 1960). The likelihood that imitative behavior will occur increases as the probability of receiving reinforcement increases (Lanzetta & Kanareff, 1959).

Beside increasing the likelihood that the specific behavior will be imitated, reinforcement of a specific imitative behavior may contribute toward the development of imitative behavior as a generalized response. For example, when Baer and Sherman (1964) taught preschool children to imitate some of a puppet's responses by directly reinforcing their imitative responses, the children also imitated other responses made by the puppet without being specifically reinforced for doing so. Similarly, young school children soon generalize their imitative behavior to models other than those at home, imitating, for example, the behaviors emitted by school models—classmates, teachers, and behavioral specialists. Such imitation appears to occur because at least some of the imitated behaviors have resulted in reinforcement for the student.

Most children entering school for the first time already have a generalized tendency to imitate. School personnel capitalize on this and help develop it. However, some children fail to become skilled imitators. Baer, Peterson, and Sherman (1967) worked with three severely retarded children who initially displayed little, if any, imitative behavior. They were able to establish generalized imitative behavior in these children after an extensive period of imitation-contingent reinforcement. Sometimes children grow up in environments that fail to foster imitative behavior. This may be particularly true of the culturally disadvantaged child who comes from a very large family. The efforts of such children toward imitation may not be noticed in the home. It should be apparent to the reader at this point that in order to develop generalized imitative behavior, many instances of imitative behavior have to be reinforced. Therefore, when individuals appear to be deficient as imitators, it makes sense to train them to imitate. By having different persons, such as teachers, classmates, parents, and relatives, reinforce diverse types of imitative behaviors in a variety of situations, imitative behavior can be developed as a generalized response.

Reinforcement of the model's behavior   Imitative behavior occurs more often when the model's behavior is reinforced than when it is not reinforced (Bandura & Kupers, 1964; Bandura, Ross, & Ross, 1963a, 1963b). The following episode illustrates alternative ways in which imitative S^D's, or *prompts,* may be used in the classroom. Suppose a student, Mike, seems to understand how to square numbers. He correctly says one day that 5^2 equals 25. Yet the next day he says that 5^2 equals 10. There are several ways the teacher can handle such a situation. She can give the appropriate response, thus acting as the model and prompting Mike to give the correct response. Or she can call upon another child, Tim. Assuming Tim gives the appropriate response, he can be reinforced. Mike can then be asked to solve the problem again. Hearing Tim praised for the correct response, Mike would then be more likely to give the correct solution. He too could then be reinforced, thereby strengthening his correct response. Mike's reinforced response would then be more likely to be imitated by the rest of the class. Thus, in the future Mike and his classmates would probably continue to respond correctly to the question of what 5^2 equals. Similar procedures could be used to increase other student behaviors, such as hanging up coats, paying attention, and so on. Imitative behavior, therefore, can be facilitated by providing a situation in which the model's behavior receives reinforcement.

Model selection　Three factors are particularly worthy of consideration in the selection of a model. The first is *prestige.* Groups of students usually contain some individual whose behavior is more likely to be imitated than others. Such students are often referred to as "prestigious," or leaders. They are usually persons whose behavior has in the past received considerable reinforcement from many sources, particularly the peer group. For instance, a student may be a good athlete, have a pleasant appearance or smile, and behave in a friendly manner. These factors may have led to his behavior receiving more than the usual amount of reinforcement. Observing this, other students would be more likely to imitate that student rather than an individual who has received little reinforcement (Bandura, Ross, & Ross, 1963a; Mayer, Rohen, & Whitley, 1969). Therefore, the teacher can capitalize on such a situation by selecting the prestigious student as a model when she wants to strengthen a specific desired behavior of other students in the group.

A second factor to consider is *similarity,* or the common characteristics or elements shared by the model and the individual who observes him. There is evidence to indicate that student observers who see or are told that they have some qualities or attributes similar to a model, such as age, sex, interests, and physical appearance, are more likely to imitate other responses of the model than are students who are not so informed (Bandura, 1968; Stotland & Hillmer, 1962; Byrne, 1969; Byrne & Griffitt, 1969; Rosekrans, 1967). Teachers and behavioral specialists, then, might enhance the likelihood of imitation occurring by pointing out common characteristics among the model and observing student or by selecting a model who is already known by the observer to be similar to himself, such as a close friend of the observer.

A third factor to consider in the selection of a model is *behavioral complexity.* According to Bandura (1965), an imitative behavior is more likely to be rapidly acquired if it possesses some components that the individual has previously learned and if the complexity of the stimulus is neither too great nor too rapidly presented. This characteristic is related to the similarity characteristic. If the behaviors of the model and the individual observing him are similar, then in all likelihood the model's behavior will not be too complex. For example, a teacher is preparing her class to take a field trip to an industrial plant. She can select a student to head the procession whom she thinks will provide an appropriate model for the rest of the class. This will work well if the other students have had prior experience in making similar field trips in the past. But suppose that this was the first such trip for many of the students. The behavioral chain consisting of walking quietly, observing closely, staying in line, and not touching anything might be too complex for them. Simply placing a good model at the head of the line would probably be insufficient preparation. A better procedure would be to break the complex behavior down into its components. In this case the children could practice imitating each of the component behaviors separately, before taking the trip. Then they would be more likely to imitate the more complex behavior of the model during the actual event.

Combined with other procedures   The provision of a model can be combined with stimulus change and procedures designed to facilitate generalization training. The teacher can first use a stimulus change, say seating Tim next to Bob, in order to increase the likelihood that Tim will imitate Bob's behavior. She can also attempt to change events or stimuli in the classroom so that they are similar to the events or stimuli that were present when a child demonstrated a desirable behavior. In this way she enhances the likelihood that the desired behavior will *generalize,* or extend, to the classroom.

Exercise 3.10
Observe how often a teacher employs modeling during a fifteen-minute period. Which facilitating factors were employed and which were not?

Exercise 3.11
Design a modeling procedure to get a six-year-old student to hang up his coat after taking it off in the classroom.

Exercise 3.12
Design a modeling procedure to get a fifteen-year-old boy to pay attention to his studies.

SUMMARY

The focus of this chapter has been the presentation of a series of procedures, other than direct positive reinforcement, designed to increase desirable classroom behaviors. The procedures include negative reinforcement, reduction of conditions that interfere with desirable classroom behavior, generalization, stimulus change, and imitation. Negative reinforcement was examined in terms of its efficacy and its practicality. It was suggested that, though negative reinforcement may be the most appropriate procedure for a given situation, its general use should be avoided. The reason offered was that aversive stimuli may themselves occasion responses that are not desirable. In the section on reducing conditions that interfere with desirable classroom behavior, several obstacles to the emission of a desired response were considered. The reader was also referred to Part IV for selection of specific procedures for the reduction or elimination of behaviors that may interfere with desirable behaviors.

Generalization was described as a process by which a behavior emitted in one situation occurs in new situations. Often such an event is desirable, since the necessity to train the same behavior repeatedly in each new situation is thereby avoided. In order to facilitate generalization, it was suggested that the elements common to both situations in which the desired behaviors occur should be emphasized.

When a behavior occurs in the presence of a set of discriminative stimuli, S^D's, it is possible to increase the behavior by presenting these stimuli. Usually the determination of the stimuli must be achieved through observation. It is possible, however, to develop S^D's by consistently arranging the presentation of a stimulus event just prior to the delivery of reinforcement. The S^D should, in time, set the occasion for the desired behaviors. The behaviors, when emitted, would then be available for reinforcement.

Imitative behavior, too, is an obvious short cut to increasing existing behaviors. Several points were discussed relating to the facilitation of imitative behavior. It was noted that reinforcement of both the imitator and the model were important factors. Persons who are prestigious, who have characteristics in common with, and whose prototype behavior is not too complex for the imitator can probably serve as appropriate models.

REFERENCES

Azrin, N. H., & Holz, W. C. Punishment. In W. K. Honig (Ed.), *Operant behavior: Areas of research and application.* New York: Appleton-Century-Crofts, 1966, 380–447.

Baer, D. M., Petersen, R. F., & Sherman, J. A. The development of imitation by reinforcing behavioral similarity to a model. *Journal of the Experimental Analysis of Behavior,* 1967, **10,** 405–417.

Baer, D. M., & Sherman, J. A. Reinforcement control of generalized imitation in young children. *Journal of Experimental Child Psychology,* 1964, **1,** 37–49.

Bandura, A. Vicarious processes: A case of no-trial learning. In L. Berkowitz (Ed.), *Advances in experimental social psychology,* Vol. II. New York: Academic Press, 1965, 1–55.

Bandura, A. Social-learning theory of identificatory processes. In D. A. Goslin & D. C. Glass (Eds.), *Handbook of socialization theory and research.* Chicago: Rand McNally, 1968.

Bandura, A., & Kupers, C. J. Transmission of patterns of self-reinforcement through modeling. *Journal of Abnormal and Social Psychology,* 1964, **69,** 1–19.

Bandura, A., Ross, D., & Ross, S. A. Imitation of film-mediated aggressive models. *Journal of Abnormal and Social Psychology,* 1963, **66,** 3–11. (a)

Bandura, A., Ross, D., & Ross, S. A. A comparative test of the status envy, social power, and secondary reinforcement theories of identificatory learning. *Journal of Abnormal and Social Psychology,* 1963, **67,** 601–607. (b)

Bandura, A., & Walters, R. H. *Social learning and personality development.* New York: Holt, Rinehart and Winston, 1963.

Byrne, B. Attitudes and attraction. In L. Berkowitz (Ed.), *Advances in experimental social psychology.* Vol. 4, New York: Academic Press, 1969.

Byrne, B., & Griffitt, W. Similarity and awareness of similarity of personality characteristics as determinants of attraction. *Journal of Experimental Research in Personality,* 1969, **3,** 179–186.

DeRath, G. W. The effects of verbal instructions on imitative aggression. *Dissertation Abstracts,* 1964, **25,** 624–625.

Holland, J., & Skinner, B. F. *The analysis of behavior.* New York: McGraw-Hill, 1961.

Kanareff, V. T., & Lanzetta, J. T. Effects of task definition and probability of reinforcement upon the acquisition and extinction of imitative responses. *Journal of Experimental Psychology,* 1960, **60,** 340–348.

Kennedy, D. A., & Thompson, I. Use of reinforcement technique with a first grade boy. *The Personnel and Guidance Journal,* 1967, **46,** 366–370.

Lanzetta, J. T., & Kanareff, V. T. The effects of a monetary reward on the acquisition of an imitative response. *Journal of Abnormal and Social Psychology,* 1959, **59,** 120–127.

Mayer, G. R., Rohen, T. H., & Whitley, A. D. Group counseling with children: A cognitive-behavioral approach. *Journal of Counseling Psychology,* 1969, **16,** 142–149.

Rosekrans, M. A. Imitation in children as a function of perceived similarity to a social model and vicarious reinforcers. *Journal of Personality and Social Psychology,* 1967, **7,** 307–315.

Stotland, E., & Hillmer, M. L., Jr. Identification, authoritarian defensiveness, and self-esteem. *Journal of Abnormal and Social Psychology,* 1962, **64,** 334–342.

PART II

TEACHING NEW BEHAVIORS

In Part I we discussed procedures for increasing the occurrence of behaviors already within the repertoire of the individual. In Part II we turn to a set of procedures designed to teach behaviors that are not part of the behavioral repertoire of the individual. A tremendous number of both academic and nonacademic school-related behaviors fall into this category, depending on the particular individual: reading for the nonreader, writing for the nonwriter, paying attention for the inattentive student, swimming for the nonswimmer, sharing for the nonsharer, and the acquisition of many other complex motor, social, and academic skills.

Strengthening such behaviors by means of simple reinforcement, or occasioning their occurrence through stimulus change, generalization training, and other previously discussed procedures, is not possible since the behaviors have never been emitted. It is not possible to reinforce an infant's language if he has never said something that resembles a comprehensible word. No amount of instructions or prompting will occasion the complete response. Neither will a young child write numbers nor a beginning cook prepare a tasty meal if such behavior or its components are not within their repertoires. First the behavior or its components must be emitted; then, and only then, can it be strengthened. Our emphasis in this section is on the presenting a set of procedures which are designed to develop new behaviors. Those procedures will include the refinement of gross behaviors, or *response differentiation;* the *shaping* of new behaviors through reinforcement of closer and closer, or successive, approximations to the goal; and the grouping together of response components to form behavioral *chains. Fading* will also be discussed as an adjunct to response differentiation, to shaping, and to chaining.

4 RESPONSE DIFFERENTIATION AND SHAPING

Objectives

Using examples not described in this chapter, you should be able to

1. Define and offer school illustrations for each of the following terms:
    a. behavioral dimensions
    b. response differentiation
    c. shaping
    d. successive approximations
    e. imitative prompt
    f. programmed instruction
2. List and give educational illustrations of the rules for the effective use of response differentiation.
3. List and give educational illustrations of the major variables that facilitate shaping.
4. Give an educational example of combining S^D's with shaping.
5. Describe what shaping contributes to programmed instruction.
6. List the advantages of teaching by means of programmed instruction.
7. List the criteria you would set in evaluating the effectiveness of an instructional program.
8. Tell how to carry out an effective shaping program and actually do so.

Teaching new behaviors by means of response differentiation and shaping involves reinforcement procedures applied in a more sophisticated manner than the simple reinforcement procedures covered in Chapters 2 and 3. How this is accomplished is the major emphasis of this chapter.

Before proceeding to that discussion, one major point needs to be reemphasized: It is very important first to specify the dimensions of the goal behavior. For the procedures included in Chapter 1, the specification of goal behaviors was quite simple. A behavior already observed in the individual's repertoire was selectively strengthened until it reached an acceptable level. When the major concern becomes one of building a new behavior, however, as it is with response differentiation and shaping, it becomes much more important to decide exactly what characteristics that behavior must have.

The *behavioral dimensions* of a response are those characteristics by which the response can be described and measured. Examples of behavioral dimensions include *frequency* (how often the behavior occurs); *intensity* (with what forcefulness); *duration* (the length of time necessary to complete a response); and *topography* (what form or shape the behavior takes). It is not enough to say that the student should be able to write the number *1*. The dimensions of that behavior must be specified. For example: The student should be able to write the number *1* each time he is instructed to do so for *X* trials (frequency), with a firm enough stroke that it can be seen (intensity). The number should be a straight line varying no more than, say, $80°-100°$ from the horizontal line on the paper. Its height should not be greater than nor less than the distance between two of the horizontal lines (topography). Without this kind of specification, some aspects of the behavior may be neglected, and an adequate performance may never be reached. For instance, without the frequency dimension specified, one correct production of the number *1* could be construed as proof that the new behavior had been learned. But it could be just as possible that the line was simply drawn by happenstance and would not be repeated under the same conditions.

Exercise 4.1

Specify a set of behavioral dimensions for the following terminal behaviors:

a. writing the letter *m*

b. preparing a social studies booklet

c. cooking a well-prepared meal

d. speaking aloud in class

RESPONSE DIFFERENTIATION

The new behaviors an individual acquires as he progresses through life come from a variety of sources. Sometimes new behaviors are refinements of more gross behaviors that are already part of his repertoire. The babbling infant begins to refine some aspects of his vocalizing so that it becomes comprehensible. The scribbling of the young child gradually becomes refined into recognizable letters and drawings. The young boy's awkward toss of a basketball becomes refined into more consistently direct shots into the hoop. The early attempts of the young cook develop from a state of mess and confusion and burnt food, to a well-prepared dish. In each of these illustrations, a set of gross responses gradually becomes restricted until it reaches a specific criterion for acceptability. *Comprehensible* words, *recognizable* letters, *direct* and *consistent* ball throws, and *well-prepared* dishes are criteria for acceptability.

RESPONSE DIFFERENTIATION DEFINED

For each of the criterion terms just discussed, it is possible to select a set of behavioral dimensions and place a set of restrictions on them. For example, *comprehensible*: The infant would have to vocalize in such a way that two independent observers would agree that each has heard the identical label applied to an object *x* out of *x* times. *Direct and consistent*: The ball must fall through the hoop *x* times within *x* tries when thrown from a distance of *x* feet. It is from such specifications that the definition of response differentiation derives: "The reinforcement of only those instances of behavior that fall within the limits and meet the restrictions and requirements set on behavioral dimensions is known as the procedure of *response differentiation* [Millenson, 1967, p. 163]." The instances of behavior falling within those limits and meeting those restrictions and requirements are the *subsets* of behavior that are reinforced.

USING RESPONSE DIFFERENTIATION EFFECTIVELY

Millenson's definition (1967) of response differentiation includes the means by which the response is refined. Some aspects of a behavior are reinforced to the exclusion of its other, nonrelevant aspects. The baby babbles a variety of sounds. His parents respond to those that sound "right" by smiling, repeating the sound, and engaging in other reinforcing behaviors. The infant's "meaningless" sounds are not greeted with the same enthusiasm. The young child's scribble that appears as a recognizable object is reinforced in a similar manner. Random scribbles yield little reinforcement. Straight and forceful tosses of a ball are reinforced by its going through the hoop and by the approval from the teacher and peers; awkward, indirect, and weak shots are not reinforced. The new cook is reinforced when she prepares tasty food that receives the approval of those who eat it.

Response differentiation will be achieved most effectively when the reinforcement of the desired subset of behaviors follows the same rules as those we discussed in the section in Chapter 2 on using reinforcement effectively. To reiterate, reinforcement should be delivered as often and as soon as possible following the emission of the desired subset of behavior. In addition, every attempt should be made to withhold reinforcement from the nonrelevant aspects of the behavior.

Exercise 4.2
a. Observe a group of students in one of the following settings:
   1. a gymnasium or athletic field
   2. a science or home economics laboratory or an art or shop class
   3. a language class
b. Give an illustration of the use of a response differentiation procedure being used in that setting.
c. Which methods used by the teacher appear to be effective and efficient?
d. What alterations would you suggest for increasing the effectiveness of the procedure?

SHAPING

We now turn to another procedure designed to form a behavior that does not exist in the individual's repertoire. There will be occasions in which a gross behavior does not contain subsets of desirable behaviors, as was described in the section about response differentiation. Perhaps the baby never makes a sound that is comprehensible or the youngster never produces a mark which resembles a letter or object. In such situations, the *shaping* procedure, which is an outgrowth of response differentiation, is applicable.

SHAPING DEFINED

The procedure for shaping a new behavior begins with a behavior as it exists and involves reinforcing slight changes in the behavior as it gradually approaches the target behavior. Thus, rather than selecting and reinforcing a subset of behaviors that is in fact the desired goal,

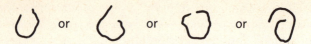

FIGURE 4.1   First attempts to enclose an area within a single line

elements, or subsets, of a behavior which *resemble* the desired behavior are selectively reinforced. For example, a youngster has never made a mark that approaches a straight line, but the teacher wants to teach him to write the number *1*. On occasion the youngster has drawn something that looked like a curvy line. If the teacher selectively reinforces the production of such a line, the production of such lines would increase. But something else will probably happen. Some of the lines will be curvy, but others will be a little straighter. Reinforced responses often vary or generalize in this manner (Reynolds, 1968). The teacher will then be in a position to selectively reinforce that subset of responses (straighter line drawing) and continue in this manner until an acceptable line is consistently produced. At the same time, old or inappropriately directed changes (curvier lines) will not be reinforced. The series of slight changes, or subsets, that are reinforced are referred to, technically, as *successive approximations. Shaping,* then, *is a procedure in which successive approximations to a goal behavior are reinforced.*

Another illustration of the procedure is teaching a child to draw a circle. At first any attempt he makes to enclose an area with a single line can be accepted (reinforced) by the teacher. His first reinforced attempt might look like any one of the illustrations in Figure 4.1. The next acceptance can be made contingent on his completely closing the figure, like those in Figure 4.2. After that, the criterion for acceptance can be gradually raised until he forms an acceptably rounded and enclosed figure. This procedure probably sounds very familiar. Teachers spend much of their time shaping, but they call it teaching. Why then use a technical term rather than the term "teaching"? Because "teaching" is

FIGURE 4.2   Later attempts to enclose an area within a single line contingent upon completely closing the figure

a broader term that includes the facilitation of many different kinds of learning, such as generalization training, combining simple responses into complex responses, and many others. "Shaping" has precise defining characteristics and better communicates what the exact procedure is.

SHAPING IN THE SCHOOL

The organization of most textbooks, workbooks, and teacher's guides and manuals is based on the assumption that, in order to acquire new academic skills, one must gradually move from previously acquired skills toward more sophisticated instructional goals. When one set of academic behaviors is acceptable at one level but a different set of behaviors is required at later levels, the academic behavior of the student is being submitted to a procedure that is very much like shaping. A handwriting workbook, for instance, can be designed along such lines. At first, letters that can be easily discriminated from other letters are presented. Then the student is guided through a series of steps in which more and more precision is required.[1] In this case, reinforcement may stem from teacher approval or, perhaps, from the student's increasing familiarity with the model or sample letters printed in the book. Usually it is a combination of both.

Shaping is frequently utilized in the development of nonacademic school-related behaviors as well. In a study by Harris, Wolf, and Baer (1967), a little boy was observed to spend almost no time climbing on the climbing frame in the school playground. It was decided that climbing on the frame was the sort of vigorous activity that would assist in his physical development. Teacher attention was selected as the contingent reinforcer.

> The teachers attended at first to the child's proximity to the frame. As he came closer, they progressed to attending only to his touching it, climbing up a little, and finally to extensive climbing. Technically, this was reinforcement of successive approximations to climbing behavior [p. 154].

Through the procedure, the boy ultimately spent more than half of each recess on the climbing frame.

Language development illustrates another area in which shaping plays an important role. Though for the most part, language is acquired by

---

[1] B. F. Skinner and S. A. Krakower (1968) have designed a series of writing workbooks that utilize a shaping procedure.

means of imitative, chained (complex combinations of simple responses), differentiated, and generalized responses, there are some circumstances in which language must be shaped. If, for instance, the child has not learned to imitate verbal samples adequately or if he has acquired some well practiced but inappropriate speech patterns, proper speech may have to be shaped. This situation can be illustrated by the early verbal learning of the infant. As has previously been described in the section on response differentiation, when the infant babbles, the parents reinforce any similarities between the baby's speech and acceptable words. At first, parents reinforce the sounds that are distant approximations to real words, such as "ook" or "kuk" for "cookie." Later, closer approximations are required for reinforcement. As the child grows older, other individuals also reinforce his improved speech patterns and help to extinguish his poor ones. They are more likely to respond to statements and requests that communicate successfully than they are to poorly and inappropriately enunciated words.

Occasionally, school children have inappropriate speech patterns. The speech therapist or, in his absence, the teacher, can use a shaping procedure to correct the deficiency. For instance, if the child pronounces the word "tree" as "fee," an approximation in the form of "tee" or "ree" can be reinforced. The "tr" sound used by itself may also occasion reinforcement. Ultimately, reinforcement can depend on the proper and consistent pronounciation of the word "tree."

Procedures similar to those we have just discussed can be used to teach a wide variety of school-related behaviors—social cooperation, attending to classwork, remaining in one's seat, and completing assignments. We shall return to some of these terminal behaviors, which are also used as illustrations in the following discussion.

Exercise 4.3

a. List one example of a shaping procedure that was used while you observed a group for Exercise 4.2.

b. Identify one or two additional goal behaviors you feel might best be handled by means of a shaping procedure in that same group.

SHAPING AND PROGRAMMED INSTRUCTION

Programmed instruction epitomizes an educational application of the shaping procedure. It is directly derived from behavioral principles that were discovered in the laboratory. In his pioneering article on the topic, Skinner (1958) discusses methods for using behavioral procedures in order to teach academic skills. He emphasizes the importance of reinforcement, primarily by means of confirmation of correct responses, as the student progresses in a steplike fashion from one academic level to the next. Usually, an instructional program starts with questions that can be easily answered by the student and proceeds gradually, to insure that the student will be reinforced with correct responses. Because the steps in an instructional program may be arranged to maximize success by a variety of methods—for example, hints or prompts and very gradual increases in difficulty—and assuming that being correct is reinforcing, the student is usually reinforced at a farily continuous rate.

The programmed instruction procedure generally follows this course: First, very simple responses are asked of the student. Correct responses are then immediately confirmed. These responses are rough approximations to the desired terminal responses. On successive trials, the text or teaching machine reinforces successively closer approximations to the criterion behavior. An instructional program may be in many forms—books, tapes, strips of paper, or microfilmed slides—and runs through finely graded steps, often referred to as *frames*. The frames proceed from simple levels to higher levels of complexity. This gradual, cumulative progression helps the student to be correct and reinforced as often as possible.

Figure 4.3 is based on a page from a programmed reading text for elementary school children (Sullivan, 1965). The student uses a strip of cardboard to cover the answer column, completing an item only after he glides the strip down to check his answer. Seeing a correct answer is assumed to be reinforcing. The advantages of shaping learning through programmed instruction, with or without the aid of a teaching machine, are numerous: (1) the material is organized and presented in a logical sequence; (2) frequent and active responding is required from the student which, in turn, expedites learning; (3) the student receives immediate feedback; and (4) the student can start at his own level and move at his own rate and is not held up or forced ahead by his classmates.

The approach to developing an effective program is empirical. Students work on a tentative program, and their performance is evaluated. If the student fails to learn, it is the fault of the program, not the student; and the items, or frames, are revised, reorganized, expanded, or reduced until most students do manage to learn the material.[2]

The programmed instruction movement was greeted with a flurry of published instructional programs. Many were carefully and appropriately prepared and empirically tested. Some, however, failed to meet the requirements for effective programming. Instructional programs must be based on the rules for effective shaping if they are to function adequately. A well-developed program is usually accompanied by data regarding its

---

[2] This topic is treated at length in Taber, Glaser, and Schaefer (1965).

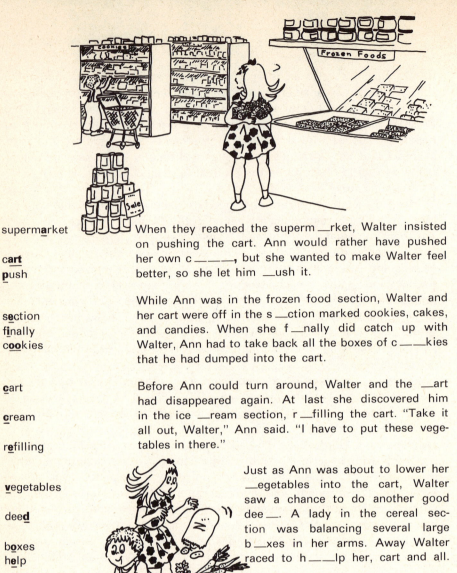

supermarket

cart
push

section
finally
cookies

cart

cream

refilling

vegetables

deed

boxes
help

2.

When they reached the superm ___rket, Walter insisted on pushing the cart. Ann would rather have pushed her own c _____, but she wanted to make Walter feel better, so she let him ___ush it.

While Ann was in the frozen food section, Walter and her cart were off in the s ___ction marked cookies, cakes, and candies. When she f___nally did catch up with Walter, Ann had to take back all the boxes of c ____kies that he had dumped into the cart.

Before Ann could turn around, Walter and the ___art had disappeared again. At last she discovered him in the ice ___ream section, r ___filling the cart. "Take it all out, Walter," Ann said. "I have to put these vegetables in there."

Just as Ann was about to lower her ___egetables into the cart, Walter saw a chance to do another good dee ___. A lady in the cereal section was balancing several large b ___xes in her arms. Away Walter raced to h ____lp her, cart and all.

Ann's vegetables landed

___ 1. in the cart.
___ 2. on the floor.
___ 3. on the shelf.

FIGURE 4.3 A sample page from the Sullivan Associates Programmed Reading Series, *Programmed Reading, Book 7*, p. 131

effectiveness with the students on whom it was developed. If the student population is adequately described, a teacher can feel safe using the program with a population that has similar characteristics. It is a good idea, however, to be sensitive to both group and individual performance on any particular instructional program. If too many errors are made or if the students become bored and distracted, the program is not performing its intended function. Its presentation should either be limited to a subpopulation of students for whom it is doing an effective job or be further revised or replaced.

USING SHAPING EFFECTIVELY

Keeping your eye on the goal   As in the use of other behavior modification procedures, the first step in shaping is a clear specification of the terminal behavior, along with the criteria for determination of success. The other requirements for the use of behavioral modification procedures specified in Chapter 1, such as the selection of an appropriate reinforcer, should also be met. A precise statement of the goal reduces the likelihood of strengthening irrelevant responses and increases the likelihood of reinforcing appropriate approximations. Suppose there is a youngster who has almost never responded to a question in an audible voice in the classroom. If the terminal goal is vaguely stated, say, "improving the responding of the student," there will likely be a failure to observe and reinforce some approximations to the desired behavior. The student, for instance, might speak loudly on the playground or shout in the hallway. In the absence of such a specific goal as, say, "speaking in class loud enough to be heard by the teacher at least once a day for five days," the approximations on the playground might well be overlooked or possibly even punished. With the specific goal in mind, however, the teacher is more likely to reinforce loud vocalizations no matter where emitted, as the first steps toward the terminal goal.

Exercise 4.4
Select a very simple terminal behavior that you want achieved for (1) yourself, (2) a student or school staff member, (3) a friend or relative, (4) a pet. Be sure that each can involve the use of a shaping procedure.
a. State each terminal behavior as precisely as possible. Be sure to include all relevant dimensions of the behavior (topography, frequency, intensity, duration); the conditions under which the behavior is, and is not, to occur; and any other restrictions or limitations that you feel should be placed on the emission of the behavior.
b. Specify one possible measure for each terminal behavior you select.

Finding a starting point   As a ceramic vase must be started from a lump of clay, so a new behavior must be shaped from an existing behavior through reinforcement of successive approximations. A starting point has to be found, even though the initial behavior may bear little or no resemblance to the final performance. Here, observing the student in the natural setting becomes very important. Through observation, one or more behaviors in which the student engages at a fairly frequent rate and which may bear at least some resemblance to the final goal behavior can be identified. Consider the illustration of shaping a student's behavior so that he completes his arithmetic papers. Suppose that observation over a period of a few days indicates that the student usually attempts the first problem, then gives up and either scribbles on his paper or crushes it. Further observation, however, demonstrates that on one occasion, when a review sheet of simple problems was handed out, the student completed about one-half of the assignment before crumpling up his paper. Two alternative starting points are suggested in this situation. (1) The teacher can start with the regular arithmetic assignment and shape from the partial completion of one problem. (2) She can start with problems similar to those found on the review sheet. The decision here can be based on a number of factors: practical considerations, such as the availability of prepared materials; the time available for the preparation of new individualized assignments; and the similarity between the starting behaviors and the terminal behavior. If the review sheet contained simple multiplication problems and the terminal goal was the solution of ten, two-decimal-place multiplication problems, the terminal and starting behaviors bear a substantial resemblance to one another. It may be preferable to drop back to the simpler review items. On the other hand, the review sheet may have contained verbal problems requiring simple computations and would, therefore, bear little resemblance to the two-place multiplication problems. In that case, it would be more advisable to select the alternative task, which bears a closer resemblance to the goal. The ideal method for determining the starting point in this particular situation would be to have the student engage in a set of graded tasks in arithmetic. When the student reaches a point at which he begins to perform poorly and fails to complete a problem, he has undoubtedly passed the ideal starting point. At that point, the level should be dropped back to the one at which the student had achieved success; and the starting point is determined.

Arithmetic is a subject area that is generally sequenced into steps of increasing difficulty. Many school-related behaviors, however, are not sequenced in so logical a fashion. Again, let us consider the case of the student who fails to speak aloud in the classroom. We have already suggested one starting point, the audible speech of the student in the playground and hallway. But suppose the student has never been observed to speak aloud anywhere in the school environment. The teacher then has to find some starting point. She might seat the student as close to her as possible, which would enable her to reinforce any approximations to speech, such as facial expressions, gestures, sighs, grunts, whispered words, or any other rudimentary behaviors resembling attempts to communicate. By reinforcing the entire group of such behaviors over many trials, their frequency should begin to increase. Whispering, for example, is one such behavior. Therefore, should the child's whispering be fairly consistently heard by the teacher, she might begin to selectively reinforce only the whispering and begin to drop out reinforcement for the other behaviors. Whispering should continue to increase in frequency, and a starting point for shaping audible speech would then have been determined.

Exercise 4.5
a. Suggest several alternative starting points for one of the terminal behaviors you selected for Exercise 4.4.
b. Select one of the alternatives and defend your selection.

Carrying out shaping We have already discussed the steplike progression shaping takes. The behaviors that intervene between the starting point and the terminal goal are broken down into a set of steps, or successive approximations. A few very important factors need to be considered at this point. How *large* should each step be? How *long* should one remain at each step before proceeding to the next? What should be done in the event that the behavior begins to disintegrate? Unfortunately, there are no specific answers to these questions. It is necessary to closely observe the behavior of the individual student. If the student is making consistent and satisfactory progress, it can be assumed that the size of each step and the amount of practice at each level has been appropriately selected. If, on the other hand, the progress begins to level off, falter, or deteriorate, the selections should be reexamined. Let us refer again to the student who was having trouble with arithmetic. Suppose the teacher had decided that she would increase the number of problems completed each day by a progression of one. On the first day the student was given and completed one problem and was reinforced. On the second day he was given two problems. He finished the first and started the second, but he failed to complete it. Reinforcement was not delivered. By the third day the student failed even to complete the first problem for that day. Quite possibly the teacher has set the requirements too high. A more successful sequence might be: (1) completing one problem each day, for five days; (2) then completing one problem and starting a second each day, for five days; (3) then completing two problems for each of five days; and so on. The situation should be arranged so that the student will be able to succeed much more often than he fails. For if he fails, reinforcement will not be forth-coming, and the behavior will begin to disintegrate. It is entirely possible that at some later time the step size could be increased. Perhaps by the time the student is consistently completing five problems correctly the next requirement might be the total completion of a sixth problem for only three, rather than five, days. This could continue until the terminal goal of ten problems completed was reached.

Let us consider now the selection of step size and the number of trials at a particular level for the child who failed to speak aloud in class. Assume that the teacher has selected the starting point—the student whispering in proximity to the teacher. Next she has to plan the sequences of steps to be followed. A good plan might begin with (1) the student remaining next to the teacher until he whispers loudly enough to be clearly understood by the teacher for five consecutive statements. Naturally the student will be reinforced for each of these utterances. The teacher might say, "_____, you've made an interesting point," and repeat it to the class. She might agree, smile, pat the child, allow him access to a preferred activity, or use any of the reinforcers that she has determined to be effective for that particular student. Once the criteria for success at the first step have been met the second step can be taken: (2) the teacher moving the student's chair back about a foot. The same criteria and procedures as those used for step (1) could again be employed. This procedure can be continued, little by little, until the student is seated across the room from the teacher. Again, the behavior must be carefully observed. If the new behavior consistently progresses, then the teacher can assume that she has selected appropriate criteria for practice and success at each level. To repeat, disintegration of the behavior suggests the need for smaller steps and more practice.

Sometimes the step sizes originally selected are too small or the student is required to remain at one particular level for too long a time. Steps that are too small become evident when the student begins to become inattentive and show other signs of boredom. This problem can also be put to an empirical test. Steps can be enlarged and practiced on each level and reduced to determine if the student's performance begins to improve. If it does, then it is apparent that the altered conditions should remain in effect. This type of situation probably occurs often in the shaping of new academic behavior. Due to the fact that each teacher has many students in her class, she often selects steps that are appropriate for the majority of her students. The few students who are capable of acquiring the new behavior in larger units and with less practice may become inattentive or engage in other than the assigned activity. In that situation, the teacher does have some alternatives: to substitute different materials for those students or, perhaps, to eliminate some of the steps or practice items for them.

Occasionally, progress seems to be going along smoothly, when the student suddenly does not seem to be making further progress. In such a situation, it is possible that too much practice has been given at one step, and the behavioral approximation has become too firmly established at that level. In order to reinstate progress, it may be necessary to make the next approximation very easy; to give a few trials of several small steps. The whispering child for example, may have been given too many reinforced opportunities to whisper at one particular distance from the teacher. Whispering then, rather than speaking aloud, may have become a more firmly established behavior than could be considered desirable. An appropriate alteration in the plan in this situation might be to move the student a couple of inches back every few days, rather than a foot at a time at greater intervals. Under those circumstances, he might be forced to whisper more and more loudly and ultimately begin to combine more audible sounds with the whispers.

Combining discriminative stimuli with shaping If a complex behavior, or its components, is not present in the repertoire of the individual, it will not be possible to occasion that behavior by means of presenting discriminative stimuli (S^D's) such as instructions or prompts. Such stimuli, however, may be used to help occasion the *approximations* to that response. Returning to the example of the child who failed to speak aloud in class, let us consider this procedure. Let's assume that the child had begun to whisper to the teacher. The teacher could use S^D's in order to occasion more frequent emissions of that response. She might say, for instance, "Good. I like the point you made" (the reinforcement) and then "Would you please say it again?" (the S^D). Or she might occasion other whispering responses by asking other questions of the student, nodding expectantly toward the student, or gesturing.

Combining imitative prompting with shaping An imitative prompt, you will recall, is a specific type of discriminative stimulus. It may occasion an imitative response, especially if the response was reinforced in the past when it resembled the topography of the model's behavior. Just as other S^D's may tend to occasion an approximation, the behavior of a model may also occasion an imitated approximation to a behavior that is too complex for direct imitation. Rather than simply waiting for the approximation to the desired behavior to be emitted, the approximation could be demonstrated to the student by a teacher or other model. This is the same procedure used by speech therapists when they attempt to shape the proper enunciation of a word. A student may be able to enunciate only one or two components of a complex word. When presented with a picture of a ball of string, the student might pronounce "fing," the "str" combination being absent from his repertoire. The components of the "str" blend are presented as a model for the student to imitate. He might first be asked to say *s* and then to repeat it a number of times; next, he is asked to say *t*, again several times; then, *st*. The procedure is continued until the response is shaped so the student combines and properly enunciates first, the three-letter blend and, finally, the whole word. Teachers use a similar procedure in shaping the various components of many academic tasks, including handwriting, computation, and reading.

Strengthening the newly acquired behavior Once a new behavior has been shaped, it resembles any other behavior that is present in the repertoire of the individual *at low strength.* It is therefore very important to take the newly achieved goal behavior and submit it to the same type of strengthening procedures that were described in Chapter 2. Reaching the terminal goal is not sufficient. The child who has begun to speak aloud in the classroom will quickly revert to whispering if his audible talking is not immediately and consistently reinforced for a great many trials. Applying the principles that relate to strengthening a behavior should increase the likelihood that the new behavior will persist. Then, once the new behavior has become pretty firmly established, procedures designed to maintain it can be used. These procedures will be discussed in Part III.

Exercise 4.6

a. Outline a series of steps designed to achieve one of the terminal goals you selected for Exercise 4.4. Include an estimate of the number of trials for each step.

b. Select a reinforcing contingency you can use in your shaping procedure. What behavioral evidence do you have to defend your choice of a reinforcer? How will you maximize the effectiveness of your reinforcement system?

c. Select an environment in which your shaping procedure will be carried out. Defend your selection of that environment.

d. Plan a system for recording your data. For each step you should be able to record the number of trials and whether the criterion for that approximation level has been met.

e. Carry out your shaping procedure. Record your data carefully. Use your data to support any changes you decide to make in carrying out the procedure.

SUMMARY

Response differentiation and shaping are designed to form behaviors that do not exist in an individual's response repertoire. Response differentiation forms a behavior by reinforcing specific behavioral dimensions that already exist in the individual's repertoire. Shaping forms a behavior by reinforcing successively closer approximations to the desired terminal behavior. Both procedures require a clear specification of the terminal behavior and its behavioral dimensions, as well as propitious use of the principles for strengthening a behavior. In addition, the shaping procedure requires careful observation to determine how large each step size should be and the duration of a particular step or successive approximation. Also, shaping can often be accomplished faster with the use of discriminative stimuli (S^D's).

REFERENCES

Harris, F. R., Wolf, M. M., & Baer, D. M. Effects of adult social reinforcement on child behavior. In S. W. Bijou & D. M. Baer (Eds.), *Child development: Readings in experimental analysis.* New York: Appleton-Century-Crofts, 1967.

Millenson, J. R. *Principles of behavioral analysis.* New York: Macmillan, 1967.

Reynolds, G. S. *A primer of operant conditioning.* Glenview, Ill.: Scott, Foresman, 1968.

Skinner, B. F. Teaching machines, *Science,* 1958, **128,** 969–977.

Skinner, B. F., & Krakower, S. A., *Handwriting with write and see.* Chicago: Lyons & Carnahan, 1968.

Sullivan Associates Program. C. D. Buchanan (Ed.) New York: McGraw-Hill, 1965.

Taber, J. K., Glaser, R., & Schaefer, H. *Learning and programmed instruction.* Reading, Mass.: Addison-Wesley, 1965.

5 CHAINING AND FADING

Objectives

Using examples not described in this chapter you should be able to:

1. Define and offer school illustrations for chaining and fading.
2. Describe the dual function that each behavior in a chain has; offer an educational illustration of the dual function.
3. List and give educational illustrations of the major variables that facilitate chaining.
4. Give educational examples of fading combined with response differentiation, shaping, and chaining.
5. List the advantages and possible limitations of fading.
6. Use chaining and fading procedures to actually teach new behaviors.

CHAINING

Essentially all school-related behaviors actually consist of sequences, or *chains,* of behaviors. The links in the chains are each composed of simpler behavioral components. For example, the behavior "going to lunch"[1] can be broken down into a set of component behaviors: lining up; leaving the classroom; walking down the hall; lining up outside the lunchroom; handing a ticket to the lunchroom monitor; picking up a tray, silverware, and napkin; placing food on the tray; going to a table; sitting down; and eating. Each of the component behaviors could be broken down into even smaller components. Eating, for instance, may be composed of: placing food on a spoon, bending arm, opening mouth, inserting spoon, removing empty spoon, chewing food, swallowing. Effective procedures designed to produce such complex behavioral sequences can enhance the quality of instruction.

CHAINING DEFINED

It may be apparent by now that chaining is accomplished by taking *simple behaviors already in the repertoire of the individual and combining them into more complex behaviors.* The teacher who wishes to teach her students to learn to look up unfamiliar words in a dictionary might be able to simply combine several behaviors that the students have already emitted in the past into the more complex chain. The students may already know how to read, locate words placed in alphabetical order, look for the answers to questions in books, and so forth. When these separate behaviors are combined in proper sequence, the complex behavior of using a dictionary will then have been established.

ESTABLISHING BEHAVIORAL CHAINS

How can a series of previously learned responses be combined and strengthened when reinforcement appears to occur only at the end of the behavioral chain? A golfer or bowler is reinforced by winning only at the end of the game. Students going to lunch are reinforced with food only after engaging in a long series of behaviors. Students using a dictionary will be reinforced by approval of the teacher only when they later spell, define, and use the words properly. Students solving a complex arithmetic problem will be reinforced only after a solution has been obtained. This might be a problem, in the light of the previous discussion on the need for immediacy of reinforcement in strengthening behavior. How is it possible that such chains do tend to become established, often

---

[1] This illustration is a modification of one presented by Reynolds (1968, p. 53).

without considerable difficulty? The answer presumably lies in conditioned reinforcement.

We learned earlier that when a stimulus or event is paired with, or directly, precedes reinforcement, it will, over time, tend to acquire reinforcing properties itself. The stimuli that acquire such reinforcing properties serve to cement the links in the chain into a complex response that can be strengthened or maintained by a single reinforcing event. The skillfully swung final putt in a game of golf and the last expert throw of a bowling ball each signal to the player that a victory or a good score is at hand. The sensation of the movement may become reinforcing in and of itself. Such stimuli reinforce the immediately preceding responses; the stance or the position of the player. Over time that stance will begin to signal that a skillful response will follow. The stance will occasion the swing or throw. It is in this manner that the stimulus components of a complex behavioral chain operate in a dual fashion, as both discriminative stimuli, which occasion the subsequent component response, and reinforcing stimuli, which reinforce the link that occurred immediately prior to it.

For a school-related illustration of the same phenomenon, take the complex behavior of coming in from recess, sitting quietly at a desk, and attending to the teacher. If sitting quietly and attending to the teacher has in the past been consistently paired with a reinforcing stimulus (S^+) in the form of approval from the teacher, the assumption of such a posture will become a signal that reinforcement is imminent; it will become a discriminative stimulus (S^D). Through further pairings with reinforcement (S^+), the discriminative stimulus (S^D) itself, "sitting quietly and attending to the teacher," will begin to reinforce (S^+) the *prior* link in the chain, "sitting down in one's seat." Through a similar process, sitting down in one's seat will become both an S^D that sets the occasion for sitting quietly and attending to the teacher *and* a conditioned reinforcer (S^+) for its prior link in the chain, say walking to one's seat, and so on. This can be illustrated, as shown in Figure 5.1.

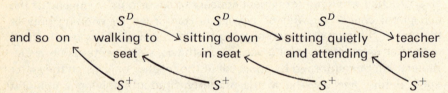

FIGURE 5.1   Example of stimulus components of a complex behavioral chain operating in a dual fashion

Each behavior in a chain, then, has a dual function. Each reinforces the response it follows and each serves as an S^D to occasion the response it precedes.

Exercise 5.1
a. From the following list of complex behaviors, break each down into a chain of five or more component responses.
b. Identify the reinforcing event that probably maintains each behavior.
c. Try to identify the stimuli in each chain which operate as both S^D's and S^+'s:

1. frying an egg
2. hammering a nail
3. getting the morning mail from the mailbox
4. hitting a baseball
5. solving a crossword puzzle
6. solving a mathematical problem

Exercise 5.2
Select one of your own favorite sports or hobbies. Take one of its component responses and break that response into a series of links, including responses, stimuli, and the crucial reinforcing event.

USING CHAINING EFFECTIVELY

Since teachers and behavioral specialists obviously expend so much of their time and energy in attempting to establish behavioral chains, it might prove helpful if we gave some consideration to a few procedures that are designed to facilitate the development of such chains. We will first discuss the wisdom of forging complex behaviors, when possible, from behavioral links already in the repertoire. Then we will consider backward chaining, or starting with the final link. This is a technique that has been used with impressive success in many animal training experiments (Holland & Skinner, 1961), and it is a potentially fruitful teaching technique. We will, finally, discuss other methods involving two procedures used in combination, such as chaining combined with the presentation of various types of prompts or with shaping. These can also be valuable aids to teaching complex school-related behaviors.

Using links already in the response repertoire A fairly basic principle for establishing chains efficiently, and one that is probably pretty obvious, is to try to form the chain from behaviors that are already part of the individual's repertoire. It is easier to teach a child to write his name if he can already write each of the component letters, than to have to shape the writing of each letter as part of that particular instructional procedure. It is easier to teach a student to perform a science experiment if he already knows how to handle the necessary laboratory equipment, than to have to teach him those component behaviors before beginning the experiment. It is probably easier for someone to get up and speak before a large audience for the first time if he already has the behaviors of looking at people when he speaks to them, organizing his materials, speaking loud enough to be heard at a distance, speaking distinctly, and using appropriate gestures, than if he had failed to acquire some of those components.

Frequently, it is possible to achieve terminal behaviors that are almost identical but are actually composed of different response components. For some people, giving an effective speech before a large audience might be composed of some behaviors different from those specified above: using an informal, conversational style rather than a more formal, tightly organized approach; showing slides rather than focusing attention on the speaker by using gestures; and so on.

Exercise 5.3

For each complex terminal behavior in the following list, specify two different sets of behavioral components which could form the links of the chain:
a. conducting an election for homecoming queen
b. building a set of book ends
c. keeping a room tidy
d. drawing a Thanksgiving Day mural
e. participating in a debate on foreign policy

When there is a close resemblance between two acceptable complex terminal behaviors, the behavior with more components fairly well established in the person's repertoire is probably the one that will be acquired more easily. Given a choice, that would be the instructional route to take.

Exercise 5.4

Which one of the pairs of component behaviors you specified in Exercise 5.3 would you or a student you know be able to acquire more easily? Why?

Starting with the final link   In Chapter 2, we discussed the development of stimuli as conditioned reinforcers. We learned that stimuli may take on conditioned reinforcing properties as a function of their being paired with either primary reinforcers or other conditioned reinforcers. The discussion emphasized that it takes many pairings of a stimulus with a reinforcer before the new stimulus will begin, of itself, to assume reinforcing properties. In the coming-in-from-recess example discussed in the section on "Establishing Behavior Chains," which link in the chain was paired most frequently with teacher approval, that is, the reinforcer? The behavior of sitting quietly and attending to the teacher, since it is the one that is emitted with the greatest proximity to, and shortest time delay from, the reinforcer, teacher approval. Sitting quietly and attending under these circumstances should, in time, operate as a reinforcing event itself. It will be a stronger reinforcer than its prior link in the chain, sitting down in the seat. We have learned that the shorter the delay between the response and the reinforcement, the more effective the reinforcement. Therefore, it is logical in training chains of responses that they be started, whenever feasible, with the final link in the chain and not at the beginning of a complex sequence. In essence, a good way to teach a complex behavior is to use *backward chaining.* Thus, in the coming-in-from-recess illustration, first the teacher could praise all instances of sitting quietly and attending. Next, the reinforcement would be made contingent on sitting down in one's seat and quietly attending. Once this chain occurs fairly frequently, the reinforcement can be made contingent on "walking in from outside and sitting down and quietly attending," and so on, until the entire chain solidifies into a complex behavior.

Now we will illustrate a backward chaining procedure that one of the authors designed to teach a six year old in a special education class to assemble a four piece wooden jigsaw puzzle. First, one of the pieces was removed and replaced in the correct position but only partially inside its space. When the child pushed the piece the rest of the way, he was congratulated for completing the puzzle and given some food. After several successful trials at that very simple level, the piece was moved to the side of the space. The child was then required to pick it up and put it in its place prior to earning reinforcement; this was repeated several times. The next step involved moving the piece off the board. When replacing that one piece was mastered and had been practiced, a second piece was added to the requirement for the chain, and the child had to replace two pieces. The same procedure was followed as with the first piece. Ultimately all four pieces were removed and the child had to complete the entire puzzle before he could be reinforced. Though the procedure was fairly time consuming, he rarely missed a reinforcer. Learning to complete that puzzle made it easier for the child to work others. Probably the most significant aspect of the training project was that "playing" with the puzzle was the first play activity that this particular child had engaged in for three years, since, for most of his working hours he had previously sat and rocked in a chair, twiddled his fingers, and made incomprehensible sounds. To have been able to perform this task appropriately, just like other children of his age, was quite a milestone.

There are several questions that might be asked regarding the advisability or necessity for teaching a complex behavior by means of a backwards chaining procedure: Is there sufficient evidence to support using this approach in all situations? Can't people learn just as well by adding on behavioral components from the beginning? The answer to both questions is unclear at this time. There has not been much research conducted with human subjects on this topic. But where the procedure has been used, especially in teaching a behavior that has been very difficult for an individual to learn, it has demonstrated its success. The fact is that most conventional instruction is organized in a "logical" sequence, beginning at the beginning and ending with the completed behavior: For example, a student is asked to write his name, "John." He writes "J" and the teacher says "Good." As he writes each succeeding letter, he is praised by the teacher. Contrast this with the backward chaining approach: *Joh* is supplied. Johnny first must fill in the last letter, then the last two letters, then the last three, then all. It is the guess of these authors, pending adequate empirical evidence, that probably both approaches would do an effective job of teaching. After all, children do manage to learn quite effectively in school. Probably the backward chaining procedure can make its greatest contribution when a student experiences difficulty in acquiring a complex behavior.

Exercise 5.5

Using the backward chaining approach, specify the steps one might follow in developing the chain of behaviors that constitute using the dictionary. Be sure to specify your terminal goal.

Using discriminative stimuli In addition to the discriminitive stimuli (S^D's) that are an integral part of the response chain, supplementary S^D's may be employed to facilitate the chaining procedure. Verbal directions, gestures, written instructions, and similar S^D's might effectively shorten the time needed to establish a fairly simple behavioral chain. For example, in our coming-in-from-recess illustration, if the teacher said (as many teachers do), "Children, please quietly walk to your seats, sit down, and look up at me," and consistently reinforced the emission of that behavioral chain, it might be acquired more rapidly than if she had simply waited for the chain to be emitted spontaneously.

Exercise 5.6

Using S^D's, specify the steps one might follow in teaching the proper functioning of a bulletin board committee.

Exercise 5.7

Expert classroom teachers often develop a set of gestures that they use as a part of their daily classroom routine. These gestures may occasion some fairly complex student behaviors. Try to visit a classroom conducted by a teacher who is regarded by her colleagues as an expert, and list how she combines S^D's and chaining.

Combining imitative prompting with chaining Children frequently do imitate behaviors that are novel for them—such as printing letters, repeating lines of poetry, doing homework and crafts projects, and so forth—as long as the behavior modeled is not too complex, and provided that most of the behavioral components are already in their repertoires. Thus, complex behavior can be occasioned by simply providing a model. Even children who fail initially to imitate can be taught to do so since imitative behavior can be shaped as a single response class. Baer, Peterson, and Sherman (1967) were able to train three severely retarded children to imitate a wide variety of simple behaviors by directly reinforcing their imitations of some of those behaviors. However, with more complex behavioral models, direct imitation may be difficult to accomplish. Acquiring the proper sequence of behaviors in a more complex chain may prove too difficult if the entire sequence is presented all at once. For example, in the coming-in-from-recess illustration, the presentation of a student model emitting the entire sequence might have been sufficient to occasion the chain by others among a group of older children. With longer or more complex chains, such as organizing and conducting a debate, however, one might have more success if the chain were broken down into shorter sequences and each of those presented as imitative prompts. The students could then first imitate each of the links in the chain. Then the chain could be gradually solidified in the manner previously described; and the segment prompts could be phased out.

Exercise 5.8

Take the complex behavior of organizing and conducting a debate. Break it down into a series of responses that you believe most sixth or seventh graders might be able to imitate. Describe the procedure you would use in training the students first to imitate each response and then to organize the responses into a chain.

Exercise 5.9

Can you think of any students who might fail to imitate the component responses you listed in Exercise 5.8? On what grounds might you account for their failure to emit the behaviors by means of imitative prompts?

At this point the reader may be asking himself, "Why not simply provide discriminative stimuli, such as directions or models, to teach all complex behavioral chains?" The answer lies partially in the fact that directions or imitative prompts may not be adequate S^D's for all students. They may not reliably occasion the desired response. Similarly, it is often the same student for whom directions are ineffective, for whom it is also difficult to find an effective model. In addition, many of the instructional and behavioral goals of teachers and school specialists are often much more complex than those we have illustrated. And the components of the particular chain may not be in the individual's response repertoire.

Chaining when links are absent from individual's response repertoire There are many examples of behavioral chains that may prove too complex to be occasioned by imitative or other discriminative prompts. For instance, teachers may select such instructional goals as the correct solution of long division problems, utilizing proper grammatical forms in writing, designing and carrying out a scientific experiment, and so forth. The guidance counselor or school psychologist may wish to assist a teacher to teach or manage her class more effectively by utilizing principles of reinforcement. Each of the components must be acquired, largely through *shaping,* strengthened through *reinforcement,* and perhaps occasioned by various S^D's or prompts. Once the components are acquired in strength, it may be possible to combine them into a chain.

Exercise 5.10

The librarian plans to teach the use of the card catalogue to a class of students who are unfamiliar with the various categories into which reading material is usually grouped. Describe the steps she might follow in training this complex chain.

Exercise 5.11

The senior class is taking its annual trip to Washington, D.C. Many of the students have never taken a long bus trip, checked into a hotel, or ordered from a menu in a restaurant before. Describe the steps that might be planned to prepare the seniors for the trip.

Exercise 5.12

The science laboratory has installed a new, expensive piece of equipment. Describe the steps the instructor might follow in order to ensure proper use of the machine.

Exercise 5.13

A school principal, at the request of a teacher, is trying to help her handle her students more effectively. She wants to acquire the practice of giving directions to the students, waiting for them to make the appropriate response, and following that with her praise or other reinforcers. The teacher, fairly new in the field, has previously only used aversive management techniques. Describe the steps that the principal might follow in assisting the teacher to acquire that chain of behaviors.

FADING

Basic to all educational planning is the notion that learned behavior should ultimately be emitted "spontaneously" rather than always as a response to a prompt or a cue. When individuals are described as "showing expertise," "being motivated," or "showing initiative," they are usually emitting behavior in the absence of obvious external cues. One student is considered an expert photographer because he can take, develop, and print pictures without external guidance. When another student goes to the dictionary to look up a word without an adult's suggesting that she do so, she is showing initiative. Another student demonstrates that he is highly motivated in biology when he performs independent experiments after school in the biology laboratory. *Fading* is one technique through which those behavioral characteristics can be developed.

FADING DEFINED

Fading is the gradual removal of discriminative stimuli (S^D's), such as prompts and cues. Once this is accomplished, the behavior is under the control of more natural or desirable S^D's. In fading, while goal behaviors or approximations to goal behaviors are consistently reinforced, the S^D's that temporarily served to occasion those behaviors are slowly and progressively diminished. The procedure is designed for the purpose of developing a terminal behavior that is emitted in the presence of only minimal or no prompting.

FADING IN THE SCHOOL

Suppose a teacher were trying to instruct a student to translate the Spanish word "gato" into the English, "cat". Many prompts could serve to occasion the English word: a picture of a cat, the sound "meow," a purring sound, the initial "ka" sound, and so on. Such prompts may help the student give the right answer, thus making him eligible for reinforcement. Continued use of such prompts, however, would probably tend to make the student dependent upon their presentation. The ultimate goal of replying "cat" when the word "gato" is presented in isolation might never be achieved, unless the prompts were eventually removed.

Motor skills can be taught more effectively by using fading techniques. For example, verbal prompts can be used initially to assist students learning how to assemble and disassemble a piece of equipment in the chemistry laboratory. The instructor can specify each step as the students progress through the task. After they have performed the task several times, the instructor can then gradually fade out the verbal cues and have the trainee perform without them.

Parallels to the above can also be seen in physical education, language, and music classrooms (Carlson & Mayer, 1971). In each situation, the instructor gradually fades out the prompts or instructions to specific verbal, motor, or physical tasks. A physical education example would be teaching a child how to catch a baseball. The instructor begins by showing the child how to receive the ball, how to hold it in a glove, and so on, while constantly praising correct responses or approximations. During subsequent sessions, the instructor gradually reduces his comments, both instructional and reinforcing. In the music class, when the students are introduced to a song, they first receive the music and the words. Once they have acquired the tune, they just need a copy of the words. Finally they need no prompts whatsoever, not even musical accompaniment. In the language classroom, verbal and written prompts are faded out in a similar manner.

As Millenson (1967) notes ". . . in the world outside the classroom, spoken and written prompts are rarely present. Thus in formal teaching it is important that prompts used at the start be dropped out before the student is regarded as trained [p. 273]." In essence, then, if prompts are not faded, they may tend to become crutches. Fading helps remove the necessity for such crutches. Yet, because fading is done gradually, it avoids a situation in which the student might encounter failure.

Exercise 5.14

Visit a classroom on a day that the teacher is planning to instruct the students in some new skill, such as handling new equipment, reciting a poem, writing in a new structural form, and so on. Describe how the teacher uses fading as a method to increase proficiency.

Exercise 5.15

Select a programmed text or a teaching machine program that has demonstrated its instructional effectiveness. Find five illustrations of the use of fading in that material.

FADING IN GUIDANCE AND COUNSELING SETTINGS

Fading often plays an important part in guidance and counseling procedures. When, for instance, a student is first asked to role-play, the role is often clearly delineated and the setting carefully set. This is done because many of the role-playing responses are not usually within the student's behavioral repertoire. Such prompts are gradually withdrawn as the student's sophistication in role-playing increases. Similarly, school counselors find that they must initially assume much more responsibility in directing counseling interviews with elementary school children than with high school children (Carlson & Mayer, 1971).

Another counseling illustration is from one of the author's case files. It demonstrates the combined use of imitation, chaining, and fading procedures with a child whose speech was very limited. Though the procedure was used on a one-to-one basis in a clinic setting, there is no reason why it couldn't be directly generalized to classroom settings.

During the early sessions, the child had failed to label a particular set of objects: "truck," "car," "boat," and "train." A terminal goal was then specified: The child was to be able to identify each object correctly and without prompts at least two consecutive times and to use the label correctly within the context of a full sentence. The first step in the training procedure was to teach each object label. The object was held up, and its name was stated: "This is a boat." The child was asked to say "boat." At first the whole word had to be supplied. When it was repeated by the child, he was reinforced with praise and a small bite of food. After many such trials, the counselor said only part of the word: "This is a bo ___." The child was then reinforced when he supplied the whole word. Each label was taught in this manner. Next, more requirements were added and, as the child achieved each goal in turn, cues were dropped. Reinforcement became contingent upon his saying "a boat," then upon "is a boat," and finally upon "That is a boat." This procedure was followed in teaching him the correct description of hundreds of objects.

Exercise 5.16

All school personnel are concerned with teaching new behaviors. For each of the personnel listed below, give a terminal behavior that each might teach more efficiently by using fading procedures:
a. classroom teacher
b. physical education teacher
c. shop teacher
d. building principal
e. school nurse
f. school psychologist
g. guidance counselor
h. superintendent of schools

USING FADING EFFECTIVELY

Finding prompts that reliably occasion desired response We have already discussed the role played by the learning history of an individual in the development of stimulus control. We learned that given stimuli tend to occasion given responses. Responses to different stimuli by different individuals may vary. One may respond "cat" to a purring sound, another may be able to read the word "cat," while another may answer "cat" when presented with a picture of one. Carefully observing the student should be of help in selecting the prompts that will reliably occasion the desired response and thus minimize the student's failures.

Gradually and progressively removing prompts   Once the desired response has been reliably occasioned by "artificial" prompts, it is a good idea to gradually and progressively remove those prompts until all are gone. The teacher training students to respond "cat" to the stimulus "gato," may initially have needed to say the whole word or have shown a picture of a cat or even a real one to get them to respond correctly. The verbal prompt could then be gradually diminished: "Ca," then "C," then just the initial lip movements. Or the picture might gradually be altered to a line drawing; to, perhaps, a pair of whiskers; and so on, until nothing is needed. Figure 5.2 illustrates such a series of diminish-

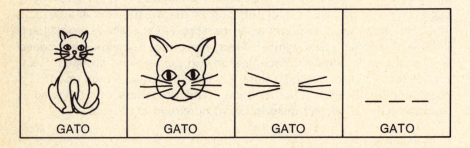

FIGURE 5.2   **Example of a series of diminishing prompts**

ing prompts. An important guideline to follow is to *prompt just barely enough to occasion the response, while avoiding abrupt reductions in the prompting.* If the student begins to make many mistakes, one can reasonably assume that the reduction has been too abrupt.

Overusing artificial prompts   A direct corollary to reducing prompts gradually is to avoid overusing artificial prompts. Too many presentations of the picture of a cat might make the student overly dependent upon that stimulus. He might attend only to the picture rather than to the verbal stimulus "gato." Sometimes children learn to "read" passages in preprimers by using the pictures to prompt their responses. This is not true reading, for, in reading, the response must be under the control of the written word stimulus and not under the control of the picture. Primary school teachers often avoid this overdependence on irrelevant cues by reproducing the text with simplified illustrations then, ultimately, without any pictures at all.

Exercise 5.17

Tell how you might use fading to teach someone to acquire the following terminal goals:

a. pronouncing "antidisestablishmentarianism"

b. a proper tennis serve, bowling throw, or golf swing

c. a simple dance step

d. ordering from a menu

e. naming all the states in the United States

f. reciting the *Preamble* to the Constitution

g. one of the goals you listed in Exercise 5.16

Combining fading with shaping We discussed, in Chapter 4, the use of discriminative stimuli (S^D's such as directions, modeled behavior, gestures, and other prompts) in shaping. We learned that the shaping procedure could be facilitated by occasioning approximations through the presentation of appropriate S^D's. It is often desirable, however, to remove those S^D's before a new step in the shaping procedure is to be initiated. This is particularly important if acquisition of approximations toward the terminal goal are to be firmly incorporated into the learner's repertoire. If a musician is to develop virtuosity in the performance of a particular musical selection, he must become less and less dependent upon the coaching of his teacher and the notations in the score. As the student of a foreign language becomes more and more proficient in conversation, he should require less and less cueing from his teacher or from his notes. In each case cues and prompts have to be faded.

Fading and shaping procedures are frequently combined in the development of programmed instructional materials. Programmers often find that when fading is used, the student makes fewer errors than he would were he required to progress without assistance. Since errors are less likely to be emitted in the first place, they are less likely to be recalled or to recur.

Skinner's and Krakower's (1968) "Write and See" instructional handwriting program illustrates how fading can be a useful tool in the hands of the educator. Ellen Reese (1966) clearly describes the program in the following passage:

The handwriting program shapes successively closer approximations of writing by immediate differential reinforcement of the correct response and by gradual attenuation of the controlling stimulus. The controlling stimulus is a letter which the child traces.

Portions of the letter are gradually faded out, and the child composes increasingly more of the letter freehand until he is writing the whole letter himself. Immediate differential reinforcement is provided by a special ink and a chemical treatment of the paper. The child writes with a pen which makes a black mark when the letter is properly formed, but which turns the paper orange when the pen moves from the prescribed pattern. The child thus knows *as he is writing* whether or not he is drawing the letter correctly, and he can immediately correct a response by moving the pen so that it makes a black mark. Under these conditions, the children learn quickly; they learn to write well; and they love it [p. 57].

Taber and Glaser (1962) used a similar approach to teach first graders to read color names. When the students saw a color, they could say its name, but they were unable to read the name of the color. Taber and Glaser then presented each color name printed in its respective color. The colored letters were gradually replaced by black letters until all were black. Reinforcement was contingent upon correct responses. What began as color naming, ended as reading names of colors.

Exercise 5.18

If you have a pet, plan to teach it a simple trick, such as lying down or sitting up on command. Specify the approximations you would train and tell how you would fade out prompts for each approximation. Carry out the training program. Record the number of correct and incorrect responses for each approximation level. By referring to your data, evaluate your fading procedure.

Exercise 5.19

Find a friend, student, relative, or colleague to serve as your subject. Select an instructional objective that is not a part of his repertoire. Prepare an instructional program including several steps, each of which more closely approximates the objective. Include fading procedures as part of the material for teaching each approximation. Try the program on your subject. Record the number of correct and incorrect responses at each step. By referring to your data, evaluate your fading procedure.

Combining fading with chaining   The S^D's that have been added to occasion the emission of each of the links of the chain must be removed before one can assert that the behavioral goal has been achieved. In the solution of long division problems, for instance, the ultimate goal would probably be for the students to carry out the entire process without any external prompts. If the teacher said, "First compare the divisor and the dividend to see which is larger," and waited for her students to do so; then said, "Now place a decimal point to the right of the dividend," and waited for her students to do so, and so, on, few would agree that the terminal behavior (being able to solve long division problems) had been acquired. The criterion for acceptable acquisition of the response chain would probably be the correct solution of a number of long division problems completed without the assistance of the teacher.

As with shaping, it is obvious that a gradual fading of the intermediate prompts in a complex chain of behaviors is necessary if the goal behavior is to be emitted smoothly and with precision. Too abrupt a removal of these S^D's would probably result in the breakdown of the behavioral chain.

Since each prompted link in a behavioral chain occupies a sequential position, there is the question of at which link should one begin to fade S^D's? Since the link of the chain that probably has the greatest strength is the last link, it seems logical that the prompt that occasions the final link of the chain is the first one that should be removed. Using the example of long division, the instruction to reduce the fraction to the smallest common denominator should be removed first. As that final link and the one immediately prior to it become fairly well cemented, the S^D for the next prior link may then be eliminated (the instruction to place the remainder over the divisor), and so on, until the entire chain is performed with perhaps only a single S^D at the beginning of the chain, such as the instruction to divide 987 by 31.

Exercise 5.20

Outline the steps you might follow in training the following behavioral chains:
a. the phrases "that is a boy," "that is a girl," "that is a dog," "that is a cat" in Spanish
b. performing a complex dance step
c. bringing completed work to a student monitor for checking

Exercise 5.21

Select a terminal goal consisting of at least a three-link chain. Specify the steps you would follow in training the chain. Be sure to include fading procedures in your teaching program. Carry out the program with a friend, student, relative, or colleague. Record your data, including the number of correct and incorrect trials for each segment and for each combination of segments. Evaluate the effectiveness of your fading procedure.

ADVANTAGES AND DISADVANTAGES OF FADING

The major advantage of the fading procedure is that it reduces students' errors as they learn. Both McCandless (1967) and Terrace (1963) indicate that if errors are allowed to occur in the acquisition of new behaviors, future errors are much more likely to occur. By minimizing initial errors, fading serves to avoid the need for eliminating subsequent errors and retraining correct responses. When applied gradually, the fading procedure reduces dependency upon such S^D's as directions and imitative prompts.

While minimizing of errors has obvious advantages in the acquisition of a specific complex behavior, the question of whether consistent error-free responding is desirable for a student has yet to be resolved experimentally. Considering errorless performance in another area, discrimination learning, Terrace (1966) states "It should be noted . . . that numerous factors would detract from the wisdom of trying to train all discriminations without errors. Perhaps the most important of these is the lack of frustration tolerance that would result from a steady diet of errorless discrimination learning [p. 335]."

SUMMARY

Chaining and fading were defined and discussed relative to their use in educational settings. Both procedures can be used to teach behaviors that are not part of an individual's response repertoire. Chaining forms behaviors by combining existing simple behaviors into a more complex behavior. Chaining probably works best when the separate behavioral components are already present in the individual's repertoire. Backward chaining, starting with the final link, can be a fruitful approach. Discriminative stimuli, such as instructions, gestures, and imitative prompts can serve to facilitate the acquisition of a complex chain.

Fading brings behavior dependent upon external prompts under the control of the individual. Fading can be performed most effectively when just enough of the right kinds of prompts are initially presented and then gradually removed. Used in this manner, fading can also serve to increase the effectiveness of given shaping and chaining procedures. In addition to reducing the individual's dependence upon external prompts, fading helps to minimize the likelihood that the individual will make errors as he learns.

REFERENCES

Baer, D. M., Peterson, R. F., & Sherman, J. A. The development of imitation by reinforcing behavioral similarity to a model. *Journal of the Experimental Analysis of Behavior,* 1967, **10,** 405–416.

Carlson, J. D., & Mayer, G. R. Fading: A behavioral procedure to increase independent behaviors. *The School Counselor,* 1971, **18,** 193–197.

Holland, J. G., & Skinner, B. F. *The analysis of behavior.* New York: McGraw-Hill, 1961.

McCandless, B. R. *Children: Behavior and development.* Hinsdale, Ill.: Dryden Press, 1967.

Millenson, J. R. *Principles of behavioral analysis.* New York: Macmillan, 1967.

Reese, E. P. *The analysis of human operant behavior.* Dubuque, Iowa: William C. Brown, Publishers, 1966.

Reynolds, G. S. *A primer of operant conditioning.* Glenview, Ill.: Scott, Foresman, 1968.

Skinner, B. F., & Krakower, S. *Handwriting with write and see.* (teacher's ed.) Chicago: Lyons & Carnahan, 1968.

Taber, J. I., & Glaser, R. An exploratory evaluation of a discriminative transfer learning program using literal prompts. *Journal of Educational Research,* 1962, **55,** 508–512.

Terrace, H. S. Stimulus control. In W. K. Honig (Ed.), *Operant behavior: Areas of research and application.* New York: Appleton-Century-Crofts, 1966.

Terrace, H. S. Discrimination learning with and without errors. *Journal of Experimental Analysis of Behavior,* 1963, **6,** 1–27.

PART III

MAINTAINING BEHAVIORS

As the body of accumulated human knowledge becomes greater and more complex, the aim of public education has had to change from attempting to teach "all there is to learn" to providing students with the background and methods for acquiring information and skills on their own. The schools can begin to teach the basic tool subjects, some general summaries of information, some basic concept-forming and problem-solving approaches, and some additional skills; but they cannot make specialists of all their students. They cannot sufficiently equip their students to function successfully in our complex society simply on the basis of what the school has been able to impart. Once out of the school environment, the student must continue to learn, to acquire more skills, and to make new applications of old ones. He must be able to do this in the absence of the contingencies that the schools have been able to place upon him. Perhaps in light of this, education needs to be judged today not only in terms of how much it is able to teach its students during their school years but also in terms of how well students are able to continue developing once they finish school. The ultimate judgment might be based on the effectiveness with which education has managed to program for the maintenance of skills that allow students to continue learning and applying what they learn beyond the years of formal schooling. When educators specify such educational aims as "preparing students to become responsible and productive citizens," they are indicating that they do recognize that formal schooling is only the beginning of an individual's education and that they hope their students have been sufficiently equipped to continue progressing after they leave the school environment.

The fact that individuals do perform in highly complex roles attests to the fact that such long-range educational aims are being fulfilled, at least to some extent. It hardly needs to be mentioned, however, that we still have a long way to go in achieving those goals for the entire population. Crime and unemployment flourish, and we suffer from an insufficient supply of skilled personnel. There is considerable room for improvement. The development of a "technology" of education that is directed toward the goal of providing for maintained performance would be a distinct contribution.

Closely related to the need for maintained performance beyond the years of formal schooling is another: the need for maintained responding, that is, maintaining behaviors acquired by the student as he progresses through school. School personnel have long been in the habit of providing for periodic review and practice before assuming that a newly acquired school behavior will maintain. Yet, often those behaviors assumed to have been permanently acquired begin to fade. In addition to trying to achieve increasingly larger numbers of objectives, the teacher finds herself spending a good deal of time reteaching material that the students should have retained. The guidance counselor and psychologist similarly find themselves repeating programs with the same students from one year to the next.

However, when perceived from a different vantage point, maintained responding is a phenomenon that should be avoided. When a student begins to respond incorrectly, emit a disruptive behavior, or do something other than that which he has been instructed to do, the last thing the teacher desires is the maintenance of that behavior. The teacher then needs to be aware of the kinds of environmental conditions that could serve to keep such undesirable responses going. With such an awareness, she is more likely to find effective ways to avoid contributing to the maintenance of undesirable classroom behaviors.

Two questions seem to evolve from a consideration of the issues we've just discussed: How can maintained responding be achieved or avoided once contingency control is reduced or removed? What procedures are likely to maintain consistent performance, steady performance, or high and low rates of performance? The chapters in Part III are concerned with the role played by schedules of reinforcement in providing partial answers to these questions.

6 INTERMITTENT REINFORCEMENT

Objectives

Using examples not described in this chapter, you should be able to

1. Define and offer school illustrations for each of the following terms:
   a. schedule of reinforcement
   b. intermittent reinforcement
2. List and give educational illustrations of the major advantages of intermittent reinforcement.
3. Describe with an educational example how one should proceed in switching from continuous reinforcement to intermittent reinforcement, first, without using supplementary reinforcers and, then, with the use of supplementary reinforcers.
4. Use intermittent reinforcement to maintain the emission of a behavior.

The issue of maintaining acquired behavior once continuous contingency applications are reduced or removed is one which has been given considerable attention by behavioral psychologists within recent years. The publication *Schedules of Reinforcement* (Ferster & Skinner, 1957) demonstrates how experimental situations can be so structured that firmly acquired animal behaviors maintain for long periods of time. This was accomplished with both noncontinuous reinforcement and in the complete absence of any reinforcement. Further research has also repeatedly demonstrated that, given certain conditions, prolonged periods of maintained responding can be achieved.[1] The conditions that have resulted in such maintained performance have to do with the manner in which the environment delivers reinforcement. More specifically, they have to do with the *schedule* of reinforcement, ". . . the rule followed by the environment . . . in determining which among the many occurrences of a response will be reinforced [Reynolds, 1968, p. 60]." (We have discussed scheduling in a different context in Chapter 2.)

More recently, human performance under various schedules of reinforcement has been investigated. Hutchinson and Azrin (1961) found that one form of schedule performance by mental hospital patients, while not identical with, did resemble similar schedule performance by several nonhuman organisms. This resemblance was also observed among mental defectives (Ellis, Barnett & Pryer, 1960) and among chronic psychotics (Lindsley, 1960). Continuing research in schedule effects with humans (Bijou & Orlando, 1961; Long, 1962, 1963; and Weiner, 1969) is making it possible to extend the conclusions reached about the behavior of infrahumans under various reinforcement schedules to similar human behavior under similar conditions. Such research is also aimed at discovering those characteristics of schedule performance that are more specific to human behavior. Because the resemblance of schedule performance between animals and humans has been found to be close, but not identical, much more experimental work with human subjects will have to be performed. Until then, only tentative statements can be made regarding the applicability of the principles of intermittent reinforcement to the performance of school children.

GENERAL CHARACTERISTICS

INTERMITTENT REINFORCEMENT DEFINED

When a behavior is being *intermittently reinforced,* it simply means that some, but not all, of the emissions of the response are being reinforced. Many specific reinforcement schedules fall under the very

---

[1] Many of the significant studies relating to maintenance of behavior through schedule control have been reported in various issues of the *Journal of the Experimental Analysis of Behavior.*

general label of "intermittent reinforcement": Joe is not given a drink of water each time he asks for one, just sometimes. Asking for a drink is being intermittently reinforced. Charles is allowed to go to the rest room only after a certain time interval since his last visit to the rest room has expired. Otherwise his requests to leave the room are denied. Charles' requests are being intermittently reinforced. Since different reinforcement schedules tend to generate performance characteristics that may differ from one another, several of the more extensively investigated schedules will be discussed individually in Chapter 7. There are, however, some generalities that hold true for many different intermittent reinforcement schedules. And these generalities will be presented in this chapter.

Exercise 6.1

Observe a class for a few hours. You will see many instances of intermittent reinforcement. List as least five illustrations.

ADVANTAGES OF INTERMITTENT REINFORCEMENT

In Chapter 2 we learned that the best way to strengthen a weak behavior is to reinforce it as often as possible, preferably continuously. Assuming that this has been done and the behavior is well-established in the repertoire of the individual, the question arises about whether such a schedule of *continuous reinforcement* (CRF) should be kept in effect. Fortunately, this is not necessary. Continuous reinforcement is neither the most effective nor the most efficient way to maintain behavior. It is actually preferable to stop reinforcing every emission of a response and switch to an intermittent reinforcement schedule.

Delaying satiation   One reason for shifting away from continuous reinforcement (CRF) is that an individual may become satiated if he receives too much reinforcement. Let us consider how long responding maintains under CRF. The response of lifting a fork to the mouth is continuously reinforced by the consequence of food in the mouth. Though unlimited quantities of food may be available, the behavior of lifting the fork will eventually stop and will not be resumed for several hours. One can assume that the individual has been satiated. Under CRF scheduling, satiation occurs fairly rapidly, especially when the reinforcers are of a primary variety, such as food, drink, or sex (Holland & Skinner, 1961). With conditioned reinforcement, satiation effects are somewhat delayed; with generalized reinforcement, they are delayed even further. But, satiation does eventually occur under very dense, or rich, reinforcement schedules. Though a preschooler continues to scribble "pictures" for an approving parent or teacher, he will stop scribbling after a while. Though the approval may have been reinforcing, its effect becomes temporarily inadequate to support the behavior, especially since continued scribbling probably requires increasing amounts of effort from the child. A child who has acquired a large number of tokens will also tend to reduce his rate of working for token reinforcement.

If the goal is to keep well-established behaviors going, it then becomes important to avoid the problem of satiation. One way to do this is to stop reinforcing the emission of each and every behavior, and reinforce each behavior intermittently instead. Fewer reinforcers will then be received for an equivalent number of responses, and the behavior will continue to be emitted before the satiation effect manifests itself. The hungry child, in the early stages of learning to use a fork, will usually drop a lot of the food. And the behavior of lifting the fork to the mouth will result in reinforcement on an intermittent schedule. Assuming that enough food reaches his mouth to maintain the attempt, many fork-lifting responses will be emitted; more lifting responses than an adult or child adept in the use of the fork would emit. Natural consequences have provided for an intermittent reinforcement schedule, and satiation effects have been delayed. The behavior (lifting the fork) maintains for a long time.

In the school setting, the shift from continuous to intermittent reinforcement can be planned into the program. We will consider how this might be accomplished in the earlier example of hand raising in the classroom. For several days or weeks the teacher has attempted to call on a student each and every time he raises his hand properly. When data inform her that his behavior is well established (talking out without permission has diminished to a near-zero rate for several days), she begins to skip calling on him occasionally. Reinforcement has shifted from continuous to intermittent reinforcement.

Maintaining performance under extinction Intermittent reinforcement provides for longer periods of maintained responding while reinforcement is being delivered. What happens when reinforcement is ultimately discontinued; that is, what happens under extinction conditions? Experimental data suggest that, again, a history of intermittent reinforcement tends to generate performance under extinction conditions that maintains longer than does a CRF history. A frequently used illustration of this phenomenon is a comparison between a person's performance with a vending machine versus his performance with a slot machine. Which performance persists longer when reinforcement is no longer forthcoming? In most cases, each time he inserts a coin into a vending machine and subsequently presses the lever, those responses are reinforced with the delivery of an item like candy. Individuals with such a CRF history on the vending machine give up quickly when the behavioral chain is no longer reinforced, that is, when the machine will no longer dispense the item. He may drop two or three more coins into the machine, but pretty soon that form of responding ceases. What of the slot machine player? He inserts coin after coin into the machine. Occasionally he hits the jackpot. A pile of coins drop into his hands. More often than not, the number of coins in the jackpot is less than the number he has already spent. Yet, even though the machine might break down and no further winnings may result, slot machine performance may tend to maintain for quite a while, usually, at least longer than vending machine performance. (If extinction conditions were maintained indefinitely, customers would give up. The slot machine would no longer be used, and the machine owner would lose business. So, slot machines are usually not intentionally programmed to withhold delivery of coins permanently. They are simply programmed to reinforce intermittently.)

Maintained performance under extinction conditions, following intermittent reinforcement, can be observed in all facets of life. Shooting at the basket with a basketball maintains for a pretty long time, as long as the player has occasionally made a basket in the past. A student's completion of his arithmetic papers maintains for a while in the absence of his receiving A's for them when he has had a history of being reinforced intermittently with good grades for his performance. The student who has won spelling contests will continue to enter the competition many times in the absence of victory before his attempts cease. Contrast these illustrations with the performance of individuals who have had histories of CRF schedules. The basketball whiz who sank just about every basket he shot for in the past would probably give up quickly (and in a fit of frustration) if after many attempts he were unable to get the ball through the hoop. For the student who received only A's on his arithmetic paper, a sudden string of papers with low grades might be devastating; he might stop working altogether. A similar reaction could beset the spelling star of the school. Having won every spelling contest in the past, defeat might produce a rapid cessation of his entering any spelling competitions.

Undesirable, as well as desirable, behaviors show similar characteristics as a function of the scheduling history. Another familiar illustration is the "spoiled" child who has been reinforced very heavily in the past by doting parents. But if the day comes when reinforcement is no longer delivered, performance stops fairly abruptly. Jack's dad, for instance, has been very lenient in lending him the family car. In fact Jack has never had his request turned down. Dad decides one day that enough is enough. Jack is failing in school, and his father wants him to get down to work instead of driving around town every evening. Jack's repeated requests for the car are refused. In a fit of temper, he stamps out of the room and refuses to engage in any conversation with his father for days. But his car-requesting behavior ceases rapidly. Had Jack's father occasionally refused him the car in the past, the likelihood would be that his car-requesting behavior would tend to persist for a much longer period of time, although his emotional reactions to the refusals would more likely be less intense.

Exercise 6.2

Select two different behaviors that are likely to be intermittently reinforced in school: one you consider to be a desirable school-related behavior; one you consider to be an undesirable school-related behavior. Watch specific students who are engaging in each of these behaviors. Record each emission of the behavior and whether it was reinforced or not. Plot the frequency of each behavior within each of several fifteen-minute periods. Then, assuming it is feasible, have the reinforcement withdrawn. Plot the frequencies of the emission of the responses for several more fifteen-minute intervals. (Be sure that all other conditions are the same for all recorded intervals.) Did the frequency of the emission of the behaviors change during extinction? If so, describe the change. How do you think the reinforcement schedule affected performance under extinction conditions?

Exercise 6.3

Consider a friend or relative for this exercise. Cite a very persistent behavior that continues to maintain even though it is apparent that the reinforcing consequences of the behavior have been removed. Try to explain the persistence on the basis of whether the schedule history was of continuous or intermittent reinforcement.

Maintaining well-established behaviors It is undoubtedly reassuring to school personnel that intermittent reinforcement maintains well-established behaviors more effectively than does CRF. It is this fact that makes the whole notion of employing behavioral procedures in the classroom a feasible one. Chaos could be the only result if a teacher were to try to continually reinforce certain specific behaviors of each of the twenty-five or thirty students in her room. First of all, she would be so busy concentrating on how to respond to whom that she'd probably forget what she was trying to teach. Secondly, in many cases it would be patently ridiculous for her to handle CRF for such a group. The hand raising example again would illustrate the potential absurdity of such a situation. The teacher decides to put Jimmy, Susie, Ralph, George, Tommy, and Ebenezer on CRF for hand raising. "How did you spend your vacation?" she asks. All six children raise their hands! Then what? It is apparent that only one child could be called upon at a time. But actually, that's fine. If all six former problem hand raisers did manage to raise their hands simultaneously, the behavior is probably becoming fairly well-established in their repertoires. They were probably ready for the switchover from continuous to intermittent reinforcement. Each child could be called on in turn. Assuming that intermittent reinforcement effectively maintains the behavior, the teacher has found a practical and efficient means of employing behavioral procedures in her classroom.

SWITCHING TO INTERMITTENT REINFORCEMENT

The reduction of *reinforcement density* (reducing the frequency with which a particular response is reinforced) is a touchy affair. If reinforcement is abruptly withheld following many emissions of a behavior that has been on CRF, the behavior may disintegrate. The individual is likely to stop emitting the behavior, and he may exhibit some unpredicted behaviors such as crying or hitting. Suppose a man failed to pay a neighborhood boy for mowing his lawn four or five times in a row. How long would the boy continue to mow the lawn after that? Suppose a school district stopped paying its personnel for five or six months. They'd probably quit. For the child who was recognized by his teacher each time he raised his hand for several consecutive days, a sudden failure to be recognized following eight or ten attempts would probably result in his ceasing to raise his hand any more. The way to avoid such disintegration is to make the changeover gradual and progressive. It is also helpful to ease the shock of reduction in reinforcement density by adding discriminative stimuli, such as reminders, and additional reinforcers. The following sections offer hints on how the changeover can be accomplished smoothly.

Gradually reducing reinforcer density A smooth changeover from continuous or very dense reinforcement schedules can be accomplished by making the reduction fairly gradual in the beginning. In a situation in which one of the authors participated, a child was being trained to name objects. For each correct response, the child was reinforced with food. Eventually the child was able to label correctly each object in a set. Clearly, the natural environment could not provide such dense reinforcement conditions. Wishing to avoid satiation effects, we decided to begin reinforcing correct responses with food on an intermittent schedule. Since functional language was very new to the child, it was very important to proceed with care. Rather than reduce the reinforcement to, say, delivering food once every third or fourth correct response, the reduction was made by *skipping* reinforcement for about one correct response out of four. As time went by, more and more trials went unreinforced until eventually the child had to label the whole set before the first food reinforcer was delivered. But this was done very gradually. It took many weeks to accomplish the reduction in reinforcement density, but the behavior maintained at a high level of performance. As training progressed, it was possible to reduce the density of reinforcement for newly acquired behaviors more rapidly. Ultimately the child could continue to function with abrupt shifts from CRF to a schedule in which only each fifth correct response was reinforced with food. Yet the behaviors maintained.

Teachers frequently make such gradual changeovers to intermittent schedules on an intuitive basis, as they do with many other behavioral procedures. The athletic coach continues to praise the members of the team as they acquire a new style of responding. The first grade teacher consistently praises her students as they print their names for the first few times. But after each performance reaches a certain level, the density of reinforcement is gradually diminished. No longer is every single response made by the athletes praised. The teacher no longer compliments each student every time he writes his name correctly. By carefully attending to this particular aspect of teaching methodology, however, the instructor can handle such changeovers with consistent precision. Sensitivity to signs of satiation and behavioral disruption can be heightened. If the emission of the behavior abruptly ceases, though dense reinforcement remains in effect, the need to reduce reinforcement density is indicated. If the emission of the behavior abruptly ceases and the disruption is accompanied by emotional-like responses at a time when a changeover from continuous to intermittent reinforcement has been made, the reduction in reinforcement density has probably been too rapid. In such situations, a hasty retreat to denser reinforcement schedules is indicated, if the desired behavior is to be reestablished.

Progressively reducing reinforcement density Once a particular behavior is no longer receiving continuous reinforcement, it becomes possible to increase the number of responses or amount of time required prior to reinforcement. In fact, animals and human beings are known in some cases to continue to emit particular behaviors in incredibly large numbers and over extremely long intervals before a single reinforcement is received. A college student may read thousands and thousands of pages before obtaining the credit for a course. He attends school for approximately seventeen years before being reinforced with a college diploma. Novelists have been known to write for years and years before selling a book, and the avid fisherman or hunter keeps at his vigil for lengths of time that confound the uninitiated. Training students in a similar kind of persistence at a task is one of the major goals of formal education. To have developed students who, on the completion of their formal schooling, continue to be productive (although financial, social, and other rewards may be infrequent) testifies to the success of an educational program. In order to achieve this goal, the schools must require their students to do progressively more work for longer time periods prior to receiving formal consequences. It is just fine to praise each sentence that a student composes in the second grade. But if a similarly high rate of reinforcement for his writing persisted through his senior year in high school, he would be in trouble. Once the contingency is removed, it is likely that the behavior (writing) will disintegrate. All the efforts made in this respect by that student's teachers will have gone for naught. Yet students do, on the whole, tend to maintain many behaviors that were acquired in school. In general, our educational system is doing well in that regard. Progressive reduction in reinforcement density is practiced, probably without awareness. But, perhaps, by placing an emphasis upon the crucial need for such progressive reductions, even more persistent student behaviors may be achieved. Perhaps educational programming needs to include in its plans not only content, teaching methods, and evaluation techniques but also the periodicity with which reinforcement will be delivered. For instance, when a new subject area is introduced at the high school level, first assignments might be evaluated daily (assuming that feedback on the assignments is reinforcing), then semiweekly, then weekly, biweekly, and so on. Reinforcement of assignments could be scheduled so that by the end of the term, long intervals in the absence of such feedback were being tolerated by the students. Or, in the early phases of training elementary school children to study independently, the teacher could circulate continuously around the room; nodding, patting, and smiling at students as they worked at their tasks. Then gradually, she could begin to circulate a little less frequently; progressively lengthening the intervals before dispensing social reinforcement for the students' study behavior. Using such an approach would necessitate a formidable time commitment by the teacher in the early phases of any new educational task. Her efforts, however, would be adequately compensated for when the class progressed to the successful completion of longer or larger assignments.

Adding S^D's Another technique for smoothing the transition from continuous to intermittent reinforcement is by supplementing the procedure with additional discriminative stimuli and reinforcers. The part played by the S^D's in occasioning behavior has been discussed in previous sections. To reiterate, S^D's, the stimuli that have been repeatedly paired with the receipt of reinforcement, suggest that a particular behavior has a probability of being reinforced. Verbal S^D's in particular can therefore serve to assist in maintaining the emission of high frequencies of behaviors or continued responding over fairly long intervals. The most obvious examples are verbal instructions such as, "As soon as you complete fifty problems, you will be excused for lunch." "After you've worked on our staff for twenty-five years, you can retire at half pay." Written instructions, gestures, signals, and so forth, can also function in a similar way. Thumbs up and a broad grin from a person in

111

the distance signals that good news will soon be forthcoming. The time interval required in reaching a particular floor at the top of a skyscraper is bridged by the changing numbers of the elevator sign. The clock on the classroom wall signals that the time for dismissal is approaching.

Teachers can use such S^D's with their students. They could, for instance, facilitate maintained responding by communicating response requirements. Signs or instructions such as, "All those who achieve 100 percent on their spelling papers will be allowed to enter the lunchroom first," or "A's will be given to all students who complete the first fifty pages in the workbook," could help to avoid the behavioral disruption that might otherwise occur during the transition to longer and larger requirements.

SUPPLEMENTING INTERMITTENT REINFORCEMENT

If one stops to think, it becomes fairly apparent that most reinforcers dispensed by human beings are accompanied by other, though perhaps weaker, reinforcers. The excellent report card is handed to the student with a smile. The winning touchdown is rewarded not only by another recorded victory for the team but also with cheers, pats on the back, a parade atop the shoulders of teammates, newspaper headlines, and sometimes even scholarships or lucrative contracts to play on professional teams. Reinforcers dispensed in the normal course of the school day usually occur in such clusters as well. Stu writes an excellent theme. The teacher gives him an A, smiles at him, has him post it on the bulletin board, asks him to submit it to the school paper, and so forth. Suppose that in Stu's case the major reinforcer was the A grade because he needs a high average in order to enter college. Nevertheless, the teacher could use the less powerful reinforcers effectively. It might be possible, for example, for her to use them to bridge the gaps between graded themes. She could maintain other examples of excellent, but ungraded, theme writing in the interim through praise, smiles, or the other weaker reinforcers she has given him before. Such supplementary reinforcers could train him to persist in creating well-written materials while the teacher initiated a program of scheduling progressively longer ratio requirements.

A transition from token to other forms of reinforcement can also serve to supplement intermittent reinforcement. Having found no other way to motivate Mervin to complete his reading workbook, his teacher used a token system. For each page completed at a level of 80 percent correct or better, Mervin received a token. The teacher paired delivery of the token with praise, smiles, head nods, and pats on the back. When he completed a multiple-page assignment, the tokens were exchanged for a certain number of minutes at the paint easel. Mervin began to perform as desired. Assignments were completed in increasing numbers. The teacher, however, had a number of concerns. The end of the school year was approaching. She felt reasonably certain that the next teacher would not continue a token system. Checking each page and delivering a token immediately upon its completion was both time consuming and would interrupt her other activities. Mervin even seemed to become tired of painting at the easel, an activity that he had earlier embraced with enthusiasm. The time for shifting to less frequent reinforcement and ultimately to removing the token reinforcement altogether was obviously at hand. Gradually and progressively the change was made. She delivered tokens following the completion of first two, then three pages, then, ultimately, at the completion of the entire assignment. The cost for time at the easel was also increased gradually so that Mervin had less and less opportunity to paint per amount of work completed. However, as often as possible, when the teacher observed that Mervin was hard at work, she would come by, compliment him for doing such a nice job, pat him on the back, and smile. Even if she were busily occupied with other students, such as listening to a group of children read aloud, she would stop periodically and compliment Mervin and other children who were hard at work. If Mervin happened to look up for a moment during a period in which he were hard at work, she would nod, smile, or wink. Such events, though perhaps only weak conditioned reinforcers, could perhaps accomplish the task of providing a smooth transition, first, to progressively longer ratios of reinforcement, then, eventually, from a token system to a program in which reinforcers more natural to the school setting could be used.

Exercise 6.4

Using the two classroom behaviors you selected for Exercise 6.2:
a. Suggest a specific program for shifting over to intermittent reinforcement for the *desirable* behavior, utilizing the guidelines offered in the preceding discussion.
b. If possible, have reinforcement reinstated and follow the maintenance program that you designed.
c. Continue observing and recording the emission of the response as you did in Exercise 6.2. Plot your results on a graph. Describe how your program worked.

Exercise 6.5

a. Offer a program for eliminating the undesirable behavior (from Exercise 6.2) by means of extinction. What particular environmental events should be avoided?
b. Try out the program.
c. Observe and record as you did in Exercise 6.2. Plot the results on a graph and describe how the program worked.

SUMMARY

Once a behavior is well-established in the repertoire of an individual, chances are that the behavior will maintain better if the density of reinforcement is reduced. This is accomplished by switching over from continuous reinforcement (CRF) to intermittent reinforcement. The achievement of such a transition prevents the individual from becoming satiated and provides him with a history that tends to maintain the behavior longer under extinction conditions. And intermittent reinforcement is, usually, more practical to administer. A smooth transition to intermittent reinforcement may be effectively accomplished by making the changeover gradual and progressive and by supplementing the procedure with additional S^D's and reinforcers.

REFERENCES

Bijou, S. W., & Orlando, R. Rapid development of multiple-schedule performances with retarded children. *Journal of the Experimental Analysis of Behavior,* 1961, **4,** 7–16.

Ellis, N. R., Barnett, C. D., & Pryer, M. W. Operant behavior in mental defectives: Exploratory studies. *Journal of the Experimental Analysis of Behavior,* 1960, **3,** 63–69.

Ferster, C. B., & Skinner, B. F. *Schedules of reinforcement.* New York: Appleton-Century-Crofts, 1957.

Holland, J. G., & Skinner, B. F. *The analysis of behavior.* New York:McGraw-Hill, 1961.

Hutchinson, R. R., & Azrin, N. H. Conditioning of mental hospital patients to fixed-ratio schedules of reinforcement. *Journal of the Experimental Analysis of Behavior,* 1961, **4,** 87–95.

Lindsley, O. R. Characteristics of the behavior of chronic psychotics as revealed by free-operant conditioning methods. *Diseases of Nervous System Monograph Supplement,* 1960, **21,** 66–78.

Long, E. R. Additional techniques for producing multiple-schedule control in children. *Journal of the Experimental Analysis of Behavior,* 1962, **5,** 443–455.

Long, E. R. Chained and tandem scheduling with children. *Journal of the Experimental Analysis of Behavior,* 1963, **6,** 459–472.

Reynolds, G. S. *A primer of operant conditioning.* Glenview, Ill.: Scott, Foresman, 1968.

Weiner, H. Controlling human fixed-interval performance. *Journal of the Experimental Analysis of Behavior,* 1969, **12,** 349–373.

7 SPECIFIC SCHEDULES OF REINFORCEMENT

Objectives

Using examples not described in this chapter you should be able to

1. Define and offer illustrations for each of the following terms:
   a. ratio schedules of reinforcement
      (i) fixed-ratio schedules
      (ii) variable-ratio schedules
   b. interval schedules of reinforcement
      (i) fixed-interval schedules
      (ii) variable-interval schedules
   c. limited hold
   d. differential reinforcement of high rates
   e. differential reinforcement of low rates
2. List and describe the characteristics of ratio schedule performance.
3. List and describe the factors that influence response rate characteristics, such as consistency under ratio schedule performance.
4. List and describe the characteristics of interval schedule performance.
5. For fixed- and variable-interval schedules, compare and contrast response rates and consistency of responding. State the reasons for the variations among them.
6. Describe the kind of history you would provide in order to schedule a rapid rate of responding and a slow rate of responding under a variable-interval schedule.

In Chapter 6 we considered the fact that intermittent reinforce-ment serves to maintain behavior in the school setting. We will now examine the ways in which specific schedules of reinforcement effect performance, because different schedules can generate performance characteristics that may differ subtly or even dramatically from one another. The rate, consistency, and opportunities for competing behaviors while the schedule is in effect, as well as after reinforcement has been discontinued, are all characteristics that are of interest to educators and behavioral specialists. The following sections will be directed toward, first, those factors as they relate to the simpler ratio and interval schedules. Next, some additional schedules that appear to have particular pertinence for school personnel will be discussed. The study of reinforcement schedules is an extremely broad discipline, and many complex combinations and permutations have been investigated. The human environment, being as complicated as it is, probably more closely approximates combinations of such complex schedules. However, a consideration of those will not be attempted in this text, not because they are unimportant or irrelevant, but because their study would go beyond the basic and into the advanced realm of behavioral analysis.

RATIO SCHEDULES

RATIO SCHEDULES DEFINED

When reinforcement is made *contingent upon the emission of a given number of responses before one response is reinforced,* the schedule is referred to as a *ratio schedule.* Sometimes the *number of responses required prior to the reinforced response is fixed at one specific number.* In that case, the schedule is called a *fixed-ratio* (FR) schedule. The classical illustration of an FR schedule comes from industry and is called "piecework." When each twentieth piece of equipment is assembled, the worker is credited with $5.00. In school, an example of an FR schedule would be giving a student a certain number of points upon his completion of, say, three pages in his workbook. (Fixed ratio schedules are often abbreviated for the sake of convenience. In the last illustration, for example, reinforcement is delivered at the ratio of three page units to one reinforcer, and the schedule can be abbreviated FR 3.) More typical of reinforcement schedules used in the schools, however, is the *variable-ratio* (VR) schedule. While the VR schedule also programs reinforcement contingent upon a response following a number of responses, *the number of required responses varies.* Typically a VR schedule is programmed in the laboratory by selecting *an average number of required responses.* For example, a pigeon is to be reinforced *on the average of* once each fifty responses (of pecking a disc). VR schedules, too, are usually abbreviated, and in the pigeon's case, the schedule would be abbreviated VR 50. Let us suppose that units in an arithmetic workbook varied in length from four to eight pages, *with an average of six pages.* If students were reinforced with points toward their final grade upon their completion of all the pages in each unit, they would be working on a VR 6 schedule.[1]

Exercise 7.1

Offer three illustrations of ratio schedules of reinforcement that are not described in the text. Tell whether the schedule is an FR (fixed ratio) or a VR (variable ratio).

a. one from a home situation
b. one from a work situation
c. one from a school setting

CHARACTERISTICS OF RATIO SCHEDULE PERFORMANCE

Ratio schedules tend to generate specific types of performance while the schedule is in effect and to generate specific performances under extinction conditions, when reinforcement is no longer delivered. With laboratory animals, performance characteristics under different ratio schedules are quite distinct and predictable (Ferster & Skinner, 1957), while with humans, such characteristics cannot be predicted with as much precision. Nonetheless, general patterns of ratio performance have manifested themselves in studies in which simple (Hutchinson & Azrin, 1961), as well as complex (Bijou & Orlando, 1961; Long, 1962; 1963), schedules of reinforcement have been tested with human subjects. Among the predictable general performance characteristics of ratio responding are *high and fairly consistent rates while the schedule is in effect* and *continued responding under, at least, the early phases of extinction conditions.* These performance characteristics will be examined in a little more detail so that the factors that appear to influence each can be identified.

High rates of responding With ratio schedules, reinforcement is contingent upon the emission of a number of responses. Therefore, the faster the individual responds, the sooner he gets reinforced. Rapid responding also allows him to accumulate more reinforcers within a given period. Naturally, individuals will tend to work rapidly under ratio schedules. A typist being paid by the page will likely work as quickly

---

[1] In reality, any student is usually operating under many different complex schedules at one time. We have simplified the material to make the discussion easier to follow.

as possible: the faster she types, the more pages she can complete within a given period, and the more money she can consequently make. Similarly, a student who is allowed out to recess upon completion of a number of assigned pages will probably make haste to finish.

However, several specific factors have been found to have an effect on rates of responding on a single task. Among those that are more relevant to educational practice are the ratio of nonreinforced-to-reinforced responses and the gradualness with which the rate reinforcement schedule is phased out. Several investigators have studied the effect of the size of the ratio requirement upon response rate. One study (Hutchinson & Azrin, 1961) conducted with human subjects, showed results similar to those found with animal subjects in two other studies (Boren, 1956; Skinner, 1938). Those general findings were that, to some maximal level, the larger the response requirement, the more rapid the response rate. Given that all pages of a spelling workbook are of equivalent length and difficulty, if a student completes two pages under an FR (fixed ratio) 2 reinforcement schedule within a specified period, he would be expected to complete a longer requirement in proportionally less time than a shorter one. For instance, one would expect that a ten-page requirement (FR 10) should take five times as long as a two-page requirement, yet the experimental findings suggest that it would be completed in less than five times that period. All other factors being equal, the writing rate per line would be higher if reinforcement were made contingent upon a six-line written requirement than upon a two-line requirement. It would therefore seem logical to conclude that high ratio requirements are effective. But individuals and tasks vary, so it would be impossible to predict when this principle may appear to break down. For, at some point the ratio requirement can become too large, and the individual may begin to pause at various, unpredictable times. Ultimately, as was indicated previously, responding can disintegrate altogether. Of course, by increasing the ratio gradually and progressively, such effects will be delayed. But eventually a point may be reached at which the steady high rate begins to slow down. At that point, the ratio can be reduced to the point at which rapid responding resumes. Then the requirement can be even more gradually increased.

Let us suppose that Mrs. Jones, a sixth grade teacher, is trying to increase her studnets' rate of completing workbook assignments. She begins by complimenting and giving each student a bonus point toward his final grade each time he finishes a workbook assignment. This has the effect of increasing the rate of completing assignments. Eventually she gives the bonus points less often but continues to compliment the students as they complete their assignments. As time goes by, she gradually diminishes both reinforcers, but the response rate goes higher. Eventually, weeks go by without her delivering any contingent reinforcers. Sporadically, the students' rate of completing assignments diminishes. Mrs. Jones then decides to reinstate the reinforcers occasionally. The class's rate of completing assignments resumes and remains at its high level.

A generalization can be extracted from this discussion: If the goal for a particular program is a high response rate, it is probably best to gradually and progressively increase the ratio requirement until the behavior reaches its peak, or the point at which the increase stops and the rate levels off and remains steady. If the rate of responding begins to disrupt, a temporary reduction in the ratio requirement should solve the problem.

Consistency of performance   Animal studies (Reynolds, 1968) have shown that a subject may tend to pause immediately following reinforcement under large FR (fixed ratio) requirements. This is not, however, a consistently observed phenomenon with human FR performance. The student assigned a fixed number of pages to complete prior to his receiving bonus points may or may not stop working for a while after receiving the points. If the required number of pages were very large, he might be more likely to pause after receiving the points than if the required number of pages were few. At least the possibility of a pause prior to the next response would exist, and the consistency of responding might thereby be disrupted. During the pause the student might engage in other behaviors than the one desired: doodling, leaving the room, daydreaming, and so on.

Variable-ratio (VR) performance, however, is almost never characterized by post reinforcement pauses. Let us take a look at an illustration of a VR reinforcement schedule. A student is being reinforced on a VR 6 schedule. Bonus points are to be delivered *on the average of* every six pages completed in the workbook. The actual reinforcement program could look like this

$$R_7 \rightarrow S^+ \qquad R_4 \rightarrow S^+ \qquad R_{10} \rightarrow S^+ \qquad R_2 \rightarrow S^+$$
$$(RRRRRRR) \rightarrow S^+ \quad (RRRR) \rightarrow S^+ \quad (RRRRRRRRRR) \rightarrow S^+ \quad (RR) \rightarrow S^+$$

Let each *R* represent the response of completing a workbook assignment. By looking at the way the responses are *distributed* just prior to reinforcement, we can see that in some cases reinforcement follows a fairly large number of responses (the R_{10}) while in other cases the reinforcer is delivered following just a few responses (R_2). The student has no way of anticipating when the next reinforcer might be delivered. It could be after the completion of one or two pages; it could be after completing as many as ten pages. Because the next reinforcement might be imminent, he quickly resumes work. There is no post reinforcement pause. Analogous to this is the situation in which the teacher collects written assignments in a random fashion, spot checking on the average of every fifth page completed by each student. A student could conceivably complete ten pages before the teacher checked one and praised him for his performance. At other times, he might have two pages in a row checked. Such a VR schedule would be likely to maintain performance at a steady rate, with hardly any pauses following reinforcement. Since VR schedules do not tend to generate pauses in performance, while FR schedules might, particularly those with high ratio requirements, VR appears to be the type of schedule that might best be employed if the objective is to maintain a consistent performance.

Continued responding in extinction Teachers and behavioral specialists can do an exellent job by making appropriate use of contingency management procedures; that is, by presenting contingencies that strengthen, shape, or weaken specific performances. But the issue of maintaining behavior following the removal of contingency management programs, as we discussed in Chapter 6, is just as crucial, if not more so. Fortunately, experimentation in the behavioral area has found that intermittent reinforcement is the key to such behavioral persistence under extinction, or nonreinforcement, conditions. Ratio schedules, in particular, have been shown to provide a reinforcement history that tends to sustain performance once reinforcement is terminated. Differences in performance, following the termination of different kinds of ratio schedules, do exist; and some of their important characteristics have been identified. School personnel will probably find it useful to become familiar with those characteristics.

Performance following the termination of an FR (fixed-ratio) schedule is characterized by bursts of responding at the same high rates that had been emitted when the schedule was in effect (Reynolds, 1968). The problem with the plan of providing for maintained high rates under extinction is that between the bursts of high rate responding, the periods of nonresponding become longer and longer. Eventually, the frequency of the bursts of responding diminishes to almost nothing, and the frequency of the periods of nonresponding increases. Ultimately the behavior may cease to be emitted at all.

Cindy's mother usually refused her daughter's initial requests for money, figuring that if Cindy really needed it she would ask for it again. Cindy had learned that money is usually forthcoming by her third request (an FR 3 schedule). On Cindy's thirteenth birthday, her mother decided that Cindy should be able to earn her own spending money. The next time Cindy came with a request for funds, her mother told her to find a babysitting job. Cindy continued to plead, but to no avail. She went away for a while and then returned ("It always worked before"). The pleading resumed. With her mother holding steadfast, the bursts of requests for money stopped before long. Had her mother relented, Cindy's requests for money would have returned to their former level almost immediately.) Another illustration of this phenomenon can be taken from the school setting. Every Friday Mrs. Smith collected her students' spelling papers and put a gold star on each 100 percent correct paper that had been neatly written. Karen loved getting gold stars. She brought them home proudly to her parents, who hugged her and acted very pleased with her accomplishments. One day Mrs. Smith ran out of stars, and she decided that the students were getting too big and did not need to receive them any more. Friday came and no star was forthcoming. Karen continued studying her spelling and writing neat papers each day for the next week or two, hoping to earn the coveted gold star. Then she would occasionally hand in a sloppy paper, which was followed with a few very neat ones. Pretty soon Karen seemed to give up. She rarely handed in carefully prepared spelling papers. The major point here, for the educator, is that after an FR schedule has been discontinued, responding in extinction may maintain for a short while, but the overall rate of responding will eventually approach zero.

A VR (variable-ratio) schedule tends to generate behavior that will maintain much longer under extinction conditions. In fact, a history of a VR schedule with a very high ratio requirement (that is, a very thin reinforcement density) for a particular response, can yield an exceedingly high and persistent performance pattern under extinction conditions. For example, Professor Potts gave a few spot quizzes early in the semester, then stopped giving them. His students did their assignments religiously "just in case." Out of approximately twenty entries, Uncle Herman had the luck to win a trip to Florida in one contest, a 5-dollar gift certificate in another, and a case of dog food in a third. And although Uncle Herman had not won a thing for many years after his streak of luck, he still spent all his spare time entering contests. Early in the seventh grade Mrs. Jones' former students were occasionally complimented by their new teacher "for being thorough scholars" when they used reference materials. Though later on in the year such compliments were no longer delivered, use of the materials remained at a high rate for a fairly long time.

In most cases, no matter what the schedule history, a response will diminish and eventually approach a zero rate when extinction conditions are maintained. This is true for VR histories as well. It is just that it takes much longer. Typical performance following the termination of VR reinforcement consists of very long, sustained, rapid bursts of responses. These are interspersed with gradually increasing periods of nonresponding, similar to those following FR schedule termination. But with VR performance, the periods of nonresponding usually begin later and occur less frequently than with FR. If Cindy's mother had given her money following an irregular number of requests, Cindy's requests would probably have persisted much longer. If Mrs. Smith had checked papers and delivered stars irregularly rather than regularly, Karen would probably have sustained the performance of her assignments for a longer period of time after the delivery of stars had been terminated.

Two important practical conclusions can be drawn from the fact that a well-established history of a thin VR schedule of reinforcement tends to generate very persistent performance under extinction conditions. (1) If the terminal goal of a program of behavior change or of an instructional sequence is the maintained emission of the response once contingencies are removed, a variable-ratio schedule of reinforcement that has been gradually and progressively thinned should best suit that purpose. (2) Conversely, an undesirable behavior should *never,* if it is possible to avoid doing so, be maintained by such a schedule. Since the schedule will tend to make it very resistant to extinction, getting rid of it will prove very difficult.

Exercise 7.2

Observe your own behavior or the behavior of a relative. Select a specific response class, such as a habit, hobby, or personality attribute. Describe the response in terms of rate, consistency, and persistence. Can you discover the reinforcers supporting the emission of the response? Try to account for the characteristics of the response on the basis of schedules of reinforcement.

Exercise 7.3

Teach a very simple skill, such as matching letters or colors, to a young child in a series of short training sessions. Reinforce each correct response on a continuous reinforcement (CRF) schedule until a specific criterion level is reached, say, eight correct responses in a row. Try a few nonreinforced test trials, then begin to thin out the schedule according to a specific predetermined program. Remove reinforcement altogether and probe (see Chapter 1) at various intervals (say, a week apart) by administering test trials. Plot your data. How well did the response maintain under reinforcement; under extinction? What changes, if any, would you make in your reinforcement schedule were you to replicate this experiment?

INTERVAL SCHEDULES

INTERVAL SCHEDULES DEFINED

We have learned that ratio schedules are related to a *specific number of responses.* Here we will learn that *interval schedules* are dependent upon the *passage of a specific period of time.* When a particular response is scheduled for reinforcement following the passage of a specific amount of time, and that *time requirement is held constant,* the schedule is labeled a *fixed-interval* (FI) schedule. For example, Carl's teacher has decided that it would be desirable for Carl to spend more time reading his assignment during social studies class and less time looking around the room and out the window. After operationally defining reading as "looking at a printed page for ten seconds," she sets an oven timer for five-minute intervals. If Carl is reading just after the timer rings, he is reinforced with a token. Otherwise, as soon as the response is emitted, following the termination of each five-minute interval, a token is delivered. FI schedules are also abbreviated, and the schedule in this illustration would be called an FI 5, or a fixed-interval five-minute schedule. An FI schedule, therefore, specifies that reinforcers are to be delivered contingent upon the emission of a particular response that occurs following the passage of a specific amount of time. Most pay schedules are FI schedules. As long as Mr. Smith is at the office, he is paid each Friday. Reinforcement is directly contingent upon the response of his coming to the pay window. If Mr. Smith is ill or out of town on Friday, his check remains available until such time as he does come to the pay window. In the school program, many events are scheduled on a regular basis: recess and lunch periods, weekly quizzes, delivery of report cards, classes in specific subjects, and many others. When the events have reinforcing properties and are delivered contingent upon a specific response, such situations represent FI schedules as they often operate in the schools. An illustrative model might look like these:

$$S \xrightarrow{\hspace{3cm}} R \xrightarrow{\hspace{3cm}} S^{+}$$

(twenty-four hours interval)　　　(line up)　　　(lunch)

As long as twenty-four hours have elapsed, the response of lining up will be reinforced with lunch.

or

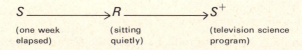

$$S \xrightarrow{\hspace{3cm}} R \xrightarrow{\hspace{3cm}} S^{+}$$

(one week elapsed)　　　(sitting quietly)　　　(television science program)

Following an interval of a week, sitting quietly is reinforced with the presentation of a television science program.

Variable-interval (VI) schedules operate in a similar manner, except that the time interval varies; that is, the time requirement is not held constant but is *a specified average.* The oven timer could have been set differently by Carl's teacher. She could, for instance, have randomly varied the intervals anywhere between zero and ten minutes. Over time, the length of the intervals would average out to about five minutes. Such a schedule would be called a VI 5, or variable-interval five-minute, schedule. For example, Mrs. Brown assigns her eighth graders to read at least one book on their own every two weeks. The students are expected to write in-class reports on their books. This assignment is given at various times during the school year, on an average of once in two weeks. For those students for whom writing and receiving a grade on a book report or successfully avoiding a failing grade is reinforcing, such a practice may operate as a VI schedule of reinforcement. Under VI scheduling, as with VR (variable ratio) scheduling, it is possible for reinforcements to be delivered very close together or very far apart. Mrs. Brown could assign the written reports as close together as two days in a row or as far apart as once in four weeks. This characteristic of VI schedules may generate performance that is different from that generated under FI schedules. In the following discussion those differences will be discussed along with a consideration of some of the general properties of interval schedule performance and how they may relate to the school setting.

Exercise 7.4

For each of the classroom episodes listed, identify the response and the schedule with which the reinforcer is delivered: CRF, FR, VR, FI, or VI; assume the contingency is reinforcing.
a. Provided that the class is sitting quietly, the teacher allows a restroom break each hour and a half.
b. Every neat paper is given a star.
c. Following the successful completion of each ten arithmetic problems, students may select a library book.
d. The teacher tells jokes and the class laughs at about half of them.
e. Mrs. Neophyte teaches reading daily. The principal drops in to observe her teaching reading on the average of three times a month.
f. Janie only gets to sit next to her boyfriend during fifth period science class each day.

Exercise 7.5

Offer an illustration drawn from your own personal life for each of the five schedules in Exercise 7.4.

CHARACTERISTICS OF INTERVAL SCHEDULE PERFORMANCE

The response characteristics generated by interval schedules are not necessarily identical for both laboratory animals and humans. Interval schedules, which generate very predictable patterns among different animals subjects (Ferster & Skinner, 1957), appear to show more variability among human subjects. Apparently such factors as instructions (Lippman & Meyer, 1967) and, more importantly, reinforcement history (Weiner, 1964) account for much of this variability. However, within the broad range of varied performances under interval reinforcement schedules, some generalizations can be drawn. Because it is possible to design a particular history for an individual with respect to a particular response, we can obtain a fairly tight amount of control of interval schedule performance (Weiner, 1969). It is possible, for instance, to generate either very rapid or very slow rates of responding under VI schedules, depending upon which prior schedules have been used with the same response. How this may be achieved will be discussed later in this chapter. Here we will make a general survey of such VI characteristics as rate, consistency of responding, and how performance maintains in extinction.

Low rates of responding An interval schedule carries only one simple requirement: The specific response must occur at least one time following the specified time interval. A pigeon can peck a disc once at the end of a required interval and receive his grain. Carl, who is on a fixed interval five-minute schedule (FI 5), could still technically receive his token as long as he spent just one ten-second period looking at his page each five minutes. For an individual on an FI schedule to respond with only one response per interval, is not typical, however. What frequently happens with a laboratory animal for instance, is that following reinforcement he pauses. Then, as the interval progresses, responding begins to accelerate. With an FI schedule, the individual is not penalized by postponement of reinforcement if he fails to respond for a while as he would be under an FR (fixed-rate) schedule. Reinforcement is postponed under an FI schedule only when the period of nonresponding is greater than the interval requirement. Carl would begin to lose out on receiving tokens only if he looked at his book less frequently than once per five minutes. So FI schedules may tend to generate lower response rates than FR schedules, though, over time, responding does usually maintain at least at a rate sufficient to allow the individual to earn his reinforcers when they become accessible.

In general, responding is more rapid under VI (variable-interval) than FI schedules. The variable nature of the VI schedule allows the individual to be reinforced at unpredictable times during each interval. Sometimes a response is reinforced near the beginning of the interval; sometimes near the middle; sometimes near the end. This unpredictability appears to keep the individual emitting responses at a fairly constant rate and, thus, has the effect of yielding more responses per time period. If Carl had no way of predicting when he would receive a token for reading, he would be more likely to keep reading, "just in case the teacher might look." But still, there is a limit, imposed by the scheduled interval, on the number of responses which can be reinforced under VI. Very high rates of responding contribute nothing to the amount of reinforcement received. Therefore rates that are greater than or equal to those found with ratio schedules are less likely. In general, interval schedule performance rates tend to be equal to or lower than ratio performance rates; but they are rarely greater than ratio performance rates.

Some factors have been identified as influencing the rapidness with which a response may be emitted under interval schedules. These include the size of the interval and the schedule history with respect to the particular response. Why the size of the required interval has an effect on the overall rate of performance should be pretty apparent. Since the individual is required to make at least one response per each designated time interval in order to receive maximal reinforcement, the shorter the required time interval, the higher the rate. Were Carl on an FI 2 schedule, he would have to read at least once each two minutes in order to earn the maximum number of tokens. On an FI 9, he would have to read only once each nine minutes for maximum pay-off. An FI schedule, then, makes it possible to easily manipulate the response rate by either shortening or lengthening the time interval.

Not quite as apparent is the reason why prior schedule history with respect to the particular response has an effect upon interval performance. Weiner (1964) has found that the rate of key-pressing responses by humans on FI schedules was markedly affected by their prior experience on the apparatus. Those subjects who had a history of receiving fixed-ratio reinforcement performed, on an FI schedule, at rates that were quite high, similar to their FR schedule performance. Other subjects who had a history of being reinforced only when they responded very slowly continued to respond very slowly when the schedule was switched to FI. Over a great many sessions, the rates among some of the subjects who responded at high FI rates began to diminish but never to the low level of their slow responding counterparts. The significance of this point for school personnel is that there is a possibility for achieving a reasonably high rate of performance under interval scheduling. Let us say that Carl's teacher, for convenience sake, prefers to use FI reinforcement. In order to avoid the potentially low rates that are known to sometimes characterize FI performance, she plans an initial phase of FR reinforcement. After all, she does not want a situation in which Carl reads for only a few ten-second intervals each five minutes. The teacher's aide agrees to help. Starting with a fairly low ratio requirement—FR 10; each reading response equals ten-seconds of looking at a page—the specific frequencies of the response are reinforced. The teacher's aid keeps track of the responses and arranges to have the tokens delivered at the appropriate time. The ratio of required responses is gradually increased to about FR 30. Then, when Carl is spending most of the time reading his assigned material, the teacher switches to an FI schedule. Ultimately the teacher can take over contingency control without assistance and remain fairly confident that the high rate of responding will maintain for quite a while. The teacher's aid could periodically shift Carl back to an FR schedule and further ensure the maintenance of the high rate.

Consistency of performance Ratio performance is, for the most part, consistent, and the ratio requirement is emitted at a steady rate. Fixed interval performance is not necessarily characterized in that manner. Because of the nature of the FI schedule, persistent responding throughout the interval is not required. What frequently happens with laboratory animals is that immediately following FI reinforcement, they tend to engage in other responses. Since grain has never been delivered immediately following a previously reinforced peck, it does not "pay" for the pigeon to resume pecking right away. Instead he pauses: struts, coos, preens, and flaps his wings before again starting the accelerating rate of disc-pecking, as the interval progresses to its end. Unlike animals, human subjects working in the laboratory tend to respond more consistently under FI schedules (Weiner, 1969). Yet, in the natural setting, instances of postreinforcement pauses can be occasionally identified. Students who are quizzed or graded at regular intervals often tend to study sporadically. As the interval progresses, studying behavior increases in an accelerating fashion. While study behavior is low, other response rates are higher: playing, dating, rushing for fraternities, and so on. During reading class, Carl could conceivably look out of the window, disrupt, get a drink, doodle, or engage in other behaviors in the early phases of the five minute interval. Yet he could still remain eligible for and receive maximal token reinforcement as long as at least one reading response occurred each five minutes.

Such inconsistency does not usually occur under variable interval schedules. Since the reinforceable response cannot be predicted, some occur close together, others, further apart, the individual tends to maintain a steady pace of responding. Two successive pecks sometimes yield grain to the pigeon, so pecking continues following reinforcement. Students, whose instructors give "surprise" quizzes also tend to keep up better with their assignments. Whether to avoid failure or to seek success, studying is maintained and they are less likely to engage in competing activities. Following a written in-class book report, Mrs. Brown's pupils would probably continue to read books on their own at a pretty constant rate, just in case she were to assign another report the next day. Since variable interval performance is typified by consistency while fixed interval performance may not be, it is probably a good idea to ultimately switch from FI to VI when consistency of performance is desired.

Continued responding in extinction   As with ratio schedules, interval schedules tend to generate responding that maintains longer in extinction than responding that has been previously maintained on continuous reinforcement (CRF). In general, if a particular response has been maintained on a schedule with a very long interval requirement, the response will probably maintain longer than if the interval was fairly short (Reynolds, 1968). This tendency again underscores the importance of using a program that progressively extends the schedule of reinforcement. To terminate the reinforcement program with Carl functioning on either an FI 5 or a VI 5 schedule, because the terminal goal of having him read his social studies assignment had been achieved, would be insufficient. A sudden withdrawal of the reinforcing contingencies might result in a disruption of the response before much time had passed. It would probably be preferable to gradually lengthen the required interval until token delivery were made contingent upon continuing to perform his reading assignment for days or perhaps even weeks. By that time, removal of the tokens would hardly be noticed.

If the intention of the behavioral specialist or teacher is to design a program that will yield responses that continue to be *consistently* emitted once the reinforcing contingencies have been removed, a variable interval would probably be the training schedule of choice. The regular responding that is characteristic of performance under VI reinforcement schedules appears to maintain itself under extinction. Laboratory animals who have been trained on VI schedules continue to respond similarly under extinction conditions. Responding maintains without pausing; though of course, over extended periods of time, the rate diminishes and ultimately ceases. On the other hand, performance under extinction following FI training tends to be interspersed with numerous periods of nonresponding prior to its ultimate cessation. In the event that a fixed-interval training schedule is selected, for practicality or convenience, it is usually possible to eventually switch over to a variable schedule prior to the removal of all reinforcing contingencies.

For example, in a program conducted by a special education teacher, a switch was made from a schedule closely resembling an FI to one similar to a VI schedule. In order to reduce a student's thumbsucking, a token was given to the student each time the bell on an oven timer rang, provided his thumb was not in his mouth. During the first phase; the timer was set at regular intervals. For the next phase, numbers from one to twenty were selected at random by drawing numbered paper slips from a bowl and replacing the slips. The numbers were listed in the order they were drawn. Each time the timer was set, the interval was the succeeding number on the list. The random selection of intervals from one to twenty thus provided a schedule that operated like a variable interval of ten minutes (VI 10).

Exercise 7.6

For each of the responses illustrated in Exercise 7.4, describe the performance characteristics you might expect as a function of the reinforcement schedules.

Exercise 7.7

Describe the characteristics of your own performance under each of the schedules you illustrated for Exercise 7.5.

VARIATIONS IN REINFORCEMENT SCHEDULES

Interval schedules can be used conveniently in the school setting. They ensure that the delivery of reinforcers contingent upon a desired response is maintained on a regular basis. Yet, with an interval schedule, it is not necessary for specific frequencies of a response to be counted before reinforcement is to be delivered. The individual in charge of managing the contingencies has only to observe the responding individual periodically. She is otherwise free to continue her other tasks. Emphasis has already been given to one potential limitation of using interval schedules: They may tend to generate low rates of responding. Yet that does not necessarily have to happen. Sometimes rapid responding characterizes the rate of an individual performing under an interval schedule. The fact is that human response rates under interval schedules tend to be variable. It is therefore difficult to predict response rates for most situations. One method for improving the control over the rate of interval performance—providing a ratio schedule history—has already been discussed. This discussion will be directed toward some schedule variations that can provide other appropriate histories to allow for greater control over subsequent responding.

LIMITED HOLD

One way of ensuring a high rate of performance under an interval schedule is to impose an additional restriction on the performance. That restriction requires that a primed response (the first response following the termination of the required interval) must be emitted within a specific time limitation or reinforcement will no longer be made available. In other words, reinforcement is only available for a brief time period. The schedule is one that many educators have probably learned to use intuitively. Grades are only given if an assignment is fulfilled within a certain time. The class is dismissed for recess as soon as the students come to order. But if they fail to come to order within a certain number of minutes, recess time will be over and the opportunity will be lost. Here is another hypothetical example: In a seventh grade social studies class, the teacher assigned her students the project of bringing in ten newspaper clippings. She did not specify a time by which they were due. The students would be able to present their current events items to the class and would receive credit toward their grades. Some students went for several weeks without fulfilling the assignment and then, toward the end of the marking period, began to bring in sheaves of clippings. The last week before report cards were to be distributed, classroom activity was overloaded with their current events presentations. The teacher was forced to postpone presenting the next planned subject unit. And, some of the students never did complete the assignment. In order to avoid such a situation during the next marking period, the teacher added a restriction: Credit would only be given once in a week, on Friday. The students had only one week in which to collect and present the news clippings. They could receive no credit if they brought the clippings in the following Monday. The opportunity for reinforcement was available for only a brief time period. Laboratory studies demonstrate that the imposition of a short *limited hold* has the effect of increasing response rates (Reynolds, 1968). In the hypothetical situation presented here, one might expect that the new policy would have a similar effect. In order to avoid losing out on the opportunity to earn credits, the students would probably bring in clippings regularly and more often. Another way, therefore, to speed up responding under interval schedules is to restrict the time during which reinforcement is made available to a brief period; to use a *limited hold contingency*.

Exercise 7.8

Some of the readers of this text are reading it for a course requirement. Others are not. Specify the contingency (or contingencies) that are maintaining your reading the material. Is there a limited hold provision? How is the presence or absence of such a restriction affecting your reading rate?

DIFFERENTIAL REINFORCEMENT OF HIGH RATES (DRH)

Still another method for providing a history of high rate responding is to use a differential reinforcement of high rates (DRH) schedule for awhile. In establishing a DRH schedule, sequences of responses are observed very closely. Reinforcement is delivered only when several responses occur in rapid succession. When pauses are interspersed, reinforcement is postponed. High rates are differentially reinforced in preference to low rates. When the mile runner completes his run in less than four minutes, the crowd cheers. Completion times greater than that are not cheered. When the student correctly completes all the problems in his workbook within a week, he is given an A. If it takes him longer, his grade is lowered to a B. Returning to the illustration of the news clippings, suppose one student were still responding at a low rate. He only brings in an occasional clipping. Then the World Series is held, and the student brings in four clippings on that subject in a row. The sequence is reinforced, not only with the earned credits but also with social reinforcers and, perhaps, even access to some preferred activity. Such powerful contingencies are repeated with that student each time he does bring in several clippings in a row. In this manner, the response rate would be more likely to increase. Once the rate reached an acceptable level, it would be possible to switch over to an interval schedule.

Exercise 7.9

Suggest three instructional objectives that you think would be rapidly achieved by means of DRH scheduling. Describe the specific procedure you would use with each.

DIFFERENTIAL REINFORCEMENT OF LOW RATES (DRL)

On occasion, certain responses need to be reduced but not necessarily eliminated. The student who writes too quickly and ends up handing in a sloppy paper, the swimmer working on perfecting his stroke, the ballet dancer who performs more rapidly than called for by the score all need to be slowed down. The student who tends to dominate class discussions is exhibiting another example of a behavior that a teacher may wish to reduce but not necessarily eliminate. She may want to keep the student participating, but just not as often. The schedule best suited for this is the differential reinforcement of low rates (DRL). If sequences of behavior which are spaced relatively far apart are reinforced differentially, the rate of responding should diminish. So, in the latter example, when the domineering student emits a response following a long period of nonresponding, the teacher could take the time to praise the student, paraphrase the comment, nod to the student, or smile. Should the student emit several comments in rapid succession, the teacher would ignore him. Assuming that the major reinforcing consequences derived from the teacher's responsiveness, such a DRL procedure might tend to reduce the rate with which the particular student participated in the discussion.

Again, since rate of performance under interval schedules is known to be significantly affected by schedule history, prior experience under

DRL could slow down subsequent response rates. Once a desired rate of responding were fairly well stabilized, it might be possible to maintain that low rate under interval scheduling. Recognizing the formerly domineering student at irregular intervals could maintain his low but consistent rate of participating in the class discussion. Like the other schedules of reinforcement, DRL provides a program for the regular delivery of reinforcement and therefore has the same advantages that other positive procedures have: Good things still continue to happen! Certainly it would be possible to slow response rates in other ways: yell at the student when he hurries, ignore him altogether, flunk him, keep reminding him to slow down, feed him tranquilizing drugs and all kinds of other possibilities. But here is a situation in which the responding individual does not lose out. He can still earn his reinforcers and go merrily on his way.

Exercise 7.10

A student constantly raises his hand in order to request a drink. Describe in words how you might use a DRL procedure in order to reduce that rate.

Exercise 7.11

Suppose you had a friend whose company you enjoyed, but she talked too much. How could you use a DRL procedure in order to reduce her verbal output?

Exercise 7.12

If you have a student, friend, or relative who emits a desirable behavior but at a rate that you consider to be too high, design a program for reducing the rate of emission. Establish a base rate by counting the frequency with which the behavior is emitted during each of several equivalent sessions. Then introduce a DRL schedule for several sessions by reinforcing your subject each time there is a pause between responses which is greater than some minimal length. Count the frequency of the responses during each of the experimental sessions. Plot your base rate and experimental data. Evaluate the effectiveness of your procedure.

SUMMARY

Ratio and interval schedules were defined and discussed as procedures for maintaining behaviors. When the behavioral program's terminal goal is the maintained emission of a response following the removal of contingencies, a variable ratio or interval schedule, which has been gradually and progressively thinned, is effective.

Response rates tend to be differentially influenced by the schedule that is selected. Ratio schedules generally produce higher rates of responding than interval schedules. However, when the objective is to maintain a behavior at a high rate while avoiding the necessity of counting responses prior to the delivery of reinforcement, an interval schedule can be planned. Provision of a ratio or differential reinforcement of high rates (DRH) schedule history or a limited hold requirement should increase the likelihood of a higher rate of performance under interval scheduling. Conversely, DRL schedules reduce response rates and probably provide the right kind of history for low rates of responding under interval schedules.

REFERENCES

Bijou, S. W., & Orlando, R. Rapid development of multiple-schedule performances with retarded children. *Journal of the Experimental Analysis of Behavior,* 1961, **4,** 7–16.

Boren, J. Response rate and resistance to extinction as functions of the fixed ratio. *Dissertation Abstracts,* 1956, **14,** 1261.

Ferster, C. B., & Skinner, B. F. *Schedules of reinforcement.* New York: Appleton-Century-Crofts, 1957.

Hutchinson, R. R., & Azrin, N. H. Conditioning of mental hospital patients to fixed-ratio schedules of reinforcement. *Journal of the Experimental Analysis of Behavior,* 1961, **4,** 87–95.

Lippman, L. G., & Meyer, M. E. Fixed-interval performance as related to instructions and to subject's verbalizations of the contingency. *Psychonomic Science,* 1967, **8,** 135–136.

Long, E. R. Additional techniques for producing multiple-schedule control in children. *Journal of the Experimental Analysis of Behavior,* 1962, **5,** 443–455.

Long, E. R. Chained and tandem scheduling with children. *Journal of the Experimental Analysis of Behavior,* 1963, **6,** 459–472.

Reynolds, G. S. *A primer of operant conditioning.* Glenview, Ill.: Scott, Foresman, 1968.

Skinner, B. F. *The behavior of organisms.* New York: Appleton-Century-Crofts, 1938.

Weiner, H. Conditioning history and human fixed-interval performance. *Journal of the Experimental Analysis of Behavior,* 1964, **7,** 383–385.

Weiner, H. Controlling human fixed-interval performance. *Journal of the Experimental Analysis of Behavior,* 1969, **12,** 349–373.

PART IV

REDUCING OR ELIMINATING THE OCCURRENCE OF UNDESIRABLE BEHAVIORS

Parts I, II, and III have emphasized procedures for increasing and maintaining behaviors that exist in some strength in the student's behavioral repertoire and the development of new student behaviors. Probably one of the greatest irritants to school personnel are student behaviors that are undesirable in the school setting. Though the designation of a particular behavior as "undesirable" is based upon a subjective impression, many behaviors would probably be so designated by most educators. Obvious among these are giving incorrect answers; engaging in non-school-related activities; or in disruptive acts such as making distracting noises, leaving one's seat at the wrong time, directing aggression toward other students or the teacher. No matter how well instruction is programmed by the teacher, efficient teaching cannot take place if she is spending most of her time attempting to cope with such problems. Nor can students function at their optimal levels if they are being distracted by their fellow students. Undesirable classroom behaviors must be reduced or eliminated if a learning atmosphere is to prevail.

The educator who sets about to reduce a particular behavior has a variety of alternative procedures available to him. He can use gestures, instructions, or other stimuli prior to the emission of the specific behavior or he can provide a particular consequence contingent upon the emission of the behavior. Part IV discusses both categories: the manipulation of prior stimulus events and alteration in the consequences of the behavior. Chapter 8 considers nonreinforcement of a response, or extinction. Chapter 9 deals with response contingent withdrawal of reinforcement, timeout, and response cost. Chapter 10 discusses the presentation of an aversive stimulus contingent upon the response, or punishment. Alterations in prior stimulus conditions alone or in combination with changes in consequences are discussed in Chapter 11. Reserved for the last chapter in Part IV is a positive approach to the reduction of undesirable behaviors, reducing behaviors by means of reinforcement.

In attempting to select a given procedure, several factors should be considered by the teacher or behavioral specialist. These include the advantages of using the procedures, techniques for maximizing their effectiveness as well as their disadvantages. Accordingly, after defining, describing, and illustrating each procedure, each of those factors are discussed. Further emphasis upon the selection of any given reductive procedure are presented in Part V.

8 EXTINCTION

Objectives

Using examples not described in this chapter, you should be able to:

1. Define and offer school illustrations of extinction.
2. List and explain, in two sentences or less, each of the advantages of using extinction.
3. List and give school illustrations of the properties of a behavior undergoing extinction.
4. List and offer school illustrations of factors known to influence the rapidity with which a behavior is eliminated through extinction.
5. List and offer school illustrations of the variables that serve to facilitate or maximize the effect of extinction.
6. List and explain, in two sentences or less, each of the disadvantages of using extinction.
7. Describe specific situations in which extinction would and would not be the behavioral procedure of choice; justify each position you take.

GENERAL CHARACTERISTICS

EXTINCTION DEFINED

Viewed as an operation, extinction is a fairly simple and straight-forward procedure, although it is not the easiest to carry out in practice. It is a procedure in which *behavior that has been reinforced previously is no longer reinforced.* Ultimately, the consistent nonreinforcement of a behavior tends to result in a reduction of that behavior to its prereinforcement level. For instance, if Clarissa fails to come to the phone every time her rejected suitor asks for her, his calls will eventually cease.

Extinction is probably used by most people at various times in their lives. This is especially true of individuals who are responsible for, and concerned with, other people's behavior. Parents, teachers, behavioral specialists, employers, and even partners in a marriage often use extinction, though probably without awareness, in attempting to reduce particular behaviors. A mother ignores her whining child in order to reduce whining. Teachers withhold good grades, praise, privileges, and other reinforcers when their students perform inappropriately. Counselors may ignore certain undesirable statements from their clients, and employers often withhold raises from employees whose performance fails to meet the job requirements. When a husband stops giving his wife money when she nags him for it, he is, in technical terms, placing that behavior on extinction.[1]

The extinction procedure is one that has been heavily researched both in the laboratory and in applied settings. Quite a bit has been learned about its properties. Therefore, after the procedure is illustrated and its advantages discussed, emphasis will be given to those properties. The variables that are known to influence the effectiveness of the extinction procedures and the disadvantages involved in using extinction will be considered as well. A recognition of those factors should assist the practitioner to utilize extinction effectively and to provide a basis for deciding when extinction is and is not a method of choice.

EXTINCTION IN SCHOOL AND COUNSELING SETTINGS

A teacher asks her class the question: "What holiday do we celebrate on the Fourth of July?" Jimmy stands up, waves his hand frantically, and shouts "I know, I know." The teacher ignores Jimmy and calls on

---

[1] Though the operations performed in the extinction procedure are often labeled "punishment" in everyday use, we are making a clear distinction between *extinction* (withholding reinforcement contingent upon behavior) and *punishment* (presenting an aversive stimulus contingent upon behavior, to be discussed in Chapter 10).

George, who has raised his hand and remains silent and in his seat. Jimmy's hand waving, calling out, and out-of-seat behavior is undergoing extinction. Archibald also volunteers an answer and is recognized by the teacher. "We celebrate the adoption of the Constitution on July Fourth." The teacher ignores Archibald's response and calls on Jennifer. "We celebrate Independence Day on July Fourth." "That's right, Jennifer. Good for you." Archibald's incorrect response is put on extinction while Jennifer's is reinforced and also serves as a model for Archibald.

In a counseling session, Roger tells the counselor about all his current aches and pains. His foot hurts; he has a headache. And last night he really felt dizzy just when it was time for him to clear the table. Assured by the doctor that Roger's complaints have no organic basis, the counselor averts his gaze and makes no response while Roger is on that particular subject. When Roger mentions that he got an A on a spelling paper, the counselor responds enthusiastically. His somatic complaints are put on extinction by the counselor. Other specific categories of verbal behavior are not.

Exercise 8.1

In one of the following settings try to find an episode in which extinction was used by a teacher, parent, or counselor:

a. a classroom
b. a playground, store, home
c. an individual or group counseling session

Describe the episode. Tell what reinforcers were withheld.

ADVANTAGES OF EXTINCTION

Effectively reducing behavior   Extinction, often used in combination with other procedures, has been found to be effective in reducing a wide variety of undesirable child behaviors. Crying (Hart, Allen, Buell, Harris, & Wolf, 1964) and glasses throwing (Wolf, Risley, & Mees, 1964) were reduced substantially when the reinforcing consequences for those responses were removed. Within the past few years there have been many reports of programs that used extinction as a means of effectively reducing undesirable classroom behaviors. Disruptive classroom behavior (Thomas, Nielson, Kuypers, & Becker, 1969; Zimmerman & Zimmerman, 1962; O'Leary & Becker, 1967), aggressive behavior (Scott, Burton, & Yarrow, 1967; Brown & Elliot, 1965), tantrums in the classroom (Carlson, Arnold, Becker, & Madsen, 1968) and nonstudy behavior (Thomas, Becker, & Armstrong, 1968; Bijou, Birnbrauer, Kidder, & Tague, 1967; Hall, Lund, & Jackson, 1968; Hall, Panyon, Rabon, & Broden, 1968) were all successfully handled in this manner. In many of these instances, a more rapid decrement in the undesirable behavior was accomplished with the simultaneous reinforcement of the desired behaviors. For instance, in one project (Bijou, et al., 1967), nonstudy behavior resulted in the loss of social reinforcement for institutionalized retardates. At the same time, appropriate study behaviors earned the subjects tokens, with which they could purchase a wide variety of tangible and edible reinforcers.

Extinction's effectiveness has also been recognized in counseling activities. One study (Krumboltz & Hosford, 1967) notes that "extinction procedures . . . have been shown to be effective counseling techniques for weakening or eliminating deviant behaviors (p. 33)." Extinction is used in counseling much the same way as it is in the classroom. Reinforcement is withheld from undesired verbalizations or other behaviors. For example, a goal of increased verbal participation was specified for five students participating in group counseling. The attention of the counselor was withdrawn whenever a student left the counseling table or failed to participate in other ways. Verbal participation was immediately reinforced with attention, interest, and positive verbal responses.

Long-lasting effect   Some of the reductive procedures under consideration in this text, such as stimulus change, reduce behavior only temporarily. If extinction is used with maximal effectiveness, its results can be enduring (Skinner, 1938). Many of the studies cited above demonstrate the long-term effectiveness of extinction. The undesirable behaviors were rarely emitted following the extinction program.

Aversive stimuli not required   Because extinction simply involves the nondelivery of reinforcement rather than the presentation of aversive consequences, it avoids the negative effects that often result from the use of aversive control. (Such effects will be discussed at greater length in Chapter 10, "Punishment".)

Exercise 8.2
Specify a simple school-related terminal goal that you think might best be achieved by means of extinction. Defend your choice of extinction as the procedure.

PROPERTIES OF EXTINCTION

When all reinforcement is permanently withheld following the emission of a specific behavior, that behavior should, over time, gradually diminish and, ultimately, cease. There are, however, some general, predictable properties that characterize a behavior as it is undergoing extinction. These include temporal aspects, a temporary increase in response rate and intensity, extinction induced aggression, and spontaneous recovery.

Behavioral reduction gradual   Extinction usually does not have an immediate effect. Once the reinforcing consequences are removed, the behavior continues to be emitted for some indeterminate amount of time before it finally ceases (Skinner, 1953). The whining child and nagging wife continue to whine and nag for a while even when such behaviors yield them no reinforcement. Jimmy would probably continue to call out many times before stopping. Archibald might continue to give the same incorrect answer several times before emitting the correct one.

Several factors are known to influence the rate with which a behavior is eliminated through extinction. These include the number of reinforced trials, the schedule with which the response has been reinforced in the past, the deprivation level of the individual, the effort needed to make the response, and the use of procedural combinations (Millenson, 1967). In general, a behavior that has been frequently emitted and reinforced in the past—an established behavior—is much more resistant to extinction than one that has been only rarely emitted and reinforced. Also, as we discussed in Part III on schedules of reinforcement, a response that has been reinforced on an intermittent schedule is more resistant to extinction than one that has been continuously reinforced. Had the teacher recognized Jimmy every time he jumped out of his seat and said "I know, I know," the behavior would probably disappear sooner when she withheld such recognition than it would had she reinforced such behavior frequently but inconsistently.

The more deprived an individual, or the longer the period of time since the individual has received a given reinforcer, the longer a behavior will be emitted under extinction conditions. This factor is especially important when the behavior has been maintained by primary reinforcement (Holland & Skinner, 1961). A hungry child whining for a cookie would emit many more responses in the absence of reinforcement than the same child would after having completed a big meal.

A response that requires considerable effort will extinguish more rapidly than one that is emitted with ease. A two year old would probably persist in the response "Cookie, cookie" much longer than in the response "Mommy, may I please have a cookie," since the latter response undoubtedly requires much more effort than the former.

When extinction is used in combination with reinforcement for an alternative or incompatible behavior, the response will diminish more rapidly. Were Jimmy frequently recognized by the teacher when he sat and raised his hand quietly, his less desirable form of responding would diminish more rapidly than if he had no such reinforceable behavioral alternative available. The same is true of extinction used in combination with punishment of the undesirable response. Were Archibald scolded for his incorrect response in addition to not receiving praise, he might tend to emit the incorrect answer less frequently in the future than if his wrong answer were simply ignored (unless, of course, scolding were the only form of attention Archibald received). We will, subsequently, discuss such combined procedures. We will consider reasons for using punishment cautiously, even though it may serve to facilitate extinction, in Chapter 10.

Exercise 8.3

If you have carried out the shaping procedure in exercise 4.6 put the response on extinction by removing the reinforcer. Count the number of times the response is emitted within a specified period of time. Continue extinction sessions consisting of equal time durations for several days. Count the frequency of the response for each session. Plot your results on a graph, like the one illustrated below:

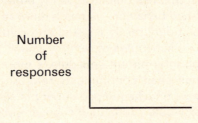

Number
of
responses

Sessions

Was there a decrease or cessation of the response? (*Note:* If you wish to reinstate the behavior, reinforce the response once again after it drops to a low level but before it disappears.)

Exercise 8.4

Do the following experiment.
a. Select a particular common language category, such as plural nouns, colors, descriptive adjectives, names of objects in the room, and so on.
b. Select a subject and ask him to recite any words that come to his mind at the rate of about one per second.
c. Have someone seated behind the subject record the number of words emitted that fall within and those that fall outside of the specified category.
d. For the first two and one half minutes watch the subject, nod slightly, smile, or say "hmm" or "uh-huh" following the emission of each word.
e. For the next two and one half minutes nod slightly, smile, or say "hmm" or "uh-huh" following the emission of all words *except those in the designated category*. For the words in the designated category, turn your head away from the subject and avert your gaze after each such emission. Say nothing. Do not nod or smile.

f. For the next two and one half minutes, repeat the procedure you followed in d.

g. Calculate a percentate for each phase of the experiment by dividing the number of words that fell within the specified category by the total number of words emitted for each phase of the experiment:

$$\frac{\text{specified category}}{\text{total words}}$$

Was there a difference?

h. Present your conclusions in a sentence or two.

Increase in rate and intensity of responding A brief increase in the rate and intensity of responding immediately following the cessation of reinforcement has been a phenomenon observed in both animals (Millenson, 1967) and humans (Kelly, 1969). This is especially likely to occur when the density of the reinforcement schedule is high. What happens when a candy machine fails to deliver? The individual pulls on the plunger more and more frequently and with greater vigor before giving up and going away. The infant whose crying is ignored for the first time will continue to scream with increasing intensity before the crying begins to subside and ultimately cease.

Inducing aggression A brief period of aggressive behavior may also accompany extinction in its early phases (Skinner, 1953, p. 69). The discontinuation of positive reinforcement has been found to produce aggression in pigeons (Azrin, Hutchinson, & Hake, 1966) and in squirrel monkeys (Hutchinson, Azrin, & Hunt, 1968). A recent study (Kelly, 1969) has demonstrated a similar response with human males. In that situation, subjects were reinforced with money for pulling a knob. The discontinuation of the delivery of the money resulted in several subjects engaging in a forceful hitting response. This is similar to the vending machine phenomenon. After the frustrated customer yanks at the lever with an increasing rate and intensity, he, not uncommonly, kicks or bangs the machine. Examples of this kind of response are also found in the school. The good student who cries in exasperation when he does not receive a good grade and the student who, used to being selected for special privileges, slams his book on the desk when another student is selected are probably exhibiting *extinction induced aggression.*

Producing spontaneous recovery Another phenomenon that has been observed in connection with extinction is the reappearance of the "extinguished" response following a time interval but without any intervening reinforcement of the response. This phenomenon is called *spontaneous recovery* (Skinner, 1953). Although this particular property is a transitory one and the frequency of the "recovered" response is very limited, recognition of its existence can save school personnel from making a wrong move. Here is an example. Reggi, thanks to his older brother, came to school with a vocabulary of off-color words which would tend to make a turnip blush. The behavioral specialist, to whom the problem was referred, observed that Reggi's use of such words seemed to be strongly maintained from various sources in the environment. The teacher frowned and scolded him, thereby attending heavily to the response. His classmates giggled and gasped; the principal lectured. Perhaps because Reggi had had little attention in the past, all of the attention from teacher, peers, and principal served to heavily reinforce his language. A full-scale extinction program was put into effect. The teacher now turned away when Reggi swore. The students were reinforced for ignoring such language, and they ultimately stopped attending to it. The principal no longer discussed the topic with Reggi. His swearing gradually subsided and ultimately appeared to have been eliminated. Then, several days later, though the response had not been reinforced, Reggi emitted a choice four-letter word. That was a crucial moment. The teacher could have decided that the whole procedure had been a failure and begun to scold Reggi again. The other reinforcers could also have been presented again and the behavior might then have assumed its former, or even greater, strength. But the teacher was prepared for the predictable minimal recovery of the behavior, and she was able to continue the extinction procedure until such recovery no longer manifested itself.

Exercise 8.5

If you have conducted the extinction procedure for Exercise 8.3, describe any instances of increase in response rate, aggression, or spontaneous recovery that you observed.

Exercise 8.6

Try to observe an extinction episode in a classroom, store, or at home. Did you observe any instances of increased response rate, aggression, or spontaneous recovery during your observation? Describe them.

USING EXTINCTION EFFECTIVELY

Identifying and withholding sources of reinforcement   Does Sam respond "rudely" in class because his peers approve, because the teacher becomes angry, because his parents smile at such responses at home, or because of all those reinforcers? Does Jack take money from the teacher's purse because the money will buy him food or items that he cannot afford? Or does he increase his prestige with his pals by bragging about his "accomplishment"? Extinction requires that all major sources of reinforcement have to be withheld. Again, the method for determining which reinforcers are maintaining the behavior is based upon empirical observation. Once the response is operationally defined, an object or event which appears to be reinforcing it is withheld for a period of time. If the behavior subsequently declines, one reinforcing contingency has probably been identified. In order to be *certain* that the reinforcer is indeed functionally related to the emission of the behavior, it can again be temporarily re-presented. If the behavior then increases and drops again when the reinforcer is withheld, a source of reinforcement has been determined. This procedure can be repeated for each of the suspected reinforcers. Once the major sources of reinforcement for a particular undesirable behavior have been identified, those contingencies should, if possible, be permanently removed. Suppose in Sam's case that all of the suspected reinforcers were demonstrated to have had a reinforcing effect upon his rude behavior in class. When the teacher withheld her anger, the behavior began to diminish. When the students, praised for ignoring Sam's response, no longer approved of that behavior, it diminished further. When Sam's parents were told of his difficulties in school, they agreed to ignore, rather than smile at, such responses. The task of the teacher and, perhaps, the behavioral specialist would be to maintain the elimination of those sources of reinforcement until the behavior ultimately disappeared. The behavioral specialist, for instance, could have periodic meetings with Sam's parents. He could show them a record of the declining frequency of rude responses and thank them for their cooperation in contributing toward the reduction of the response. The teacher's behavior might be maintained in a similar way for a while. Ulimately the reinforcement of having a better behaved student would probably be sufficient to maintain the teacher's behavior.

A point worthy of repetition here is the importance of guarding against allowing occasional reinforcers to slip in unnoticed during an extinction procedure, since this would provide an intermittent schedule of reinforcement. The more often such uncontrolled reinforcement occurs, the longer the behavior tends to persist. Were Sam's best friend, unbeknown to the teacher, to give Sam a signal of approbation for a rude response, the behavior would take longer to extinguish. The same would be true if the teacher happened to be tired or upset one day and became angry before she was able to control her outburst. This kind of thing does happen and understandably so. But by structuring the environment, for instance, by praising peers who ignore rudeness, and guarding against such events, one can increase the efficiency of the extinction procedure.

Maintaining extinction conditions for a sufficient time The short burst of high-rate responding which often occurs when extinction is first put into effect can often be very discouraging. When the teacher decided to ignore Reggi's colorful language, he responded by bursting forth with a stream of epithets, the meaning of which the teacher did not even know until she was an adult. She might well have branded the technique of ignoring the undesirable behavior a failure. But, was it? The only way she could find out would be to ride the crest of the wave for a while (and hope that the other students are no more sophisticated than she was at their age) and see if it began to subside. Assuming the teacher's frowning and scolding were the reinforcing events, the behavior would ultimately diminish. At such a time, data collection can be a tremendous asset. The frequency of Reggi's emission of off-color words per day could be tallied, perhaps with the help of a golf counter. If the data showed a small but steady decrease in the response rate, there would then be room for optimism. Sometimes the decrease is so gradual that it would escape notice in the absence of recorded data. The basic point of this discussion, however, is that the temporary increase can be anticipated. Knowing that it is a predictable phenomenon should help the practitioner not to abandon the extinction program.

Combining extinction with other procedures Although extinction used by itself is a very effective method for reducing an undesirable behavior, it is probably a good idea to combine its use with other procedures. Chapters 9 and 10 discuss combining extinction with timeout, response cost, and punishment. Here the emphasis will be on providing reinforcing consequences for alternative responses while a particular undesirable response is undergoing extinction. There are two reasons for providing reinforcement for alternative responses, which are probably apparent to the reader by now. One reason concerns the tendency of living organisms to emit behavior until some reinforcing consequence occurs. The other has to do with the idea of "killing two birds with one stone."

Because extinction implies the discontinuation, or withholding, of reinforcement for a particular response, it is important to determine if the individual has "sufficient" reinforcement available to him from other sources. When Sam's rude responses were no longer yielding him teacher attention, the teacher would have to make sure that Sam did not lose out on receiving her attention altogether. For if Sam could find no constructive way to get the teacher to notice him, he would probably continue trying different (even destructive) things until one worked. And that other way might be worse than rudeness. He could, for instance, begin slamming books against his desk or hitting other children. The point, then, is that the individual whose specific behavior is undergoing extinction should receive lots of reinforcement for desirable behaviors. Sam could be praised or smiled at for completing assignments. He could be given extra privileges for responding politely, and so on.

By planning the reinforcement of desirable behaviors simultaneously with the extinction of undesirable behaviors, a constructive outcome can be achieved: the desired behavior should increase. When the desired behavior *interferes* or is *incompatible*[2] with the undesirable behavior, reinforcement of that desired behavior should speed up the process even more. Putting Sam on extinction for rude language should ultimately lead to the diminution of that response, but reinforcement of polite language will simultaneously increase it and reduce the rudeness. Both polite and rude responses cannot be emitted at the same time. Two things, then, are being accomplished at once.

Exercise 8.7

For the terminal goal that you selected for Exercise 8.2 (or for one you specify now), describe all the steps you would take in attempting to maximize the effectiveness of your extinction procedure.

Exercise 8.8

If it is feasible, carry out the procedure outlined for Exercise 8.7. Be sure to first collect sufficient operant level data (the frequency of the response within a particular time interval—see Chapter 1) against which to measure the decrease in behavior. After a substantial decrease has occurred, re-present the reinforcer once or twice. Describe what happens. Once again remove the reinforcer. Continue until the behavior has reached the level specified for the terminal goal. Plot your data on a graph (see Exercise 8.3 for an illustration of a graph).

Exercise 8.9

For any of your classroom, counseling, or other recent observations:
a. describe how the individual who used extinction made use of techniques for maximizing the effects of the procedure
b. which techniques were not used
c. describe what happened to the undesirable behavior

DISADVANTAGES OF EXINCTION

Many of the disadvantages of the extinction procedure have been implied in the discussion of the properties of extinction. We will now consider them more fully.

Delayed effects The elimination of a response through extinction takes time and this can present problems under some circumstances.

---

[2] This point is elaborated upon in Chapter 12.

A child's responding with rude behavior might be tolerable for a longer time than his responding with running out into a street full of traffic. The child himself might be extinguished before the response were eliminated. A response suggesting imminent danger to the child himself or to others must be stopped immediately. Unless some additional fast-acting procedure, such as punishment or stimulus change, is combined with it, extinction would not be the method of choice in such circumstances.

Temporarily increasing rate, intensity, and aggression Because the increase in rate and intensity and the display of aggression often emitted during the early stages of the extinction program are of a temporary nature, they should present no serious disadvantage to the practitioner. There are times, however, when such displays are less than desirable. It would not be a good idea for a teacher to start an extinction program on a day when the school board is making its annual visit to the school, nor start on the morning after she has hosted a big party. The early stages of the extinction program require lots of patience, and personal pressures such as those could make it difficult for the teacher to maintain her patience. Later, as the temporary behaviors begin to diminish substantially, and the practitioner is reinforced for her efforts, things become much easier and less patience is necessary.

Identifying and controlling reinforcing consequences Sometimes reinforcing consequences are fairly obvious to the observer. At other times, they are not. Sometimes it takes considerable painstaking investigation in order to discover what reinforcers are maintaining the behaviors. Identification of the reinforcing consequences is particularly difficult in the case of responses that are being maintained on very thin reinforcement schedules. The reinforcer may be presented so seldom that it may fail to be noticed by the observer. The mother of a fourteen-year-old girl came to the school's behavioral specialist much distraught. Her daughter's personality had changed drastically. From a happy, outgoing girl who was always busily engaged in all kinds of activities with her friends, she had turned into a social isolate. She sat around the house and refused to go out with her friends. Even phone conversations were generally short. When her mother asked for an explanation, the girl said, "I don't feel like going out," or "Those kids bore me." Sufficiently concerned, the behavioral specialist helped to search for the cause of the problem. Was the girl sick? Was she undergoing a depressive neurosis? He asked the mother to observe her daughter more closely. One day her classmate Jim called for help with an algebra problem. The mother noticed that her daughter's face lit up and saw the spark of enthusiasm return. On thinking back, the mother remembered that Jim had occasionally called for help in algebra in the past. Suddenly, the potential reinforcer is apparent. Had the mother not been near by when the girl answered the phone, the episode might have gone unnoticed. Let's assume for the moment that the phone call from Jim was the event that intermittently reinforced the girl's remaining at home. This could possibly, with some ingenuity, be supported with more formal observation—she went out with her friends on days when no algebra homework was assigned to Jim and when he was absent from class. The next problem then would be to determine whether the behavioral specialist or the mother has control of the reinforcing consequences. Not as things stand. It would, of course, be possible to ask Jim not to call, to ask him to call at a specific time, to set up a regular tutoring session, to remove the phone, or do lots of other such things. Probably wisely, the behavioral specialist and mother decided that they should not interfere in the situation, assuming that it would, in time, pass. The daughter was left to wait at home by the phone. Extinction was not programmed. At those occasional times when she did go out, her mother gave her some extra money to spend at the movies, hoping thereby to reinforce her going out with her friends.

Many teachers often find it difficult to control the reinforcing consequences when they are being delivered by classmates. Various boisterous and hyperactive behaviors often receive peer reinforcement in the form of smiles, giggles, and imitation. Such behaviors may be fine on the playground, but they often interfere with classroom learning. There are several ways a teacher might achieve extinction conditions when the behavior is being reinforced by classmates. One of the most obvious is for the teacher to reinforce the student's classmates for not attending to the disruptive behavior. For example, whenever a classmate withheld his attention from the disruptive antics the teacher would reinforce him with praise or with some social or tangible event or object known to be reinforcing to him. This student's behavior of ignoring the disruptive antics, then, would serve as a positively reinforced model for the rest of the class. (The reader may wish to review the section in Chapter 3 on model selection.) Other students might imitate that student's behavior and thus provide the teacher with the opportunity for reinforcing their behaviors of withholding attention to disruptive behavior. As their ignoring behavior continued to receive reinforcement, extinction conditions would be gradually achieved.

In other situations in which control of the reinforcing contingencies is difficult, discriminative stimuli (S^D's) combined with reinforcement and modeling can assist in achieving extinction conditions. For example, let's suppose Mike is very hyperactive. The teacher can discuss the situation with Mike and the class or with several students she wishes to use as models. The teacher can point out that Mike wants to do well (receive reinforcement) and not get into trouble (not receive punishment), and asks the students how they can help. Once it is clear to the students that they are helping Mike get into trouble by attending to his antics a plan can be worked out to "help" Mike rather than get him into trouble. The students can agree to ignore his acting-out behavior and praise him for accomplishing his work. The teacher can reinforce the students (models) for following the program and can also reinforce Mike for any improvements in his behaviors. By so doing, the teacher serves as a model, which the class can imitate, and the class receives reinforcement along with Mike for the improved behaviors.

Patterson (1965) achieved extinction conditions and successfully reduced the hyperactive behavior of a nine-year-old boy through a similar approach. Earl's behavior consisted of excessive in-and-out-of-seat movements, excessive talking, and hitting. Patterson's approach was to set up a situation in which Earl and his classmates obtained candy or pennies from a "magic teaching machine" whenever Earl displayed ten seconds of attending behavior. His classmates were also rewarded for withholding their attention during his antics. Thus, by reinforcing students for not attending to disruptive behavior, the teacher rapidly obtained extinction conditions and received reinforcement himself due to the more favorable classroom environment.

Sometimes it is impossible to remove reinforcing consequences. Some behaviors have their own built-in reinforcers. As long as a thief is not caught, he is reinforced for stealing with the attainment of material goods. It would be pretty difficult to *remove* the reinforcing consequences of speeding in a car (it gets one places faster), cheating on examinations (if it yields one higher grades), drinking lots of alcohol, eating lots of sweets, or engaging in sexual activities. Therefore, when the identification or control of the reinforcing contingencies is very difficult or impossible, it is preferable to turn to other methods for reducing the undesirable behavior. These will be discussed in Chapters 9–12.

Exercise 8.10
Did you note any behaviors during a recent observation for which you feel an extinction procedure would be inappropriate. Why?

Exercise 8.11
Describe any problems you have encountered in using an extinction procedure.

SUMMARY

Extinction can be a very effective procedure for reducing undesirable school-related behaviors. Used by itself or in combination with other procedures, it has demonstrated its effectiveness in a wide variety of situations. Though the behavioral reduction achieved by means of extinction may take time to accomplish, the effect can be long lasting. Efficient use of extinction requires the removal of all reinforcing consequences for the undesirable behavior. The process can be speeded up if desirable behaviors are reinforced simultaneously with the extinction of undesirable behaviors. If it is not possible to remove the reinforcing contingencies for a specific response, an alternative reductive technique should be used.

REFERENCES

Azrin, N. H., Hutchinson, R. R., & Hake, D. J., Extinction-induced aggression. *Journal of the Experimental Analysis of Behavior,* 1966, **9,** 191–204.

Bijou, S. W., Birnbrauer, T. S., Kidder, J. D., & Tague, C. Programmed instruction as an approach to teaching of reading, writing, and arithmetic to retarded children. In S. W. Bijou & D. M. Baer (Eds.), *Child development: Readings in experimental analysis.* New York: Appleton-Century-Crofts, 1967.

Brown, P., & Elliott, R. Control of aggression in a nursery school class. *Journal of Experimental Child Psychology,* 1965, **2,** 103–107.

Carlson, C. S., Arnold, C. R., Becker, W. C., & Madsen, G. H. The elimination of tantrum behavior of a child in an elementary classroom. *Behavior Research and Therapy,* 1968, **6,** 117–120.

Hall, R. V., Lund, D., & Jackson, D. Effects of teacher attention on study behaviors. *Journal of Applied Behavior Analysis,* 1968, **1,** 1–12.

Hall, R. V., Panyan, M., Rabon, D., & Broden, M. Instructing beginning teachers in reinforcement procedures which improve classroom control. *Journal of Applied Behavior Analysis,* 1968, **1,** 315–322.

Hart, B. M., Allen, K. E., Buell, J. S., Harris, F. R., & Wolf, M. M. Effects of social reinforcement on operant crying. *Journal of Experimental Child Psychology,* 1964, **1,** 145–153.

Holland, J. G., & Skinner, B. F. *The analysis of behavior.* New York: McGraw-Hill, 1961.

Hutchinson, R. R., Azrin, N. H., & Hunt, G. M. Attack produced by intermittent reinforcement of a concurrent operant response. *Journal of the Experimental Analysis of Behavior,* 1968, **11,** 489–495.

Kelly, J. F. Extinction induced aggressive in humans. Unpublished masters thesis, Southern Illinois University, 1969.

Krumboltz, J. D., & Hosford, R. Behavioral counseling in the elementary school. *Elementary School Guidance and Counseling,* 1967, **1,** 27–40.

Millenson, J. R. *Principles of behavior analysis.* New York: Macmillan, 1967.

O'Leary, K. D., & Becker, W. C. Behavior modification of an adjustment class: A token reinforcement program. *Exceptional Children,* 1967, **33,** 637–642.

Patterson, G. R. An application of conditioning techniques to the control of a hyperactive child. In L. P. Ullman & L. Krasner (Eds.), *Case studies in behavior modification.* New York: Holt, Rinehart and Winston, 1965.

Reynolds, G. S. *A primer of operant conditioning.* Glenview, Ill.: Scott, Foresman, 1968.

Scott, P. M., Burton, R. V., & Yarrow, M. R. Social reinforcement under natural conditions. *Child Development,* **38,** 1967, 53–63.

Skinner, B. F. *The behavior of organisms.* New York: Appleton-Century-Crofts, 1938.

Skinner, B. F. *Science and human behavior.* New York: Free Press, 1953.

Thomas, D. R., Becker, W. C., & Armstrong, M. Production and elimination of disruptive classroom behavior by systematically varying teacher's behavior. *Journal of Applied Behavior Analysis,* 1968, **1,** 35–45.

Thomas, D. R., Nielsen, L. J., Kuypers, D. S., & Becker, W. C. Contributions of social reinforcement and remedial instruction in the elimination of a classroom behavior problem. Unpublished manuscript, University of Illinois, 1969.

Wolf, M. M., Risley, T. R., & Mees, H. L. Application of operant conditioning procedures to the behavior problems of an autistic child. *Behavioral Research and Therapy,* 1964, **1,** 303–312.

Zimmerman, E. H., & Zimmerman, J. The alteration of behavior in a classroom situation. *Journal of the Experimental Analysis of Behavior,* 1962, **5,** 59–60.

9

PROCEDURES FOR RESPONSE CONTINGENT WITHDRAWAL OF REINFORCEMENT

Objectives

Using illustrations not described in this chapter, you should be able to:

1. Define and offer school illustrations of
   a. timeout
   b. response cost
2. Define and illustrate the differences between extinction, timeout, and response cost.
3. List and discuss the advantages and disadvantages of timeout.
4. List and offer illustrations of the factors that influence the effectiveness of using timeout.
5. Describe specific situations in which timeout (a) used by itself and (b) combined with other behavioral procedures would and would not be the best behavioral procedure; justify your positions.
6. List and discuss the advantages and disadvantages of response cost.
7. Tell how to use response cost effectively.
8. Describe specific situations in which response cost would and would not be the best behavioral procedure; justify your positions.

We will discuss two procedures in this chapter, *timeout* and *response cost.* Both involve changes in the environment contingent upon the emission of an undesirable behavior. In both cases the behavior is followed by the *withdrawal* of reinforcing stimuli. In contrast with these, Chapter 10, "Punishment," will deal with the *presentation* of aversive stimuli contingent upon the emission of the behavior.

TIMEOUT

TIMEOUT DEFINED

Timeout is a procedure through which *access to the sources of reinforcement are removed for a particular time period contingent upon the emission of a response.*[1] Timeout is similar to extinction, since it too involves nonreinforcement. In extinction, however, the reinforcing stimuli are simply withheld; they are no longer delivered contingent upon a response. Clarissa's suitor stops calling her because she never comes to the phone when he calls. Cookies are withheld from the crying, demanding child; and crying and demanding lead to no change in the environment (no cookies are delivered). The extinction situation is diagrammed:

Extinction

$$R \underset{\substack{\text{(phoning}\\\text{Clarissa)}}}{\underline{\hspace{3cm}}} /\!\!\longrightarrow$$

phoning Clarissa leads to no change in the environment

$$R \underset{\substack{\text{(crying}\\\text{and demanding)}}}{\underline{\hspace{3cm}}} /\!\!\longrightarrow$$

The response of crying and demanding leads to no change in the environment.

With timeout, however, something does occur in the environment, contingent upon the response. What happens is the *removal* of the opportunity to receive reinforcement. Either the behaving individual is removed from the reinforcing environment or the reinforcing environment is removed from him for some stipulated duration. Using the same example of the crying child, timeout can be illustrated by the child's being re-

---

[1] This definition is a variation of one offered by Reese (1966) combined with Ferster and Skinner's (1957) laboratory derived definition.

moved from the kitchen for a specific time *(t)*, in this case, for ten minutes, contingent upon crying for cookies. The opportunity to cry for cookies, therefore, no longer exists for that ten-minute period. (Another possibility would be the mother contingently removing herself and the box of cookies from the kitchen, thereby leaving the child in a nonreinforcing environment.) Diagrammed, the timeout situation looks like this:

$$\text{Timeout} \qquad R \xrightarrow{\hspace{3cm}} S$$
$$\underset{\substack{\text{(crying} \\ \text{demanding)}}}{} \qquad \underset{\substack{\text{(removal from room} \\ \text{for ten minutes)}}}{}$$

The subject is removed from the reinforcing environment for an amount of time.

TIMEOUT IN THE SCHOOL

A student throws a paper clip. The teacher sends him to stand in the cloak room for twenty minutes. An entire class becomes rowdy. The children are all instructed to put their heads down for a brief period of time. A student sasses the gym teacher. The student is sent to sit in the principal's office for the rest of the gym period. A group of students in the senior class paint the statue of the school's namesake in psychedelic colors. They are expelled from school for a week. A student pushes in the lunch line. He is made to stay in class for a half hour after dismissal. All of these contingencies are illustrations of timeout procedures as they are sometimes used in the school setting. The reader himself can probably provide further illustrations of similar timeout procedures, since they are so commonly used in schools.

Exercise 9.1

Offer an illustration of a timeout procedure from one of your classroom observations.

ADVANTAGES OF TIMEOUT

Effectively reducing behavior   When a classroom management procedure is frequently used by school personnel, there's a good chance that the use of the procedure reinforces the users sufficiently often. Educators are behaving individuals too. Those procedures that reinforce them are maintained. Those which are reinforced intermittently probably maintain even longer. Because of its widespread use, one can then assume that timeout works, at least intermittently, in the school setting.

Support for the assumption that timeout can be an effective reductive procedure derives from many studies reported in the literature. Among them are some which relate to the reduction of undesirable child behaviors. Unable to control the disruptive behavior of delinquent boys around a pool table with other techniques, Tyler and Brown (1967) reported that a brief confinement in a "timeout" room was a useful procedure in reducing their misbehavior. Another study (Wolf, Risley, & Mees, 1964) reported on the use of a timeout procedure with an autistic boy. Each time a temper tantrum occurred, they isolated the child from his peers and aids by placing him in a room for a few moments longer than the duration of the tantrum. His temper tantrums were virtually eliminated. A similar procedure with the same child was effectively used to reduce tantrums and pinching in school (Wolf, Risley, Johnston, Harris, & Allen, 1967). Zeilberger, Sampen, and Sloane (1968) reported using a timeout procedure with a four-and-a-half-year-old nursery school child by the name of Rorey. Rorey's objectionable behaviors were screaming, fighting, disobeying, and bossing in the home situation. The parents requested assistance from the school's behavioral specialist. They were subsequently instructed to follow, under the specialist's supervision, the following treatment:

1. Immediately after Rorey acts aggressively or disobediently, take him to the timeout (TO) room. (One of the family bedrooms was modified for this use by having toys and other items of interest to a child removed.)

2. As Rorey is taken to the TO room for aggressive behavior, say "you cannot stay here if you fight." As Rorey is taken to the TO room for disobedient behavior, say "you cannot stay here if you do not do what you are told." Make no other comments.

3. Place Rorey in the TO room swiftly and without conversation other than the above. Place him inside and shut and hook the door.

4. Leave Rorey in the TO room for two minutes. If he tantrums or cries, time the two minutes from the end of the last tantrum or cry.

5. When the time is up take Rorey out of the TO room and back to his regular activities without further comment on the episode, i.e., in a matter-of-fact manner.

6. Do not give Rorey explanations of the program, of what you do, of his behavior, or engage in discussions of these topics with him. If you desire to do this, have such discussions at times when the undesired behaviors have not occurred, such as later in the evening. Keep these brief and at a minimum.

7. Ignore undesirable behavior which does not merit going to the TO room. "Ignore" means you should not comment upon such behavior, not attend to it by suddenly looking around when it occurs.

8. Ignore aggressive or disobedient behavior which you find out about in retrospect. If you are present, treat disobedient behavior to other adults the same as disobedient behavior to you.

9. Reinforce desirable cooperative play frequently (at least once

every five minutes) without interrupting it. Comments, such as "my, you're all having a good time" are sufficient, although direct praise which does not interrupt the play is acceptable.

10. Always reward Rorey when he obeys.

11. Special treats, such as cold drinks, cookies, or new toys or activities, should be brought out after periods of desirable play. It is always tempting to introduce such activities at times when they will interrupt undesirable play, but in the long run this strengthens the undesired behavior.

12. Follow the program 24 hours a day [p. 49].*

The employment of the this timeout procedure, which was combined with the use of prompts (step 2), extinction (steps 7 and 8), and reinforcement (steps 9, 10, and 11), decreased Rorey's objectionable behaviors.

The scope and limitations of the timeout procedure need further investigation, but timeout does appear to be a very potent reductive technique.

USING TIMEOUT EFFECTIVELY

Removing all reinforcers A teacher decided that she would try a timeout procedure with one of her students. Each time the child pushed or hit another child, he was told simply but firmly, "You cannot push. You must leave." Nothing more was said. (Further conversation might be reinforcing.) He was then immediately placed on a chair in the hall outside the classroom for five minutes. Things went along fine for a while. Pushing and hitting began to subside. Then the improvement seemed to stop. When she investigated, the teacher found that several times when the child had been seated out in the hall, the principal came by. Each time he had stopped, he asked the youngster why he was out in the hall, and gave him a sympathetic pep talk on the importance of getting along well with other children. Having never in the past received any attention from the principal, the child's undesirable behavior was probably being reinforced by the well-intentioned, kindly toned lecture. A conference between the teacher and the principal cleared up the situation. The principal no longer stopped to chat when the child was on timeout in the hall. The undesirable behavior began to subside again. Timeout was again in effect and performing its function.

One of the authors had a similar experience while teaching in an inner-

---

*Reprinted by permission from J. Zeilberger, S. E. Sampen, and H. N. Sloane, Modification of a child's problem behaviors in the home with the mother as a therapist. *Journal of Applied Behavior Analysis,* 1968, **1,** 49. Copyright 1968 by the Society for the Experimental Analysis of Behavior, Inc.

city school. Children who misbehaved while preparing for dismissal were told to return to their classroom and remain after school for a while. Though this procedure was effective with some of the children, for others the reverse seemed to be the case. Some of the children actually appeared to solicit the "timeout." An analysis of their situation hinted that perhaps remaining in the classroom, watching the teacher decorate the room and engage in other of her duties, may actually have been reinforcing. A switch in procedure showed that this was probably the case. For these students, the teacher used staying after school and helping the teacher as a reinforcer for desirable classroom performance. This proved to be a powerful incentive for several of the students.

As we discussed in Chapter 8, "Extinction," it is often difficult to identify and remove all the reinforcers in a situation. However, a good environmental arrangement could help. One method for providing a reasonably effective timeout environment is to place the child in a location in which he has neither visual nor physical access to people or materials. Some practitioners have used an empty office; others have used a seat behind a screen. In cases in which the child has been violent towards others, such as in mental hospital wards, rooms without furniture or breakable windows have been used. That kind of environment would probably be too drastic for the normal school setting. Simply seating the child by himself with his chair turned away from the other children should be a sufficiently effective environmental arrangement.

Avoiding timeout from an aversive situation Timeout from positive reinforcement can effectively reduce a behavior only if the individual's *environment changes from one in which reinforcement is available to one in which it is not.* The procedure will not work effectively if the environment switches from one in which *aversive* stimuli abound to one in which the aversive stimuli are removed. Mary, who violently disliked a particular subject, soon found that causing a disturbance when the subject was being taught would result in her being asked to leave the classroom. Thus, the teacher inadvertently negatively reinforced Mary's disruptive behavior.

Maintaining timeout consistently Most people who have experience in working with children know the importance of a consistent method of handling a particular situation. We have already discussed the need for consistently maintaining reinforcement and extinction conditions. With timeout, as well, a consistent approach is probably a good idea (Zimmerman & Baydan, 1963). If some emissions of a particular behavior are treated with a timeout contingency and others are not, the behavior is being intermittently reinforced. For instance, suppose the child who pushed and hit other children was not contingently placed in timeout every time he emitted the undesirable behavior. By successfully avoiding timeout (an aversive situation) he would be negatively reinforced. Also, being able to hit others with few and irregular negative consequences would be a pretty reinforcing state of affairs for a while.

Keeping duration relatively short Logic might tell us that if a little timeout works pretty well, a lot of timeout would work very well. Evidence suggests that this is correct but only to a point (Zimmerman & Baydan, 1963; Zimmerman & Ferster, 1963). It appears that beyond a certain duration, longer timeouts provide no further reductive effect and, sometimes, even seem to disrupt behavior. Additionally, there is some evidence suggesting that short timeouts are very effective. For example, in one study (Tyler, 1965) the timeout period lasted fifteen minutes; in two others (Wolf et al., 1964, 1967) an autistic boy was isolated for brief periods of time, usually for a few minutes longer than the duration of any ongoing tantrum. In each case the undesirable behavior was reduced significantly. In another study (Bostow & Bailey, 1969) severe disruptive and aggressive behavior by two hospitalized retarded adults were reduced by using a two-minute timeout duration, paired with differential reinforcement of desirable behaviors. Long timeout durations can actually be risky. During long durations, the individual could adapt to the timeout situation, and the procedure would lose its effectiveness. Isolated for long periods of time, a child might acquire new means for receiving reinforcement: self-stimulation, fantasizing and so forth. Long timeout periods present other problems. Some individuals would, for instance, be hesitant to enforce many lengthy timeouts on a child. A situation would therefore exist in which a student's incorrect behavior would be inconsistently subjected to the timeout procedure, and this would serve to defeat the effectiveness of the procedure. Lengthy timeouts can also interfere with a student's learning. Suppose that every time a particular student engaged in some specific behavioral category, he was sent to the principal's office for two hours. He could (and probably would) miss the lessons given during that time. Since short timeout periods can be effective, there is no need to use long, and potentially disruptive timeout durations.

Providing desirable alternative behaviors The provision of a desirable alternative behavior can substantially alter the effects of a timeout procedure. When such an alternative is made available, the behavioral reduction can occur more quickly and thoroughly. One study (Holz, Azrin, & Ayllon, 1963) demonstrated this phenomenon with human subjects. When only one response was available to the subjects, timeout had only a minor reductive effect upon the rate of their performance. When a second response was made available to the subjects, the response receiving periodic contingent timeout was almost immediately eliminated. This idea can easily be transferred into the school situation. Let us assume that the painting of a symbolic object has become a traditional senior class prank. If only one major symbol is available, the statue of the school's namesake, it will probably be painted. But suppose, on the other hand, a large wall or billboard in the high school's main entry hall were made available to the senior class and the students were allowed to decorate it to their hearts' content. The statue would have a better chance of escaping unscathed. The chamber of commerce in a local community does something similar to this around Halloween. Store windows in the community are made available to the children to decorate. Contests are held for various artistic categories, and the children busily get to work decorating the windows. As a result, vandalism in the stores hardly occurs in that community on Halloween night.

Exercise 9.2
a. Assume there is a child who frequently throws objects around the classroom as soon as the teacher turns her back to write on the board. This is very disruptive to the functioning of the class. A timeout contingency is selected. Given a typical public school setting, offer at least one plan for the design of a practical timeout environment.
b. Justify the environmental design you have chosen by referring to the major points regarding the effective use of the timeout procedure.

Exercise 9.3
Evaluate the effectiveness of the timeout procedure you observed for Exercise 9.1. What changes, if any, would you make in that particular procedure? Why?

DISADVANTAGES OF TIMEOUT

An aversive contingency The timeout procedure involves the withdrawal of the reinforcing environment. It is, therefore, probably an aversive contingency for most individuals. Stimuli which are paired with the timeout situation, such as the teacher pointing toward the timeout room with a frown on her face, may also acquire aversive properties. Ferster and Skinner (1957) have shown how a timeout-correlated stimulus can function as a punishing (that is, aversive) stimulus. An individual will usually work to avoid or escape from such stimuli. Most educators prefer students to be motivated *toward* the achievement of positive goals (accurate reading comprehension, the acquisition of scientific information, and other forms of school "achievement") rather than *away* from aversive circumstances, (such as a nonreinforcing environment). Timeout is, ultimately, a negative procedure.

A nonconstructive contingency Used in the absence of other procedures, such as the reinforcement of alternative desirable behaviors, timeout aims only at getting rid of behaviors. Education is devoted to the building of behavioral repertoires rather than the destruction of them. And such nonconstructive approaches can be justified in only certain situations. If, for instance, the behavior of a student interferes with the ongoing class activity or presents danger to others or himself, a timeout procedure would be justified. In less serious instances, a more positive approach would be preferable.

Exercise 9.4

Did you observe any negative consequences of the timeout procedure you observed for Exercise 9.1? Describe them.

Exercise 9.5

For the student with whom the timeout procedure was used, offer alternative methods for reducing the undesirable behavior. Discuss the pros and cons of using each alternative.

RESPONSE COST

RESPONSE COST DEFINED

Response cost refers to the *contingent withdrawal of specified amounts of reinforcers,* rather than the contingent withdrawal of reinforcement for a specified period of *time* (as in the timeout procedure). Both procedures are similar since both involve the contingent withdrawal of a reinforcer. Removal of a certain number of tokens, the imposition of a fine, or a cut in salary contingent upon a specific behavior are illustrations of response cost. Diagrammed, an illustration of response cost (a fine equal to x dollars) contingent upon a response (speeding) would look like this:

Response Cost $\qquad R \xrightarrow[\text{(speeding)}]{} S_{\text{($25 fine)}}$

A *quantity* of reinforcers are withdrawn.

It is possible to apply response cost to primary reinforcers, for instance, a parent removing her child's dessert contingent upon some misbehavior. Because of the nature of the response cost procedure, its use in the school setting is usually limited to the withdrawal of conditioned reinforcers such as grades, points, or tokens. In order to remove specified amounts of a reinforcer, the individual must have ". . . some level of positive reinforcement . . . available in order to provide the opportunity for . . . withdrawing that reinforcement [Azrin & Holz, 1966, p. 392]."

Little would be accomplished by imposing a fine on someone who had no money, and it would be impossible to remove a primary reinforcer that had already been consumed.

RESPONSE COST IN THE SCHOOL

Typical uses of the response cost procedure in the schools are removing points toward a grade or lowering a student's letter grade contingent upon some undesirable performance. As token systems are being utilized with more frequency, another typical response cost procedure is the removal of tokens contingent upon specific behaviors. In one of the author's classroom experiments, tokens were removed contingent upon a student's walking around and disrupting the other children as they worked.

Exercise 9.6

Did you notice any use of response cost contingencies in any of your classroom observations? If so, describe them. If not, describe a situation involving yourself or a friend in which response cost was used.

ADVANTAGES OF RESPONSE COST

Strong and rapid behavioral reduction   Although used by our society fairly often, response cost has been the subject of very little basic research. However, several studies have been conducted (Weiner 1964, 1969) dealing with human performance under response cost contingencies. Weiner has found that response cost can have a very strong and rapid effect in reducing certain types of performances, but that the effect is far from universal. Apparently, the reinforcement history of the individual has a tremendous influence upon the manner in which response cost effects his performance. What this suggests is that it is often necessary to determine empirically for each individual whether or not a particular cost technique does indeed act to reduce his performance.

Convenient approach   Response cost can be a very convenient system, especially when used in conjunction with point and token systems. The incorrect behavior is emitted; a token or point is removed immediately, quietly, and with little physical effort. As a matter of fact, it is suspected that since response cost can be used so conveniently, it is probably used more often than it should be. For instance, George giggles and the teacher says, "O.K. George. You giggled. That will cost you 100 points!" Used with discretion, however, response cost could be one very efficient technique for getting rid of behaviors with minimal disruption of ongoing activities. It would be easier to take a few points away from George when he giggled than to remove him from the room, scold him, or change his seat.

USING RESPONSE COST EFFECTIVELY

Allowing for build-up of reinforcement reserve   For a response cost system to be able to work, it is necessary to allow the individual to build up a reinforcer reserve. Assume that a token system has been instituted in a class. First the students would have to be given the opportunity to accumulate lots of tokens. This usually happens as a matter of course when a token system is introduced, for such systems are usually employed when weak behaviors are not sufficiently strengthened by the more usual reinforcers. Also, the best way to strengthen weak behaviors, as we have already discussed, is to present reinforcement often. After the reserve had been accumulated it would be possible to penalize certain performances by means of the contingent removal of a specific number of tokens. Response cost would probably have its strongest effect after a student has had an opportunity to cash in some of the tokens for the back-up reinforcers. The student might then work to avoid loss of the tokens. Such losses, contingent upon specific behaviors, could then serve to reduce further occurrences of those behaviors. Whatever the response cost system employed, however, this principle should hold. If, for instance, points toward a grade are used as reinforcers, the student should have the opportunity to earn sufficient numbers of points before any of them are withdrawn.

Penalize sparingly   Azrin and Holz (1966) make the analogy between response cost and electric shock in terms of the rapidness and relative permanence of the behavioral reduction which each consequence appears to achieve. It may also be possible that very expensive response cost functions similarly to intense shock in still another way. Not only might the costly penalty reduce the specific behavior upon which it was levied but it might also have the same effect upon a wide range of ongoing behavior. Fine the waiter too heavily for breakage, and he quits his job. Take too many tokens away, and the student gives up completely. Reduce his letter grade by three, and the high school junior sees no reason to work at all. The approach that seems to work best is to allow the individual to accumulate and retain enough conditioned reinforcers so that he can have access to stronger backup reinforcers on some regular basis. The waiter should be able to end up with enough money to care for himself and his family. The student needs to retain enough tokens to buy access to the back-up reinforcers a sufficient number of times. The high school junior, motivated by aspirations to college admission, needs to maintain an average sufficient to allow him to be accepted into college if he is to remain motivated.

Communicating the rules of the game   When the individual is informed of the specific contingencies that are working upon his performance, he becomes more involved in determining the outcome of the situation. If students are told that certain accomplishments will lead to specific gains and that other performances will lead to specific losses, they themselves are participating in the contingency system. It is even possible for a group of students to share in setting the response cost penalty values. Individuals can also impose contingencies upon themselves in order to achieve the goal they seek. A student desiring college acceptance can impose response cost contingencies upon himself in order to achieve the necessary grade level. For instance, for every hour of television watching beyond the first two, he donates one dollar to a charity. This type of self-management is a good step in the direction of self-control.[2]

More importantly, cost rules that are consistently implemented provide the student with a set of discriminative stimuli (S^D's): such and such behaviors will be penalized, others will not. The student can learn to make the discrimination more rapidly when the rules are available to him. The rules function as other cues do in the development of differential responses. Many teachers who use classroom token systems post such rules on the walls for all the students to see. These serve as a prompt that certain behaviors will lead to loss of specific amounts of reinforcement. Used in that manner, those stimuli function to suppress the undesirable behaviors.

Combining with other procedures   Because it frequently serves as a device for conveniently and rapidly reducing specific behaviors, response cost can be used as a *temporary* reductive technique. By suppressing a set of undesirable behaviors, the likelihood that the individual will begin to engage in more desirable behaviors should increase. It will then be possible to strengthen those behaviors. Ultimately, with the increasingly frequent emission of the desirable behaviors, it should be possible to drop out the cost contingency. The continuous emission of a very high frequency of desirable behaviors will not allow the individual the opportunity to engage in a high frequency of undesirable behaviors. This is what was done with a student whose noisy out-of-seat behavior disrupted other children in the class. Initially the decision had been to give the

---

[2] Part I of Skinner's *Cumulative Record* (1961) deals with such philosophical issues as freedom and self-control.

student a point following each five minutes of in-seat behavior. This accomplished very little because he almost never remained seated for five minutes. Two alternatives were then considered: lower the time requirement for token reinforcement or place a response cost contingency upon the behavior. Because the first alternative would have required too much of a time involvement for the teacher, response cost was instituted. Each time the student left his seat without permission, he lost one point. Simultaneously, he also received one point for each five minutes of in-seat behavior. In-seat behavior increased sufficiently under those circumstances, and eventually it was rarely necessary to invoke the cost penalty. It should ultimately have been possible to dispense with the cost contingency altogether.

Exercise 9.7

Evaluate and discuss the effectiveness of the response cost procedure you described for Exercise 9.6.

Exercise 9.8

Suppose you decided to use a token system for a group of students working on remedial material in a specific subject area. Under what circumstances would you deduct tokens? How would you introduce and carry out the cost system? Support your decision.

DISADVANTAGES OF RESPONSE COST

Several of the disadvantages of the response cost procedure have already been given in the foregoing discussion. The fact that the procedure does not have a universally reductive effect, probably due to differences in reinforcement history, and the need for a reserve of conditioned reinforcers have already been discussed. The danger of using penalties that are too large has also been mentioned. In addition, response cost, as do other aversive contingencies, probably tends to occasion aggressive and escape behavior. When dessert is taken away from children, tantrums often result. Fines, penalties, and other forms of response cost appear to result in responses of a similar, though perhaps subtler, nature with older children and adults. The employee may throw darts at a picture of his boss; the student may hang his college president in effigy. Penalized with reductions in grades *too* often, the student may drop out of school altogether.

Exercise 9.10

Did the subject display any negative reactions to the response cost procedure you described for Exercise 9.6? Discuss them.

SUMMARY

Timeout from positive reinforcement is a procedure that has frequently demonstrated its effectiveness in reducing undesirable behavior. By completely and consistently removing the opportunity to obtain reinforcement contingent upon the undesirable behavior while the opportunity to earn reinforcement for alternative desirable behaviors is provided at other times, timeout can achieve its goal quite effectively. Used by itself, however, timeout is neither positive nor constructive. Such applications of the procedure should probably be limited to serious situations in which alternative reductive techniques would not do the job as expediently.

Although the effects of response cost can differ from individual to individual, it is a procedure that has been found to quickly and conveniently reduce undesirable behaviors in many instances. In order to make effective use of the procedure, the subject should be allowed to first accumulate a reinforcement reserve, the costs should be kept to a minimum, the rules of the game should be communicated to the subject, and reinforcement of desirable behaviors should be combined with the procedure response cost when possible. Response cost, since it is a negative approach, tends to stimulate aggressive and escape behavior. For that reason, it should be used sparingly and usually as a temporary expedient.

REFERENCES

Azrin, N. H., & Holz, W. C. Punishment. In W. R. Honig (Ed.), *Operant behavior: Areas of research and application.* New York: Appleton-Century-Crofts, 1966.

Bostow, D. E., & Bailey, J. Modifications of severe disruptive and aggressive behavior using brief timeout and reinforcement procedures. *Journal of Applied Behavior Analysis,* 1969, **2,** 21–38.

Ferster, C. B., & Skinner, B. F. *Schedules of reinforcement.* New York: Appleton-Century-Crofts, 1957.

Holz, W. C., Azrin, N. H., & Ayllon, T. Elimination of behavior of mental patients by response-produced extinction. *Journal of the Experimental Analysis of Behavior,* 1963, **6,** 407–412.

Reese, E. P. *The analysis of human operant behavior.* Dubuque: William C. Brown, Publishers, 1966.

Skinner, B. F. *Cumulative record* (enlarged ed.). New York: Appleton-Century-Crofts, 1961.

Tyler, V. O., & Brown, G. D. The use of swift, brief isolation as a group control device for institutionalized delinquents. *Behavior Research and Therapy,* 1967, **5,** 1–9.

Tyler, V. O., Jr. Exploring the use of operant techniques in the rehabilitation of delinquent boys. Paper presented at the American Psychological Association, Chicago, September, 1965.

Weiner, H. Controlling human fixed-interval's performance. *Journal of the Experimental Analysis of Behavior,* 1969, **12,** 349–373.

Weiner, H. Response cost effects during extinction following fixed-interval reinforcement with humans. *Journal of the Experimental Analysis of Behavior,* 1964, **7,** 333–335.

Wolf, M. M., Risley, T. R., Johnson, M., Harris, F., & Allen, E. Application of operant conditioning procedures to the behavior problems of an autistic child a follow-up and extension. *Behavior Research and Therapy,* 1967, **5,** 103–112.

Wolf, M. M., Risley, T. R., & Mees, H. L. Application of operant conditioning procedures to the behavior problems of an autistic child. *Behavior Research and Therapy,* 1964, **1,** 303–312.

Zeilberger, J., Sampen, S. E., & Sloane, H. N. Modification of a child's problem behaviors in the home with the mother as a therapist. *Journal of Applied Behavior Analysis,* 1968, **1,** 47–54.

Zimmerman, J., & Baydan, N. T. Punishment of $S^\triangle$ responding of humans in conditional matching-to-sample by timeout. *Journal of the Experimental Analysis of Behavior,* 1963, **6,** 589–597.

Zimmerman, J., & Ferster, C. B. Intermittent punishment of $S^\triangle$ responding in matching-to-sample. *Journal of the Experimental Analysis of Behavior,* 1963, **6,** 349–356.

10 PUNISHMENT*

Objectives

Using illustrations not described in this chapter, you should be able to

1. Define and offer school illustrations for each of the following terms:
   a. punishment
   b. aversive stimulus
   c. punishing stimulus
2. Compare, contrast, and illustrate the various types of aversive stimuli described in the chapter.
3. Define and illustrate the differences between timeout, response cost, and punishment.
4. List and discuss the advantages of using punishment.
5. List, discuss, and illustrate the factors that influence the effectiveness of a punishment procedure.
6. List and discuss the disadvantages of using punishment.
7. Describe specific situations in which punishment would and would not be the behavioral procedure of choice and justify your positions.

---

*This chapter is an expansion of an article, The use of punishment in modifying student behavior, by Mayer, G. R., Sulzer, B., and Cody, J. J., that appeared in the *Journal of Special Education,* 1968, **2,** 323–328.

One of the most sensitive issues in a great many communities in America is the subject of school discipline. What is usually meant by discipline is the application of punishment, frequently corporal punishment. Parents usually cluster into angry factions on the subject. One group is for the use of punishment thinking that the schools should be teaching children respect for authority. The other group does not want any "strangers" administering corporal punishment to their children.

School personnel find themselves in an equally perplexing situation regarding the use of punishment in the classroom. Some authorities feel that to "spare the rod spoils the child." Authorities at the other extreme preach the gospel of permissiveness and allowing for "self expression." Protagonists of all of these extreme positions assert that what they advocate is best for the child. This leaves teachers and other school personnel with something of a dilemma. One article (Morse, 1959) has stated, "faced with this dilemma, the vast majority of teachers are eager to find helpful guidelines for their work with resistant pupils [p. 109]."

The intention of this chapter, however, is not to provide philosophical or emotional support for or against the use of punishment. Rather, the major thrust will be to present the empirical evidence that is available on this topic and assume that the professional will place the information into his own frame of ethical reference. In other words, the reader will not be told what is right and wrong about the use of punishment; he will be informed of the variables that appear to make punishment an effective procedure as well as the behavioral results and side effects that have been identified as accompanying punishment.

Even though the information to be presented in this chapter is empirically derived, it still must be regarded as tentative since punishment techniques have seldom been researched in a classroom setting. This is probably due to the serious ethical and practical issues arising from such studies. Here, then, is one section in which conclusions are primarily based on extrapolations from laboratory studies. However, if teachers, behavioral specialists, and other educators become familiar with these research findings and the possible implications for the school setting, their decisions regarding punishment practices should rest on ground firmer than simply feeling and "intuition."

GENERAL CHARACTERISTICS

PUNISHMENT DEFINED

The term "punishment" has many connotations. Some see it as a physical pain applied by one or more individuals to another individual or group. For example, a mother wishes to convince her son that it is naughty for him to pull the tablecloth off the table. She slaps the child's hands vigorously in order to make him really feel the slap. She apparently feels that it is the pain that enhances the probability of his learning that tablecloth snatching is bad.

Others seem to view punishment as a psychological "hurt" administered to an individual or a group. An example of this notion is the teacher who holds a child before the class in public ridicule. Apparently the teacher believes that the best way to teach the student that he has done something wrong and that it should not be done again is to shame or embarrass the child, or to hurt him psychologically.

Further, an event may be described as punishing by the person who administers it while the recipient does not actually feel punished. For example, adults are likely to identify a behavior such as spanking as a punishing activity. Yet, a child might solicit spankings because of the concurrent reinforcement he would get in the form of the attention that he gains. Spanking in that case would not necessarily be punishing.

In other situations, different interpretations can be attached to the term "punishment." Because of ambiguity of the term, some effort is needed to clarify it before we can conduct a meaningful discussion. The definition selected here is designed to eliminate subjectivity. It is an operational definition that paraphrases one offered by Azrin and Holz (1966). *Punishment is a procedure in which the presentation of a stimulus contingent upon a behavior reduces the rate with which the behavior is emitted.* Punishment can be said to have occurred only if the individual's rate of emitting the dependent behavior has been demonstrably reduced. Punishment, like reinforcement, is defined solely by its effect upon behavior. Any procedure is therefore identified as punishing, if a contingent stimulus event reduces a given behavioral rate. If a teacher reprimands a pupil when he interrupts the class and the interruptions are eliminated, then the reprimand was punishing. If, however, the behavior continues with the same or greater regularity, the event was not punishing. In fact, if the interrupting behavior increases in rate, the reprimand was reinforcing rather than punishing.

PUNISHMENT COMPARED TO TIMEOUT AND RESPONSE COST

In many ways the effects of punishment, timeout, and response cost (see Chapter 9) are similar. But the punishment procedure differs from the others because it includes the *presentation* of an aversive stimulus to reduce a behavior's rate of emission rather than the *withdrawal* of the reinforcing contingencies. Removing a student from the classroom for five minutes for clowning would be a timeout procedure; fining him ten points would be response cost. The presentation of a verbal reprimand ("No"), a slap, or even a smile could be termed "punishment" for a particular student if their contingent application to the student's behavior resulted in the reduction of that behavior. Diagrammed, the operations that identify each situation would look like this:

Timeout

$$R \xrightarrow{\text{(clowning)}} S_{\text{(five minutes out of room)}}$$

The student is removed from the room; the reinforcing environment is *withdrawn*.

Response Cost

$$R \xrightarrow{\text{(clowning)}} S_{\text{(ten-point fine)}}$$

A quantity of reinforcers are *withdrawn*.

Punishment

$$R \xrightarrow{\text{(clowning)}} S^{-}_{\text{("No")}}$$

An aversive stimulus is *presented*.

AVERSIVE STIMULI

The stimulus that functions as a punisher may be labeled an *aversive stimulus.* In most cases, when a given stimulus functions as a punisher it also functions as a stimulus that the individual will actively work to avoid. Though there are some occasional exceptions to that rule (Church, 1963; Solomon, 1964), the term "aversive stimulus" will be used in this text to apply to both classes of stimuli.

Primary aversive stimuli Some types of stimuli have a universally punishing effect. Physical trauma, electric shocks of high intensity, very bright lights, and very loud sounds are examples of these. Any of those intense stimuli that are administered contingent upon a specific behavior will generally serve to reduce its rate of emission unless the individual has become adapted to the aversive stimulus. When a small child is severely spanked for dashing out into the street, he will be less likely to do so in the future. If a person received a relatively strong shock by touching the frayed part of an electric cord, he would be less likely to touch a frayed cord again. The same would be true of a child who was burned by touching a hot stove. Stimuli that are aversive in the absence of any prior learning history (such as those just described) are called *primary aversive stimuli.*

Using primary aversive stimuli in the school raises several ethical and practical issues. The child who returns home from school with a set of bruises as a result of physical punishment might well give his parents grounds for legal action against the school. Certainly one would at least have grounds for questioning the ethics of such a procedure.

It will become apparent in the subsequent discussion that if punishment is to be lastingly effective, it must be administered with a strong intensity. A student might well become bruised, then, as a result of physical punishment. Yet many children are often paddled without receiving visible bruises. The following excerpt from a recent book (Skinner, 1968) graphically illustrates the point.

> The cane is still with us, and efforts to abolish it are vigorously opposed. In Great Britain a split leather strap for whipping students called a taws can be obtained from suppliers who advertise in educational journals, one of whom is said to sell three thousand annually. (The taws has the advantage, shared by the rubber trunchion, of leaving no incriminating marks) [p. 96].

Why do school personnel continue to use such forms of corporal punishment? Their behavior is maintained, as with most behavior, by reinforcement. Even mild punishment results in a rapid (but not necessarily an enduring) cessation of the ongoing behavior (Azrin & Holz, 1966). In Chapter 3 we learned that terminating an aversive stimulus is reinforcing. Many of the behaviors that school personnel wish to reduce are aversive to them. Even mild punishment will briefly and quickly reduce that behavior. This then produces an ideal reinforcing event for the individual administering the punishment. The negative side effects of a punishment procedure will not become manifest for quite a while; they may never become apparent to the user. Thus the person who is unaware of the principles of behavior will, in the absence of any more desirable alternative reductive technique, continue to periodically paddle, spank, or otherwise inflict pain upon students.

Conditioned aversive stimuli   Much in the same way that a formerly neutral stimulus acquired reinforcing properties (see Chapter 2), some stimuli acquire aversive properties. The aversive properties may be conditioned as a result of their being presented just prior to, or along with, the delivery of the primary aversive stimulus. A good example of a conditioned aversive stimulus is the word "no" spoken in a loud, sharp tone. This no has in all likelihood been paired for most individuals with the delivery of a primary aversive stimulus. A mother yells "No!" as the child touches the hot stove. Both the loudness of the sound and the burning heat of the stove contribute to the child's being brought under the control of that stimulus. Behaviors followed by loud, sharp no's will probably be diminished, at least temporarily. As long as the no is at least occasionally paired with a strong aversive stimulus, it should continue to function as a conditioned aversive stimulus. Other examples of conditioned aversive stimuli are frowns; gestures, such as shaking a finger; or motions, such as the clenched fist or swinging hand that usually occur prior to the delivery of spanks or blows.

Conditioned aversive stimuli and the school   The use of conditioned aversive stimuli in the school is fairly common. Because they too serve to reduce ongoing behaviors rapidly, their use also serves to negatively reinforce school personnel. Teachers find that shouting, "no," frowning, or gesturing negatively often serves to accomplish their purpose. Yet often a teacher has a student who fails to respond to her disciplinary measures. For that particular youngster, a specific stimulus may not have been conditioned to become aversive. For him, there may be other unidentified conditioned aversive stimuli, or he may respond only to primary aversive stimuli. At that point, the teacher could inquire about the desirability of training that youngster to respond to such a stimulus. This probably could be accomplished in much the same way that she sets about to condition a reinforcer. But would the procedure be justifiable and worth the time and effort? There are many factors to be considered in making this judgement. The subsequent material on the subject of punishment might suggest that, considering all the undesirable consequences of punishment, the effort would be hardly worth it, and the teacher would be better advised to concentrate on the development of some more constructive alternative techniques.

Stimuli that signal nondelivery of reinforcement   Frequently, when a behavior is punished, the individual also fails to receive reinforcement; and many of the primary and conditioned aversive stimuli create that situation. However, it is not always necessarily the case that the punished behavior goes totally unreinforced. A student who is fresh to his teacher may indeed be punished by the teacher, yet he may simultaneously be reinforced by the smiles, giggles, and nods of some of his fellow students. Conversely, there may be some stimuli that, though not paired with the presentation of aversive, or strong conditioned aversive, stimuli, may still be paired with extinction, response cost, or timeout. Here we are considering the situation in which a stimulus (whether "punishing" or not) serves to signal a period of nonreinforcement. Discriminated stimuli that have been paired with the nondelivery of reinforcement (often referred to as $S^\triangle$'s) begin to acquire aversive properties (Azrin & Holz, 1966). A teacher may instruct a student to move his chair to the back of the room, where the likelihood of receiving attention or other reinforcers from his peers is substantially reduced. The verbal instruction becomes aversive under those circumstances. A more mildly stated "no" following an incorrect response to a question may also become aversive if teacher reinforcement has never accompanied the incorrect responses. The groan of the coach as the pitcher prepares to throw the ball incorrectly or the wail of the crowd as the pop fly glides toward the fielder's glove are other illustrations of these kinds of stimuli. The coach's groan signals the fact that he will not approve of the pitch; the wail of the crowd signals the fact that they will not cheer the batter.

Thus, stimuli need not necessarily be paired with only primary or strongly conditioned aversive stimuli in order to become aversive. If they have been repeatedly paired with the nondelivery of reinforcement they can also become aversive. An illustration of this situation can be diagrammed like this:

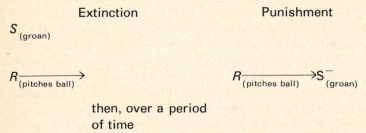

               Extinction   Punishment

$S_{(groan)}$

$R_{(pitches\ ball)} \longrightarrow$ $R_{(pitches\ ball)} \longrightarrow S^-_{(groan)}$

                   then, over a period
                   of time

In the presence of the groan,   The groan acquires aversive prop-
pitches are not approved.   erties so that its contingent
                              delivery will reduce the rate of
                              that pitching response form.

In addition, a stimulus, such as a warning or a threat, repeatedly paired with, or presented just prior to, timeout or response cost may, as mentioned above, become a conditioned aversive stimulus.

Exercise 10.1
a. Observe a class or a group of parents and children for several hours. List any student or child behaviors that appeared to be undesirable to the teacher or parent.
b. Describe how the teacher or parent handled those behaviors.
c. Describe instances of the use of punishment. What aversive stimuli were used? What effect did the procedure have upon the desirable behavior?

ADVANTAGES OF PUNISHMENT

Immediately stopping the behavior Punishment used with maximal effectiveness has the advantage of immediately stopping a behavior and reducing the behavior's future occurrence for a long period of time (Azrin, 1960; Masserman, 1946). Situations exist in which the need for immediate modification of a student's behavior is apparent, such as in instances where there is danger to an individual. For instance, immediate action must be taken to stop a child from running into a busy street or a student from getting into position to push another child over a guard rail. In addition to using restraint, using an intense punishing stimulus, such as a loud, sharp verbal reprimand or a slap, may be appropriate.

Facilitating discrimination Punishment of specific behaviors is informative to students. Marshall (1965) has reviewed considerable evidence indicating that punishment of a response under specific circumstances is "informative" to the individual since it helps him learn to discriminate acceptable from nonacceptable behaviors more rapidly. For example, shouting is usually not acceptable in the classroom, though it may be on the playground. Thus, a conditioned aversive stimulus such as a frown, gesture, or "no" used to communicate to the child that such behavior is unacceptable in the classroom may help him to make such a discrimination. To further assist the child in learning the discrimination, the teacher may provide a direction (discriminative stimulus) such as "While you are in the classroom, please speak softly." To further illustrate with an academic example, a child might respond "five" to the problem of "How much is two plus two?" Again, the teacher's response of "no" helps the child "realize" that his answer is unacceptable. A presentation of the correct response, four, would further facilitate the discrimination.

Instructive to classmates Punishment of one student's behavior may reduce the probability that other members of the class will imitate the behavior. When such a "model" is punished for a misbehavior, others are less likely to imitate his behavior in that situation. The behavior is more likely to be imitated in a situation in which it is either followed by no consequences or by reinforcement (Bandura, 1965b; 1965c). For example, if a student throws a glider or spitball in the classroom and that behavior is punished, the classmates are less likely to imitate the behavior. If the behavior was not punished, the classmates might be more apt to join in the fun of spitball throwing. Thus, through observing a classmate model being punished for a particular behavior, others in the class learn the conditions under which punishment is likely to be forthcoming.

Teachers can help students to achieve better control by clearly specifying which student behaviors are acceptable and which are not (Marshall, 1965). The students gain greater behavioral control since they learn to discriminate those behaviors that are acceptable from those that are unacceptable. The following excerpt from a counseling interview with a fourth grade girl, conducted by one of the authors, illustrates this point by describing how a student-teacher mishandled her students when they were not in their seats as they were supposed to be.

STUDENT: Well, the thing is, if the teacher lets them [the students] rile up the whole schoolroom and then makes them just slowly slow down, there will be just a mess. You know what I mean?

COUNSELOR: Kind of joke around with them, kind of edge them into their seats . . .

STUDENT: Yes, kid them, you know, kid them into getting into their seats and you will never get any place with them. But if you tell them, "Children, it's time to get to your seats" (in a firm, authoritative voice), they are all sitting in their seats, waiting for you to tell them what to do.

Exercise 10.2

Referring to the punishment procedure you observed for exercise 10.1, were you able to observe any advantages that resulted from its application?

USING PUNISHMENT EFFECTIVELY

In this section we will be concerned with a number of variables that have been identified as influencing punishment's effectiveness. The specification of these variables has primarily been derived from an article by Azrin and Holz (1966). In general, those variables are related to the manner and situation in which the aversive stimuli are presented. They include escape opportunities, temporal and schedule properties, intensity of the stimulus, and the effect of combining punishment with other procedures, such as reinforcement and extinction.

Preventing escape   Escape is one of the natural reactions to the presentation of aversive stimuli. If the student succeeds in leaving the situation, the opportunity to apply any procedure is, of course, lost. Punishment can therefore only be effective in reducing the occurrence of misbehaviors when the environment is so arranged that an *unauthorized escape,* such as the student leaving school while being reprimanded, *does not occur* (Dinsmoor & Campbell, 1956; Azrin, Hake, Holz, & Hutchinson, 1965).

Applying consistently and immediately   Punishment is also more effective when the punishing stimulus is applied every time the misbehavior occurs and as soon as possible following the emission of the behavior (Azrin, 1956; Azrin, Holz, & Hake, 1963; Zimmerman & Ferster, 1963). For example, if a student's misbehavior is hitting another child, the aversive stimulus should be applied immediately and every time the child does so. Such a procedure should reduce the behavior quickly and should help the child to more rapidly discriminate that hitting others is not an acceptable behavior in the classroom. However, extended periods of punishment should be avoided or the effectiveness of the punishment will be reduced (Azrin, 1958). For example, students soon become adept at "tuning out" a mother or teacher who constantly nags. Similarly, frequent spankings tend to lose their effect. Thus, it would be best to use procedures other than punishment for any but the most serious infractions, or the student might adapt to the overused aversive stimulus.

Maximizing intensity Punishment is far less effective when the intensity with which the aversive stimulus is presented is increased gradually than when it is introduced at full intensity (Azrin & Holz, 1966). The use of low intensity punishment, though followed by an initial reduction in the behavior, usually results in a recovery of the behavior. Individuals appear to adapt easily to aversive stimuli of low intensity and to those that gradually increase in intensity. But the effects of intense or severe punishment appear to be more enduring. Thus, in a specific instance, a hard slap on the hand may be more effective in stopping a particular behavior for a long period of time than would weak slaps or several slaps of increasing vigor. A firmly stated "no" seems more effective than a shake of the head followed by increasingly stronger head shakes and louder and louder no's.

It is less necessary, however, to use intense punishment to eliminate behaviors that are not well established in the person's behavioral repertoire. As mentioned in previous chapters, a variable that determines the strength of a behavior is the frequency and schedule with which the behavior has been reinforced. A behavior that is not well established will obviously be easier to eliminate than one that is well established. Therefore, one would expect that mild punishment would be sufficient to eliminate weak behaviors. Conversely, probably only very intense punishment would serve to reduce the occurrence of well-established behaviors. For example, if a child misspelled a word or mishandled delicate equipment for the first time, mild punishment such as a simple "no" or head shake would probably be effective in eliminating the behavior. However, if the student constantly misspelled a word or consistently mishandled delicate equipment, mild punishment would probably be less effective in eliminating those behaviors than would intense punishment.

Combining with extinction Punishment combined with extinction results in a more rapid elimination of the behavior than when either punishment or extinction is used alone (Azrin & Holz, 1961; 1966). Thus, if a rapid elimination of a behavior is sought, it is a good idea to include, along with the delivery of a contingent aversive stimulus, the removal of the reinforcers maintaining that behavior and make them contingent upon only desirable alternative behaviors. We have noted that a stimulus acquires conditioned aversive properties when it becomes a signal indicating that no reinforcement is forthcoming. Such conditioning would be retarded if the individual had been simultaneously reinforced. Similarly, the effectiveness of a punishment procedure will be reduced if the emission of the behavior is followed by the delivery of both aversive and reinforcing stimuli. The student whose disruptive behavior yields him not only an aversive scolding but also the approval of his classmates will continue to disrupt in the future to a greater extent than if the peer approval were absent. In this instance, the task of the teacher would be to somehow reduce the emission of peer approval. She might use any of the procedures previously discussed. For instance, she might praise the few students who did not demonstrate approval, thereby reinforcing incompatible behaviors and providing positive models. She might use stimulus change, such as moving the offending student to a location where his actions could not be observed and, thereby, occasion peer approval or try some other procedures.

Sometimes it is extremely difficult to remove reinforcement for engaging in a specific behavior. This is particularly true when the behavior provides its own source of immediate reinforcement. The behavior may then persist even though it may be punished. Two rather dramatic examples of this type of situation are stealing and such sexual activities as masturbating. (Remember, the issue of "right" and "wrong" is not being discussed here but simply procedures designed to reduce any preselected behaviors). Both of these behaviors yield very rapid and often very strong reinforcement. Punishment in both instances is usually delayed and intermittent and, as a result, not too effective. (This might explain why, in the case of stealing, the American system of criminal justice is so often ineffective and why the recidivism rate is high.) For both stealing and masturbation, it would be better to utilize an alternative reductive method. In the case of stealing, it would be a good idea to provide opportunities for the individual to achieve, from other sources, equivalent or stronger reinforcement. This might be accomplished by offering alternative socially desirable behaviors, say training in a skill that is both intrinsically reinforcing and remunerative. As long as a thief has no socially acceptable way to earn the things in life he covets, he will continue to steal. Behaviors such as masturbation could also be reduced by reinforcing incompatible responses. While the student is playing a vigorous game of basketball or assembling complicated equipment it would be difficult for him to also masturbate. Of course, with the latter behavior, individuals soon learn that certain stimulus situations are more likely to occasion punishment than others. The discrimination is often rapidly acquired. The behavior may not stop but it will not be emitted in a situation in which it is likely to be punished.

Occasionally one notices an individual continuing to engage in a behavior although he appears to be consistently and immediately punished for doing so. In fact, the same stimuli may function as aversive stimuli for that individual under other circumstances. The situation is the apparently paradoxical one often labeled *masochism.* What usually occurs here is a chain of events that sometimes terminate with positive reinforcement. Some individuals fail to be reinforced in the more usual ways, such as through accomplishments, work, and so forth. They may ultimately receive reinforcement only by first engaging in a behavior, then being punished, then being reinforced. Take the example of the child whose mother is frequently occupied with other things and often fails to pay attention to him. But, when the child hurts himself, pokes his younger brother, or accidentally breaks a lamp, his mother rushes over to him and yells at or spanks him. And then, in a moment of remorse, she cuddles him and says she is sorry for punishing him. The child soon learns that one sure way to get his mother's attention is to hurt himself or to do something naughty. School children are often seen engaging in similar types of behavioral chains. The teacher only pays attention to the student when he misbehaves. Misbehavior, although punished, will persist if it is the only way in which the student can receive reinforcement.

The foregoing examples illustrate how difficult it might be to remove all sources of reinforcement for a punished behavior. As long as such sources of reinforcement remain, the behavior will be very difficult to eliminate by means of punishment alone. It will not be possible to effectively combine it with extinction.

Combining with reinforcement of alternative behaviors We have already mentioned that very intense punishment will reduce well-established undesirable behaviors more effectively than milder intensities of punishment. Milder punishment will generally reduce the behavior only temporarily. It is, however, possible to use milder punishment in order to obtain a more lasting reduction of the behavior when the individual is simultaneously given access to an alternative reinforceable behavior (Azrin & Holz, 1966). Since the use of intense punishment is usually neither feasible nor ethical, this combined procedure may prove more attractive to school personnel who desire the rapid and long-lasting effects of punishment but who are unwilling to use strong aversive stimuli. Mild aversive stimuli, such as a "no," frown, or a head shake, might be sufficient to stop the occurrence of a behavior *provided* that the individual already has alternative desirable behaviors in his repertoire and the environment offers him access to, and reinforcement for, engaging in those alternative behaviors. For example, a student may give the wrong answer to a question or handle some laboratory equipment carelessly or start to hit another student. A simple "no" or a head shake would probably be sufficient to stop that behavior from recurring provided that he has been reinforced for engaging in desirable responses. To facilitate the effect, such alternatives should be made explicitly clear to the student: "No, either times eight is not 65, it is one less, or ____." "No, don't lift a microscope by the lens piece. Place your hand beneath the base." "No, you may not hit the children when they tease you, but you may tell me, and I'll take care of it." The verbal directions, in and of themselves, will have an effect only if the teacher does make certain to reinforce the student for giving the right answer, handling the equipment properly, or informing her when he is being teased.

DISADVANTAGES OF PUNISHMENT

Although effectively administered punishment is a technique that serves to reduce behavior quickly for long periods of time and seems to decrease the probability that observers will imitate the punished behavior, there are some undesirable reactions that have been observed to occur as a consequence of punishment.[1] These include generalization, withdrawal, aggression, classmate reactions, and negative self-statements.

Causing generalization   Generalization is a phenomenon that occurs with both reinforcement and punishment. We have discussed generalization at length in Chapter 3, but let us refresh our memories. Stimulus generalization occurs in this manner: the organism responds in a similar manner to stimuli that are similar to the stimulus that was present when the behavior was originally learned. Humans are generalizing when eating is occasioned by the sight of food on a plate, a menu, a colorful picture of food, or the odor of food.

Behaviors associated with a punishing stimulus may also generalize to other stimuli. One study (Watson & Rayner, 1920) is a classic example in which an eleven-month-old child's conditioned fear of a rat generalized to all furry objects. Punishment in school for a specific behavior may also produce responses that temporarily generalize. For example the student may respond to being scolded for speaking out of turn with aggression toward, or withdrawal from, the teacher, the principal, the subject he was studying, the school, and so forth. Or he may stop responding altogether—not speaking, writing, reading, or working for a time. Ultimately, the fact that the punishment was delivered for a specific act may be discriminated. But this takes time and careful planning by the teacher. *The student needs to be informed that he has been punished for a specific act. Considerable positive reinforcement for various desirable behaviors should help him to make the necessary distinctions.*

Causing withdrawal   Students may withdraw in response to punishment. The literature has indicated repeatedly that an organism will escape from a punishing situation if the possibility of escape exists (Azrin, Hake, Holz, & Hutchinson, 1965). A good illustration of this

---

[1] Skinner (1968) has discussed many of the pitfalls of punishment.

phenomenon is found in old comedy film clichés in which exaggerated descriptions of lawful behavioral events were shown. The husband who was nagged by his wife stomped out of the house. The child who was severely scolded packed his hobo pack and headed around the corner. The employee who was criticized by his boss quit. In the real world, the elementary school student who is repeatedly being reprimanded may become "sick," cut class, or attempt to drop out of school altogether. Escape also may be figurative rather than literal. For example, the student might doodle or hum while the teacher is criticizing him. In either case, the social process is disrupted. Communication breaks down.

Causing aggression   Students may become aggressive in response to the presentation of aversive stimuli. Azrin, Hutchinson, and Hake (1963) have shown that upon delivery of shock, normally friendly monkeys will begin to fight vigorously. Azrin (1964) has shown similar responses to aversive stimulation by a wide variety of organisms. Again, the use of the analogy of the film cliché illustrates the principles that have been isolated in the laboratory. For example, the Keystone Cops and Laurel and Hardy films often dramatized the development of a simple nonintentional accident into a grand melee. Many instances of punishment-related aggression exist in normal daily life. The child who is accidentally nudged often responds by hitting. The berated husband who does not actually or figuratively leave the situation often begins to argue in response. The small child when spanked by a parent will often go and hit a smaller sibling, a punching bag, his parent, or any handy item. In our highly socialized culture, many have learned to express aggression subtly rather than overtly. The student who makes "wise" remarks and the teacher who is sarcastic have found means to express their aggression in a more acceptable fashion. Aggression, whether overt or disguised, does interfere with normal social functioning (Azrin & Holz, 1966).

Producing peer reactions   Peer reactions to punishment or the effect of punishment on classmates may pose a problem. Investigators (Bandura & Walters, 1963; Bandura, 1965a) have presented considerable evidence indicating that even though observers are not likely to imitate the delivery of punishment under some stimulus conditions, they may imitate it at other times and places. Thus, public punishment of a student, such as a slap or a loud or sarcastic verbal reprimand, should be employed cautiously. It is possible that classmates will observe the punishment and they, themselves, do the same thing at some later time. Thus, teachers may, by using certain classroom discipline techniques, actually be teaching aggressive behaviors. Likewise, it has been reported (Bandura, 1965a) that even though students who observe a behavior being punished may not be likely to imitate such behavior under the same stimulus conditions, they may do so under different ones. For example, they may imitate such behaviors as swearing, cheating, or stealing when the teacher is not around. Thus, the teacher may not wish to publicly punish behaviors not previously contained in classmates repertoires, since the undesirable behaviors would then be called to their attention and possibly imitated.

When a teacher continually singles out a student and punishes him, he may become a stimulus to be avoided or ridiculed. Thus, peer reactions may pose a serious problem particularly to the well-being of the punished student. However, such negative effects might be reduced by a teacher giving the student a chance to make up for his misbehavior or by offering an acceptable alternative. Giving the student an opportunity for receiving praise is likely to positively reinstate him with his classmates. For example, the teacher might ask the student to help her perform some prestigeful job, like grading or handing out papers, or to be in charge of a class activity or event when he is behaving particularly well.

Punishment may also occasion peer support or sympathy for the punished child: the "underdog" effect. Thus, peer reinforcement would be working against the effects of the punishment, perhaps resulting in an eventual increase, rather than decrease, of the undesired behavior. When such an effect is observed it would be well for the teacher to change her approach. She might discuss the situation with the class seeking their support, select a different punisher which would not occasion the underdog effect, or select another reductive procedure.

Causing negative self-statements   The use of punishment may negatively influence the statements a student makes about himself or his school as measured by his responses on paper-and-pencil tests. Thus, after being punished, what he says about himself or about the school is more likely to be negative, particularly if the aversive stimuli are directed at him rather than at the behavior ("You're a bad boy," or "Jim hasn't grown up yet. He still behaves like a two year old?"). The importance of this point cannot be overlooked. Studies such as one by Wattenberg and Clifford (1964) have indicated that what a student says about himself is related to school achievement. Other studies (Flanders, 1965; Ludwig & Maehr, 1967; Staines, 1958) have also indicated that comments by teachers directed to the child rather than to his behavior modified the students' self-reports or self-concepts in the direction of the comments. Thus, if aversive stimuli must be used they should never be directed at the child ("You're a bad boy.") but at the behavior ("No, don't hit Jane."). Such a procedure helps the child to discriminate that it is a specific behavior that is unacceptable to the teacher and not all of his behaviors.

Again, it is desirable to encourage alternative behaviors that would provide an opportunity for positive reinforcement. This opportunity for reinforcement helps students discriminate which *specific* behaviors are tolerated and which are not. For example the teacher punishes Jim when he hits Jane; then she makes a point of reinforcing him when he does his classwork, cleans the blackboard, and for many other such activities as possible. Furthermore, reinforcement in the form of teacher praise is likely not only to occasion and strengthen desired behaviors but to also increase positive, and reduce negative, statements made by the student about himself and school (Bandura, Grusec, & Manlove, 1965; Brehm & Cohen, 1962; Davidson & Lang, 1960; Flanders, 1965).

Exercise 10.3
a. Referring to the punishment procedure you observed for Exercise 10.1, describe the state of each of the following variables during the presentation of the aversive stimulus
    1. opportunity for escape
    2. frequency
    3. delay
    4. intensity
    5. combination with extinction
    6. combination with reinforcement of alternative behaviors
b. Did you see any reoccurrence of the punished behavior during your observation for exercise 10.1? If so, how long did it take before it reoccurred? How can you relate the reoccurrence of the behavior to the variables listed above?
c. Did you observe any undesirable reactions to the punishment procedure in exercise 10.1? Describe these reactions.

Exercise 10.4
    Disagreement is often a form of punishment. Mr. Smith is a school psychologist who frequently strongly disagrees with teachers over the procedures they use. Drawing on your knowledge of punishment, predict how the teachers would react to Mr. Smith's disagreements with them.

SUMMARY

    Punishment is one of several methods for reducing or eliminating undesirable behaviors. It is a procedure that, if used properly, serves to reduce the occurrence of a specific behavior quickly and for a long time. It can be "informative" and may decrease the probability that an observer will perform the punished behavior under similar conditions.

There are many disadvantages to the use of punishment in the schools. Primary aversive stimuli and other forms of severe punishment are generally inappropriate for the school setting except, perhaps, in situations in which there is imminent danger to the child or to other children. Conditioned aversive stimuli can be, and are being, used in the schools. However, school personnel must be aware that punishment can produce various types of negative side effects. Though the use of punishment can be an effective classroom management procedure, evidence suggests that using it with *maximal* effectiveness would be difficult in many situations. Practical, moral, and ethical considerations often countermand the use of intense punishment. Alternative procedures for reducing student behaviors should always be considered. The decision to use punishment or other procedures to reduce undesirable classroom behaviors must depend upon a variety of considerations: the seriousness of the misbehavior, its frequency of occurrence, time factors, the public nature of the act, patience, ethics, practicality, and as always, contingency control.

In the event that a punishment procedure is selected, the punishment should be *employed cautiously* and its effects carefully observed. Desirable reinforceable alternatives should be available to the student while reinforcement is completely removed from the undesirable behavior. Behavioral specialists can assist teachers by means of classroom observations, informal conferences, and in-service training programs to be constantly aware of the effect that their own behavior is having on student behavior. Furthermore, such consultants should help prepare teachers to anticipate and handle the negative consequences of punishment that can arise.

REFERENCES

Azrin, N. H. Effects of two intermittent schedules of immediate and non-immediate punishment. *Journal of Psychology,* 1956, **42,** 3–21.

Azrin, N. H. Some effects of noise on human behavior. *Journal of Experimental Analysis of Behavior,* 1958, **1,** 183–200.

Azrin, N. H. Effects of punishment intensity during variable-interval reinforcement. *Journal of the Experimental Analysis of Behavior,* 1960, **3,** 123–142.

Azrin, N. H. Aggressive responses of paired animals. Paper read at Symposium on Medical Aspects of Stress. Walter Reed Institute of Research, Washington, April, 1964.

Azrin, N. H., Hake, D. F., Holz, W. C., & Hutchinson, R. R. Motivational aspects of escape from punishment. *Journal of the Experimental Analysis of Behavior,* 1965, **8,** 31–44.

Azrin, N. H., & Holz, W. C. Punishment during fixed-interval reinforcement. *Journal of the Experimental Analysis of Behavior,* 1961, **4,** 343–347.

Azrin, N. H., & Holz, W. C. Punishment. In W. A. Honig (Ed.), *Operant behavior: Areas of research and application.* New York: Appleton-Century-Crofts, 1966.

Azrin, N. H., Holz, W. C., & Hake, D. F. Fixed-ratio punishment. *Journal of the Experimental Analysis of Behavior,* 1963, **6,** 141–148.

Azrin, N. H., Hutchinson, R. R., & Hake, D. F. Pain-induced fighting in the squirrel monkey. *Journal of the Experimental Analysis of Behavior,* 1963, **6,** 620.

Bandura, A. Behavioral modification through modeling procedures. In L. Krasner & L. P. Ullman, (Eds.), *Research in behavior modification.* New York: Holt, Rinehart and Winston, 1965. (a)

Bandura, A. Influence of models' reinforcement contingencies on the acquisition of imitative responses. *Journal of Personality and Social Psychology,* 1965, **1,** 589–595. (b)

Bandura, A. Vicarious processes: A case of no-trial learning. In L. Berkowitz (Ed.), *Advances in experimental social psychology.* New York: Academic Press, 1965. Vol. 2, pp. 1–55. (c)

Bandura, A., Grusec, J., & Manlove, F. Some social determinants of self-monitoring reinforcement systems. *Journal of Personality and Social Psychology,* 1967, **5,** 449–455.

Bandura, A., & Walters, R. H. *Social learning and personality development.* New York: Holt, Rinehart and Winston, 1963. Pp. 223–236.

Brehm, J. W., and Cohen, A. R. *Explorations in cognitive dissonance.* New York: Wiley, 1962.

Church, R. M. The varied effects of punishment on behavior. *Psychological Review,* 1963, **70,** 369–402.

Davidson, H. R., & Lang, G. Children's perception of their teachers feelings toward them related to self-perception, school achievement and behavior. *Journal of Experimental Education,* 1960, **29,** 107–188.

Dinsmoor, J. A., & Campbell, S. L. Escape-from-shock-training following exposure to inescapable shock. *Psychological Reports,* 1956, **2,** 43–49.

Flanders, N. A. Teacher influence, pupil attitudes, and achievement. *Cooperative Research Monograph No. 12,* U.S. Department of Health, Education, and Welfare, Office of Education, Washington, D.C., 1965, 126.

Ludwig, J. D., & Maehr, N. L. Changes in self-concept and stated behavioral preferences. *Child Development,* 1967, **35,** 453–468.

Marshall, H. H. The effect of punishment on children: A review of the literature and a suggested hypothesis. *The Journal of Genetic Psychology,* 1965, **106,** 23–33.

Masserman, J. H. *Principles of dynamic psychiatry.* Philadelphia: Saunders, 1946.

Mayer, G. R., Sulzer, B., & Cody, J. J. The use of punishment in modifying student behavior. *Journal of Special Education,* 1968, **2,** 323–328.

Morse, W. C. The school's responsibility for discipline. *Phi Delta Kappan,* 1959, **41,** 109–113.

Skinner, B. F. Why teachers fail. *The Saturday Review,* 1965.

Solomon, R. L. Punishment. *American Psychologist,* 1964, **19,** 239–253.

Staines, J. W. The self-picture as a factor in the classroom. *British Journal of Educational Psychology,* 1958, **28,** 97–111.

Wattenberg, W. W., & Clifford, C. Relation of self-concepts to beginning achievement in reading. *Child Development,* 1964, **35,** 461–467.

Watson, J. B., & Rayner, R. Conditioned emotional reactions. *Journal of Experimental Psychology,* 1920, **3,** 1–14.

Zimmerman, J., & Ferster, C. B. Intermittent punishment of $S^{\triangle}$ responding in matching-to-sample. *Journal of the Experimental Analysis of Behavior,* 1963, **6,** 349–356.

11

DIFFERENTIAL REINFORCEMENT, STIMULUS CONTROL AND STIMULUS CHANGE

Objectives

Using examples not described in this chapter you should be able to

1. Define and offer school illustrations for each of the following terms:
   a. differential reinforcement
   b. stimulus control
   c. discriminative stimulus (S^D)
   d. S delta ($S^\triangle$)
   e. discrimination
   f. stimulus change
2. Tell how differential reinforcement can be used to teach students to discriminate in the classroom; in the counseling setting.
3. Specify the variables that influence the rate with which behaviors are brought under the control of discriminative stimuli.
4. Tell how to use differential reinforcement effectively.
5. Design an "errorless" instructional program to teach a discrimination.
6. Discuss and illustrate ways in which other procedures may be effectively combined with differential reinforcement.
7. Specify and illustrate the advantages and disadvantages of using stimulus change.
8. List three considerations in planning an effective stimulus change procedure.

The ideal class as conceived by many teachers would probably consist of a group of students who had acquired "maturity," or "social sensitivity." The students would know how to behave under particular circumstances. Should a guest speaker address them, they would listen politely. When a group discussion was held, they would enter it enthusiastically. When the teacher gave a set of verbal directions, those directions would be carried out as specified. How does such "maturity" come about? How does student behavior come under the control of the environment? How is it that even very subtle changes in environmental stimuli evoke or occasion some responses and inhibit others? Environmental stimuli develop such qualities for each individual as a result of his experiences in interacting with that environment. Maturity of the type described here is not simply a matter of becoming like a fruit, riper and sweeter with the passage of time. It is more a function of responding under certain conditions and with particular consequences. In other words, maturity is not synonymous with age. It is what happens to the individual as he grows older that makes the difference.

This chapter will discuss reducing behavior by means of differential reinforcement, *the procedure through which environmental stimuli gain control over behavior.* After discussing how such stimulus control is achieved, we will discuss reducing behavior by means of stimulus change, *a method of changing behavior by making changes in the environment prior to the emission of the behavior.*

DIFFERENTIAL REINFORCEMENT FOR STIMULUS CONTROL

We have touched on differential reinforcement as a procedure previously: in the section on stimulus change in Chapter 3 and in the section on response differentiation in Chapter 4. Our major emphasis in this chapter will be on the use of differential reinforcement in achieving stimulus control for purposes of reducing undesirable behavior.

DIFFERENTIAL REINFORCEMENT FOR STIMULUS CONTROL DEFINED

What set of events allows certain stimuli to control behavior; to acquire the property of occasioning a particular response? How do other sets of stimuli acquire the function of inhibiting particular responses? The set of events can be labeled "differential reinforcement"; it works this way in the natural environment: Sometimes a particular response is reinforced. Sometimes it is not. Whether it is or is not reinforced depends upon the conditions that exist at the time within the environment. When a particular response is regularly reinforced in the presence of a particular stimulus or stimuli, but not reinforced in the presence of other stimuli, each of the stimuli begin to take on discriminative properties. The stimuli present during reinforcement, the S^D's, begin to signal that the particular response emitted in their presence has a chance of being reinforced. The stimuli present during nonreinforcement, the S deltas ($S^\triangle$'s), begin to signal that under those conditions, the response has no chance of being reinforced. In science class Trudi knows that she has a good chance of receiving teacher approval if she questions the appropriateness of a conclusion made by the author of her text book by offering a logical counterconclusion. In social studies class, however, she has learned that her teacher will not approve of such questioning. The natural differential reinforcing consequences in her environment have taught Trudi to *discriminate* the acceptable behavior for each class. A diagram of these events looks like this:

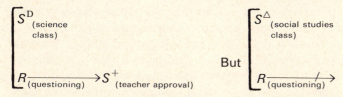

In the presence of science class, questions receive teacher approval.

But

In the presence of social studies class, questions do not receive teacher approval.

In this text, we are concerned with *programming* the acquisition of such discriminations. When the goal becomes one of teaching students to respond differently under different circumstances, the appropriate procedure to use is differential reinforcement: *regularly reinforce the given behavior in the presence of specific stimuli; place the behavior on extinction in the presence of other specific stimuli.* To summarize, then, *stimulus control* is achieved by differentially reinforcing a given response in the presence of some stimuli; not reinforcing in the presence of others. When an individual behaves differently under different stimulus conditions, or acts as if his behavior is under the control of those stimuli, we say he has learned to discriminate.

DIFFERENTIAL REINFORCEMENT IN THE SCHOOL

Susie has just entered school. At home she plays loudly and boisterously with her brothers and sisters. When she attends school, she plays just as loudly on the playground and in the classroom during reading class. The teacher has observed Susie sitting quietly on occasion. The teacher wants Susie to discriminate between the playground setting and the reading class. More specifically, she would like to reduce Susie's loud and boisterous behavior during reading class and substitute sitting quietly under those circumstances. Elsworth makes a "b" sound every time he sees the letters *b, p, q,* and *d.* The teacher wants him to reduce his errors. She wants him to make the correct phonic sound for each letter. He must be able to discriminate the differences between each letter. Lennie, in listing the events that led up to the Civil War, includes the arrival of carpetbaggers in the South and the Reconstruction Laws. The teacher wants to eliminate such responses. She wants Lennie to learn to discriminate events prior to the Civil War and events following it.

Students are taught to discriminate by means of differential reinforcement. The desired response is reinforced only in the presence of very specific stimuli. It is not reinforced in the presence of other stimuli. We will use the three situations just mentioned to illustrate. Susie's teacher approaches her, smiles at her, and waves while Susie whoops it up on the playground. When Susie starts to make loud noises in reading class, the teacher moves away and averts her glance. When Elsworth says "b" in the presence of *b,* the teacher says "good" or "right." When he says "b" in the presence of *p, q,* and *d,* she ignores him and calls on another child. In order to train Lennie to discriminate events leading up to the Civil War from those that occurred following the war, he gets reinforced only when he responds correctly in the presence of the verbal S^D's: "Which were prior events?" "Which were subsequent events?"

Behavioral specialists are often called upon to help students to learn to discriminate. Students like Susie are occasionally referred to guidance or other school personnel because of their disruptive behaviors. The behavioral specialist may help such children to more clearly identify the differences in the stimulus configurations so that the disruptive behaviors are less likely to occur in inappropriate settings. The behavioral specialist may also function in a consulting role, assisting the teacher to teach her students to make appropriate discriminations. The suggestions for using differential reinforcement effectively should be useful for all school personnel.

Exercise 11.1

The most popular restaurant in town is closed on Mondays. Every day but Monday it displays an "Open" sign. On Monday "Closed" is displayed. Tell which sign is an S^D and which is an $S^\triangle$. Tell how those signs acquired the property of occasioning the clientele's behavior of trying, or not trying, to enter the restaurant.

Exercise 11.2

Both S^D's and $S^\triangle$'s abound in our environment. Set aside a particular day and look around your environment once each hour. List as many discriminative stimuli as you can, including signs, signals, gestures, instructions, and so forth. Tell which are S^D's and which are $S^\triangle$'s. Describe how each of those stimuli may have acquired discriminative properties for your behavior.

Exercise 11.3

Visit a classroom. List five sets of stimuli that you observe acting as S^D's and five sets of stimuli that you observe acting as $S^\triangle$'s.

USING DIFFERENTIAL REINFORCEMENT EFFECTIVELY

Several variables are known to effect the rate with which an individual learns to behave appropriately under the appropriate stimuli. Those include the reinforcement and extinction procedures used, the error history of the individual, the characteristics of the discriminative stimuli, and the use of differential reinforcement in combination with other reductive procedures. The following discussion considers what can be done with those variables in order to make the differential reinforcement procedure more effective.

Using effective reinforcement and extinction procedures The most obvious guideline for using differential reinforcement effectively is to follow all the rules for effective reinforcement when the desired behavior is emitted in the presence of the appropriate stimuli and all the rules for effective extinction when that behavior is emitted in the presence of inappropriate stimuli. For example, Elsworth, who is having trouble with the "b" sound, would be immediately reinforced every time he said "b" in the presence of *b* with a reinforcer known to be appropriate for him. Every time he responded inappropriately in the presence of *b,* all reinforcers would be withheld. Once the appropriate responses were regularly emitted, reinforcement would be delivered on an intermittent schedule, which would be gradually and progressively lengthened.

Minimizing frequency of incorrect responses Prior history of the response plays an important role in the development of discriminative control. The more frequently a response has been emitted and reinforced in the past, the more resistant it is to extinction (Millenson, 1967). Errors or inappropriate behaviors that are frequently reinforced are more difficult to eliminate than those that have been reinforced only rarely. If the teacher had attended to Susie in the past when she misbehaved, it would take longer to reduce the misbehavior than if attention had never been paid to that behavior. Conscientious teachers probably help their students to learn academic material more rapidly by observing their student's performance closely, so that incorrect responses are not allowed to be inadvertently reinforced.

If frequently reinforced inappropriate responses impede the acquisition of correct discriminations, an obvious approach would be to try to discover methods for reducing the likelihood that an incorrect response will be emitted in the first place. Fortunately, some recent behavioral research has yielded a technique that trains individuals to discriminate while keeping errors to a minimum. Terrace (1966) taught pigeons to discriminate (respond differently in the presence of) horizontal and vertical lines. Sidman and Stoddard (1967) taught retarded subjects to discriminate very subtle differences between circles and elipses; Hively (1962) taught normal children to discriminate abstract geometric forms from one another. The method used in each case was to manipulate the characteristics of the S^D's. The subject was provided with only one S^D, the S^D in the presence of which he was to respond. Responses in the presence of the S^D were reinforced. As responding in the presence of the S^D continued, an alternate stimulus was gradually faded in. The alternate stimulus, the $S^\triangle$, was designed to signal a nonreinforced trial. In the early phases of the training, the $S^\triangle$ was presented very briefly. Its characteristics, such as color and shape, were very different from the S^D. As training progressed, the $S^\triangle$ began to resemble the S^D more and more. Yet, for the most part, the subjects continued to respond only in the presence of the S^D, not in the presence of the $S^\triangle$'s. Ultimately, very difficult discriminations, for example, of an S^D, from a ○ (circle) an $S^\triangle$ of an 0 (ellipse), were being performed essentially without error. Incorrect responses were not acquired. There was no need to extinguish them. Such an "errorless" discrimination training procedure has an additional advantage. Since it is not necessary to subject the incorrect response to an extinction or punishment procedure, the negative side effects of using such procedures are avoided. For example, extinction-induced aggression and the short increase in response rate during the early stages of extinction do not take place.

An errorless discrimination procedure, then, is one technique that school personnel can use in order to avoid or minimize inappropriate responses from students. Let us illustrate how this procedure might be used in training Elsworth to discriminate *b* from *d* without making errors in the first place. First the *b* is presented. The teacher says, "This letter makes a 'b' sound. Say 'b.' Good." She presents the letter again, and the students say "b." She says "good." As the "b" sound becomes reliably emitted with only the visual prompt, the *d* is gradually faded in as a visual prompt. Remember, the $S^\triangle$ must be very different from the S^D. Yet *d* and *b* are topographically very similar, so the *d* should be made to look very different from the *b* by some artificial means. The *d* could, for instance, be drawn in a different color or with a patterned background; it could be presented in such a way that the one difference, the loop to the left is emphasized; and so forth. These artificial differences would, of course, have to be gradually faded out in time. Otherwise, the teacher would run the risk that the student would learn to differentiate, not on the basis of the form of the letter, but on the basis of the artificial props. Fading

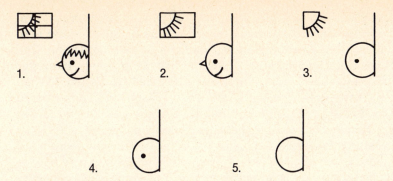

FIGURE 11.1   Example of a set of $S^\triangle$ sequences

should force the student's attention to the relevant differences between the two letters. Fig. 11.1 illustrates one possible set of $S^\triangle$ sequences.

Creative teachers have used techniques like these throughout their careers because they find that their students learn efficiently when such gimmicks are used. Here is another instance in which scientific support is lent to effective teaching practices that have been around longer than a field called "behavior modification."

Exercise 11.4

Observe a class in which the teacher is attempting to teach the students to learn to discriminate between two different stimuli.

a. Tell how the teacher responds following the emission of each correct and each incorrect response.

b. Describe any instances in which the teacher attempts to facilitate the discrimination by either emphasizing $S^D - S^\triangle$ differences or by fading in the $S^\triangle$ gradually.

Exercise 11.5

Select one of the following objectives. Using an errorless discrimination training technique, outline the steps you would follow in teaching a student to reach the objective.

a. The student will discriminate water from alcohol.

b. The student will discriminate woolen cloth from cotton cloth.

c. The student will discriminate a jig saw from a sabre saw.

d. The student will behave differently on the debate team than he does during a lecture (specify actual behaviors for each).

e. The student will discriminate when the teacher is kidding and when he is serious (operationalize "kidding" and "serious").

f. Offer your own objective.

Supplementary stimuli   To further facilitate the acquisition of dis-

193

criminations, still other stimuli such as signs, signals, written and oral directions, and comments can be added. They may be added along with prior stimuli or concurrently with the delivery of reinforcement. One example is the use of verbal stimuli. As the teacher presents the letter *d*, she says, "Remember, this is the letter that faces to the left." When a student correctly identifies the *b*, she says, "Good, you remembered that the *b* faces to right." Prior to a talk by a guest speaker, a teacher might say, "Remember; during the guest's lecture, we sit quietly so as not to disturb the others who are listening." After the lecture, to which the class listened attentively, "You people certainly know how to be polite when visitors come to speak to you. You were being considerate of the others in the audience." The class will, hopefully, begin to increase the amount of time during which it listens attentively. The teacher will then be able to assist the students to generalize the desired response to other similar situations. "Remember how quiet you were when the guest speaker visited the class? Let's try to behave the same way at the planetarium lecture." Then, at the planetarium, "I see you did remember how to listen politely."

Exercise 11.6
    Describe instances in your classroom observation in which the teacher used supplementary stimuli in order to facilitate the acquisition of a discrimination.

Combining with other reductive procedures It is possible to use differential reinforcement in combination with other reductive procedures. Such procedures are applied contingent upon responding in the presence of $S^\triangle$, while responses in the presence of S^D are reinforced. We have already discussed applying extinction to responses in the presence of $S^\triangle$. Consideration can be given, however, to using response cost, timeout, and punishment contingent upon the emission of "incorrect" responses. For instance, when Sandra talks out during a lecture a few points could be deducted from her grade or she could be sent out of the room or scolded. Such procedures, if they are known to be effective with her, will probably hasten her acquisition of the discrimination that talking should not occur during lectures but is acceptable in other situations, such as on the playground. Sandra's talking out during lectures will probably diminish faster than if she were simply ignored when she did so. It must always be borne in mind, however, that negative contingencies such as response contingent withdrawal of reinforcement and punishment may have some undesirable side effects. These should be reviewed prior to making a decision regarding combining such reductive techniques with differential reinforcement.

Exercise 11.7

Teach someone to engage in a particular behavior under discriminative control. He should respond only when an S^D is presented, but not when an $S^\triangle$ is presented. Describe your procedure. Be sure to include several base rate sessions. Keep a record of the number of trials, number of responses emitted in the presence of the S^D, and the number of responses emitted in the presence of the $S^\triangle$. Plot each response category session on a graph. Figure A illustrates such a graph. (The reader may want to refer to the discussions in Chapter 1 on collecting data, plotting graphs, and so on.)

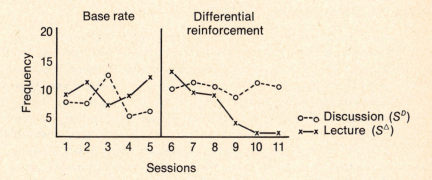

FIGURE A Number of times Sandra calls out during discussions and lectures (fictional data)

Exercise 11.8

Referring back to your observation for Exercise 11.4, discuss whether or not any supplementary contingencies were used along with differential reinforcement. Describe any side effects that you observed.

When an effective differential reinforcement procedure is used to bring a particular response under the control of a particular stimulus, the ultimate result should be a situation in which that stimulus either begins to call forth or occasion the response or, by signaling nonreinforcement, begins to "inhibit" the response. It then becomes possible to change behavior by presenting or removing such stimuli. That procedure for changing stimuli is the subject of the ensuing discussion.

STIMULUS CHANGE

In Chapter 3, we described stimulus change as follows: "When it is observed that a specific behavior tends to occur in the presence of a set of discriminative stimuli, it becomes possible to rapidly increase the occurrence of the behavior by providing those discriminative stimuli (the S^D's)." The converse also holds true. *When it is observed that a specific behavior does* not *occur in the presence of a set of discriminative stimuli, it becomes possible to temporarily reduce the occurrence of the behavior by providing those discriminative stimuli (the $S^{\triangle}$'s).* This latter point is what we will be emphasizing in this section.

REDUCING BEHAVIOR BY CHANGING STIMULI

Stimulus change procedures are frequently used by school personnel. The following examples will be familiar to many of the readers: Mike was observed to poke John whenever close enough to do so. However, he was not observed to poke any of the other children in class. Under such conditions, changing the stimulus, John, by separating the two boys eliminated the poking behavior. Suppose, in another situation, it were observed that the verbal stimulus "don't cheat" was invariably followed by an increase by the class in peeking at neighbor's papers, while the words "I know you can all be trusted to do your own work" was followed by independent work. Replacement of the words "don't cheat" with "I know you can all be trusted to do your own work" would probably result in a decrease or elimination of the "peeking" behavior. Or, in another example, a teacher found that a student spent lots of time doodling and rocking back and forth on his chair when he was provided with the regular social studies text. This behavior was never emitted when he had access to the *Britannica Junior Encyclopedia* or *National Geographic.* By frequently presenting those types of materials rather than the assigned text, the teacher decreased the amount of time during which the student doodled and rocked in his chair.

Exercise 11.9
a. Go to the supermarket and watch some children and their parents. Describe an episode in which a parent used stimulus change in order to reduce her child's undesirable behavior. Be sure to identify the S^D's that appeared to occasion the undesirable response and the $S^{\triangle}$'s that appeared to inhibit the response.
b. Do the same in a school setting.

ADVANTAGES OF STIMULUS CHANGE

Once a particular stimulus has been consistently observed either to inhibit or occasion a behavior by an individual, that stimulus may be used to achieve a *rapid* behavioral change. Presentation of the $S^{\triangle}$ should lead to a rapid cessation of the ongoing behavior. Presentation of the appropriate S^D should produce a change from an undesirable to a desirable behavior. When the altered stimulus conditions not only inhibit the undesirable response but simultaneously *do* occasion a desirable response, stimulus change can be a very *constructive* procedure. In one case, a frown from the teacher may inhibit a student's whispering to his friend. On the other hand, an assignment to do research on a subject of interest to the student might have the effect of not only reducing the whispering but also increasing the amount of information acquired by the student.

Stimulus change can also serve as a *preventive* technique. When it appears that the student is at the brink of, but not actually engaging in, an undesirable behavior, a change in stimulus conditions may serve to prevent the emission of that behavior. The term "antiseptic bouncing" (Redl & Wineman, 1957) is often applied when stimulus change is used preventitively. One study (Long & Newman, 1961) suggests that when it appears that a student is becoming tense or being irritated by other students or when it appears that he might become the instigator of a possible contagious effect, he could be antiseptically bounced. For example, if he started to get the giggles and this showed signs of spreading, the student might be given a note to deliver to the principal's office or be sent out for a drink of water. Upon returning, the student would, hopefully, have regained control and he would have been stopped from emitting the incorrect behavior.

USING STIMULUS CHANGE EFFECTIVELY

Observing systematically Because objects and events in the environment acquire discriminative properties as a result of the individual's experience in reference to those stimuli, it is very important to closely observe the behavior of each individual before attempting a stimulus change procedure. If a teacher plans to change the stimulus conditions from those that occasion a particular response to either those that inhibit the response or those that occasion different responses, she must identify the stimuli that act as discriminative stimuli for the individuals involved. Teachers frequently encounter students who fail to follow directions; students for whom verbal instructions

197

fail to operate as $S^{\triangle}$'s or S^{D}'s. One of their tasks, in addition to the slower process of bringing the behavior under discriminative control by means of differential reinforcement, is to seek out already available $S^{\triangle}$'s and S^{D}'s. These latter stimuli can then be used temporarily until S^{D}'s, such as the verbal instructions, begin to have a reliable effect. For example, whenever the teacher said "Stop making noise so we can get ready for dismissal," Margaret almost always began to whistle and shuffle her feet. The teacher began to closely watch Margaret's behavior. She observed Margaret to quiet down after she said "Sit down," and slowly counted to three. That S^{D} could then be used temporarily until a different S^{D}, such as the teacher's instructing her to quiet down, could be brought under discriminative control for Margaret. When educational experts caution teachers to "know" each individual student and to "start where the student *is*," it is probably this point that they have in mind. For educators have known for a long time that individual students operate differently under different conditions; that a technique that works well with one student will not necessarily work with another. Here, what has been offered is a partial explanation of why this may be so, along with a method for altering this state of affairs.

Exercise 11.10

During a classroom observation, watch one or two students very closely. Identify discriminative stimuli that appear to control their behavior. Try to list several S^{D}'s and $S^{\triangle}$'s for each. Do those same S^{D}'s and $S^{\triangle}$'s operate in a similar fashion for all of the students in the group? Discuss this.

Avoiding stimulus change as a reinforcer for undesirable behavior In a previous discussion, we mentioned that novelty, or stimulus change, often serves as a reinforcing event. Many forms of stimuli, such as new materials, a different setting, or different activities may have strong reinforcing properties. If these stimuli are presented immediately following the emission of an undesirable behavior, the behavior, while decreasing rapidly for the moment, may in fact be increased in the long run. This is especially likely to happen when those reinforcers are not available at any other times. If the student who rocked and doodled while reading the assigned social studies text were given his preferred reading materials only at a time when he was in the process of engaging in those undesirable activities, he would probably quickly learn that chair rocking and doodling would lead to his being given the materials he likes. Undoubtedly, the frequency of doodling and chair rocking would increase over time. Several factors, then, have to be considered: Is it possible to institute the stimulus change each and every time the undesired behavior is emitted so that the undesired behavior is consistently nipped in the bud, irrespective of potential reinforcement? Would it be preferable to delay the immediate effects of stimulus change by waiting for a time when the student is again performing as he should and then changing the stimulus? Or should one take a strict prevention approach? It would seem that either of the latter two alternatives might be more practical. In the illustration under consideration, the teacher could use presentation of the *Britannica* or the *National Geographic* contingent upon the student's accomplishing at least some specified minimum amount of work with the assigned text and at a time when he is not rocking; or she could give the student a different assignment in the first place. She could, for instance, ask him to prepare a report, based on one of those sources, that is related to the assigned topic.

Exercise 11.11

For either of the observations you made for Exercise 11.9, supply the following information:

a. What, exactly, was the child or student doing at the moment when the stimuli were altered?

b. What evidence, if any, was there that the new stimulus might be a reinforcing stimulus?

c. What was the immediate result of the procedure?

d. Try to guess what some of the long-term effects might be.

e. What procedural alterations, if any, would you suggest?

Combining stimulus change with reinforcement Although stimulus change used by itself may achieve only a temporary reduction in an undesirable behavior, it may set the stage for the reinforcement of alternative desirable behaviors. When an S^D that occasions a desirable behavior is substituted for a stimulus that occasions undesirable behavior, it becomes possible to begin to reinforce and thereby increase the frequency of the desired behavior. When a normally disruptive student is working quietly and attending closely to the materials before him, the teacher will have an opportunity to reinforce him. She can praise his work, have him present it to the class, comment upon his good work habits, smile, nod, wink, pat him, or use any other reinforcers known to be effective with that student in order to maintain the quiet work behavior.

Exercise 11.12

At the end of his English lesson, Mr. Olson writes the homework assignment on the board. All the students in the room except Eric take out their notebooks and copy the assignment. Eric begins to pack up his materials to get ready to leave for his next class. But when Mr. Olson says in a loud voice, "Eric, take out your notebook and copy your assignment," Eric follows the instruction. What can Mr. Olson do to stop Eric from rustling his materials at the end of the class and to teach him to copy the assignments without prompting?

DISADVANTAGES OF STIMULUS CHANGE

Stimulus change has an immediate effect and provides an opportunity to teach and strengthen desirable behaviors. However, if such desirable behaviors are not strengthened, returning to the original stimulus conditions often results in the rapid recovery of the eliminated response (Azrin & Holz, 1966). We will discuss an earlier example to illustrate. Separating Mike and John leads to an immediate reduction in poking behavior. But, seat Mike within reach of John, and poking may well resume. Were a proctor to come in to the class we discussed previously and say "Don't cheat," peeking would probably increase. The effects of stimulus change are temporary unless it is used in combination with other procedures. Changed stimuli also may adventitiously serve to reinforce the undesirable behavior.

Exercise 11.13

Describe any episode in which you observed one of the disadvantages of using stimulus change. What would you have suggested to ameliorate the problem?

SUMMARY

Stimulus control can be used as one general approach to the reduction of undesirable behaviors. If a particular previous stimulus reliably occasions the nonemission of a specific response, that stimulus, an $S^\triangle$, can be presented and the behavior should be quickly reduced. If a different S^D reliably occasions the emission of a desired response, its presentation can serve to reduce an undesirable behavior by supplanting it with the desired response. In order to use such a procedure, the individual must be under stimulus control. He must have learned how to discriminate between the appropriate S^D's and $S^\triangle$'s. Such discriminations are acquired through differential reinforcement. When inappropriate or erroneous responses are kept to a minimum, differential reinforcement can produce more effective results. Inappropriate responding may be minimized or even avoided through careful alterations in S^D conditions. Once such stimulus control has developed, stimulus change can then be used. Though stimulus change used by itself has a temporary effect, it provides an opportunity for reinforcing the desired response once it has been occasioned through the presentation of the discriminative stimuli.

REFERENCES

Azrin, N. H., & Holz, W. C. Punishment. In W. K. Honig (Ed.), *Operant behavior: Areas of research and application.* New York: Appleton-Century-Crofts, 1966.

Hively, W. Programming stimuli in matching to sample. *Journal of the Experimental Analysis of Behavior,* 1962, **5,** 279–298.

Long, N. J., & Newman, R. G. A differential approach to the management of surface behavior of children in school. *Teachers' Handling of Children in Conflict,* Bulletin of the School of Education, Indiana University, 1961, **37,** 47–61.

Millenson, J. R. *Principles of behavior analysis.* New York: Macmillan, 1967.

Redl, F., & Wineman, D. *The aggressive child.* New York: Free Press, 1957.

Sidman, M., & Stoddard, L. T. The effectiveness of fading in programming a simultaneous form discrimination for retarded children. *Journal of the Experimental Analysis of Behavior,* 1967, **10,** 3–16.

Terrace, H. S. Stimulus control. In W. K. Honig (Ed.), *Operant behavior: Areas of research and application.* New York: Appleton-Century-Crofts, 1966.

12 REDUCING BEHAVIOR THROUGH REINFORCEMENT

Objectives

Using examples not described in this chapter you should be able to

1. Define and offer school illustrations for each of the following terms:
   a. satiation
   b. differential reinforcement of other behaviors (DRO)
   c. behavioral contrast
   d. reinforcement of incompatible behavior
2. Tell the major advantage and the major disadvantages of a satiation procedure.
3. Describe and illustrate the factors that influence the time it takes for satiation to begin to show its effect.
4. List and discuss two major advantages and disadvantages of the DRO procedure.
5. List, discuss, and offer school illustrations of the four major advantages of using the reinforcement of incompatible behaviors procedure.
6. List three guidelines for selecting the "incompatible" behavior.
7. List, discuss, and illustrate the factors that influence the effectiveness of the reinforcement of incompatible behaviors procedure.
8. Carry out an effective reinforcing incompatible behaviors procedure.
9. List the chief disadvantage of reinforcing incompatible behavior.

The following procedures take a different approach to reducing behavior. While in Chapters 8–10 we generally emphasized the application of negative contingencies to the undesirable behavior, we will now show how behavioral reduction can be achieved by using positive reinforcement. The first such approach, *satiation,* involves repeated reinforcement delivered contingent upon the emission of the undesirable behavior. The second, *differential reinforcement* of other behaviors, which is a reinforcement schedule, provides for the regular delivery of reinforcement contingent upon the nonemission of the undesirable behavior. The third, *reinforcing incompatible behaviors,* allows reinforcement to perform the function of reducing undesirable behavior by strengthening desirable alternatives. All three procedures have one major advantage in common: because all depend upon the application of reinforcement, they all serve to emphasize how even something as distasteful as trying to get rid of problem behaviors can be approached constructively.

SATIATION

Earlier in the text, (Chapter 2), satiation was mentioned as one of the phenomena that accompany the repeated presentation of reinforcement. Here our concern will be with harnessing that effect; using reinforcement for the specific purpose of achieving a reduction of the rate with which a behavior is emitted.

SATIATION DEFINED

The satiation procedure involves a very simple operation: continued reinforcing of the response. When the rate with which the behavior is emitted begins to level off, and eventually slows to a halt, satiation is said to have occurred. Satiation, then, can be defined as *the behavioral reduction that is achieved through the repeated presentation of a reinforcing object or event contingent upon the emission of the behavior.* The examples of satiation that occur naturally are known to everyone. Eating ceases when the individual has "eaten enough." Even the bridge or fishing enthusiast will eventually stop his activity in the face of continued reinforcement. In the following section, situations in which satiation is designed into a behavior modification program will be illustrated.

ADVANTAGES OF SATIATION

The major advantage in using a satiation procedure has already been indicated: it is a positive approach. The individual who conducts the procedure is not forced into a situation in which he has to withhold or withdraw reinforcement or present an aversive stimulus. He has, simply, to provide for continuous presentation of, or accessibility to, reinforcement.

Tommy has found that when he voluntarily burps in class, everyone giggles. His teacher wants to get rid of that disruption and decides to use satiation. She says "Very good, Tommy. You really can burp. Do it again." Tommy burps again. Again the class giggles and the teacher repeats her comments. This is continued until Tommy apparently begins to tire of the whole operation. For the rest of the day no more voluntary burping is emitted. The next day, Tommy tries again. The situation is handled in the same manner as it was on the previous day. This time the rate of voluntary burps diminishes sooner. With this treatment, Tommy's rate of burping drops down very low. The procedure has been, at least temporarily, successful.

USING SATIATION EFFECTIVELY

Providing for large quantities of immediate reinforcement Eddie had a clever father. When Eddie was discovered, at age twelve, to be sneaking smokes behind the barn, his father bought him a whole package of cigarettes. He offered them to Eddie and said, "If you want to smoke, go ahead," and lit one for him. As soon as Eddie had finished smoking the first, he was offered a second; then a third. Eddie got nauseous and dizzy and asked his father if he could stop. His father said "Just finish that one. I bought it just for you." Eddie did and for the next ten years he never smoked.

Behavioral reduction by means of satiation is often *temporary.* The smoking episode probably demonstrated a longer lasting satiation effect than is found in most situations. Even the individual who gets up from the banquet table and swears that he will never eat again, usually skips no more than a meal or two. Many variables probably influence the time it takes for satiation to begin to show its effects: the characteristics of the response, deprivation conditions, the type and quantity of reinforcers, and the opportunity for alternative responses.

Considering response characteristics If the individual has to use lots of effort in order to emit a given response, like cutting and chewing a tough piece of steak, lifting heavy objects, or running fast, he will "tire" and satiate sooner. Responses that are easier to emit, such as looking out of the window, whispering, or frowning would subside more slowly. An alternative reductive procedure would probably have a longer lasting effect with the latter behaviors.

When deciding to use a satiation procedure the individual must consider whether he can live with the emission of the undesirable response for a while. People who could put up with such responses as voluntary burping, minor cutting up, use of off-color or swear words, and other similar responses, could not so easily tolerate other responses. Most teachers would hardly try to use satiation for responses such as punching other students or the teacher, using dangerous equipment, or making noises loudly and continuously enough to disrupt the entire class. In any case, each individual involved in carrying out a behavior change procedure must assess his own tolerance for the specific undesirable response. Each will have to judge whether he can tolerate the response for a time before a satiation procedure is attempted.

Exercise 12.1

Of the many undesirable responses you may have observed in your classroom observations, select one or two that you feel might be effectively handled by means of a satiation procedure. Explain why you think satiation would be a good technique to use with those responses.

Considering deprivation conditions   In general, the more an individual is deprived of a given reinforcer, the higher his rate of responding once that reinforcer is delivered. A person who has just eaten a complete meal will satiate on French pastries if they are the only food available sooner than would someone who had not eaten for six or eight hours. The child who has only rarely received attention from his teacher will emit a response that obtains her attention more frequently than if the child had received lots of teacher attention. The type of reinforcer also interacts with deprivation conditions in terms of the time it takes to achieve a reduction in behavior. The reduction occurs sooner with primary reinforcement than with conditioned reinforcement. Responses that are reinforced by such stimuli as food, water, or sex will diminish sooner than responses that are reinforced by such stimuli as praise and attention. However, too much conditioned reinforcement can also be encountered; too much praise and attention can also diminish responses (Holland & Skinner, 1961).

Opportunity for alternative responses   As a direct corollary of the situation under deprivation, a satiation procedure applied to the undesirable behavior will probably work faster and last longer if the individual has an opportunity to receive the same reinforcer for alternative responses. For this would provide a situation in which the individual would be less deprived of the particular reinforcer. If a student is successful on the football field and receives lots of peer approval, peer approval for disrupting in class will probably maintain that behavior for a shorter period of time than if disrupting in class were his only way of obtaining that approval.

Exercise 12.2

Select one of the responses you listed in Exercise 12.1 and design a satiation procedure in order to reduce the emission of the response. Outline each of the steps you would follow.

DISADVANTAGES OF SATIATION

The two major disadvantages in using a satiation procedure have been mentioned in the previous discussion: (1) satiation effects are frequently temporary and (2) the individual using the procedure has to be able to tolerate the response for a while. Satiation is probably best reserved for reducing not very serious undesirable behaviors.

DIFFERENTIAL REINFORCEMENT
OF OTHER BEHAVIOR
(DRO)

We will now discuss how a reinforcement schedule can be planned as part of a program designed to reduce an undesirable behavior. Like satiation, the differential reinforcement of other behaviors (DRO) schedule also approaches the goal of behavioral reduction in a positive manner.

DRO DEFINED AND ILLUSTRATED

Differential reinforcement of other behaviors is a variant of the differential reinforcement procedure we discussed in Chapter 11; but DRO is specifically directed toward the reduction of a particular behavior. "The DRO schedule refers to a procedure in which a reinforcer follows any performance the [individual] emits except a particular one (Ferster, 1968, p. 524)." In laboratory practice, a DRO schedule usually includes the programming of reinforcement that is delivered on some specific schedule, say, fixed interval or fixed ratio, *except* when the individual engages in a particular response. For instance, food may be regularly delivered when the subject engages in any behavior other than pressing one particular bar. In the applied situation, delivery of reinforcement also follows some prescribed pattern. The subject receives reinforcement *except* when he engages in a particular behavior.

An illustration of this would be telling a music student that he is doing fine, nodding or smiling every ten seconds, *except* when he plays an incorrect note. Or, say, the teacher is called to the office and puts a monitor in charge of the class. The monitor is asked to watch the clock, and every thirty seconds he is to place a mark on the blackboard which represents an extra minute of recess, *except* if any of the students are out of their seats at that time. Frank has a habit that annoys his teacher. He embellishes many of his school papers with pictures, symbols, and other kinds of doodles. She uses a system of giving him a star for every paper *other than* the ones containing those embellishments. Differential reinforcement of other behaviors (DRO) is the procedure being used in each of those cases.

ADVANTAGES OF DRO

Rapidly reducing behavior   DRO enables the individual to be reinforced for engaging in a universe of behaviors, with the one specified exception. It is usually a very powerful procedure. The individual has all sorts of options available to him, and he usually takes one of them. As a result, the one nonreinforceable behavior begins to drop out quite rapidly (Reynolds, 1961). If there is a behavior that needs to be reduced quickly and at all costs, such as self-destructive or aggressive behavior, and such procedural choices as stimulus change and punishment must be rejected, DRO might accomplish the aim effectively.

Because of its very powerful reductive effect, DRO is frequently used to demonstrate the effectiveness of a reinforcer in an experimental situation. DRO tends to show a stronger effect than simple extinction. Baer, Peterson and Sherman (1967), for instance, performed a study in which they taught profoundly retarded children to imitate. First the children were reinforced with food and praise for engaging in imitative behaviors. Imitative behavior increased substantially. In order to demonstrate that the reinforcing contingencies were responsible for the change, a DRO phase was instituted. Reinforcement then became contingent upon a period of time in which imitative behavior was not emitted. Imitative behavior plunged rapidly under DRO. When imitation-contingent behavior was reinstituted, the children again began to imitate and at a high rate.

Positive approach   DRO is a positive approach. The individual can earn reinforcement regularly by simply not emitting a behavior. The schedule ensures that regular reinforcement is made available. No aversive stimuli are required.

USING DRO EFFECTIVELY

DRO is a differential reinforcement procedure. The techniques that apply to increasing the effectiveness of differential reinforcement apply to DRO as well. In addition, since the nature of the differential reinforcement of other behaviors procedure requires that reinforcement is contingent upon nonresponding, careful reinforcement scheduling becomes very important. The ratio of responses or interval of time during which the undesirable behavior is not to be emitted should be specified in advance. In order to assure the greatest likelihood of success for the individual, the ratio requirements should be kept low or the time intervals should be kept short at first. This will allow the student to earn frequent reinforcement. After the undesirable behavior begins to diminish in rate, the intervals can be gradually extended. For example, a student has been observed to frequently suck his thumb in class. The children tease him for this. The child, his parents, and the dentist all wish to eliminate the behavior. A DRO procedure is put into effect. An observer watches the student. Following every one-minute interval during which thumb sucking is not emitted, the student is given a token that he can exchange for some preselected back-up reinforcer. The delivery of the token is paired with smiles, praise, and other conditioned reinforcers. When the frequency of thumb sucking diminishes by, say 50 percent, the interval is lengthened to, say, two minutes. This pattern can continue until the terminal goal is reached.

DISADVANTAGES OF DRO

"Other" behavior could be worse   All behaviors, other than the one to be eliminated, are equally reinforceable under DRO conditions. This could conceivably mean that one could find oneself in the position of reinforcing an "other" behavior that is just as bad or, perhaps, even worse than the behavior to be eliminated. Teacher attention is delivered to Leroy every five minutes, provided that he has not tapped the desk top with his pencil. It just so happens that he is drawing a picture instead of solving an arithmetic problem at the very moment that the teacher attends to him. Picture drawing might, as a result, increase. This sort of problem would be more apt to manifest itself among students who have a high frequency of many undesirable behaviors in their repertoires. It would seem best then, when working with students who frequently emit many problem behaviors, to turn to one of two alternatives: either put the most serious of the undesirable behaviors on DRO, assuming that a sufficient number of reinforceable intervals will be available to allow the program a chance to work, or to elect another reductive procedure.

Behavioral contrast   If a specific behavior is placed on a DRO schedule, it becomes very important to ensure that the behavior does not receive reinforcement at other times. If a particular behavior is placed on DRO under some stimulus conditions, it is possible that the undesirable response rate, while decreasing under the condition paired with DRO, might increase under the other condition. Evidence for this fact derives from a study performed by Reynolds (1961). In that study, pigeons were reinforced for key pecking under one discriminative stimulus (S^D) and *were reinforced for non-key pecking (DRO) under a different S^D*. Though the rate of key pecking under the DRO-correlated stimulus was practically eliminated, responding under the reinforced-response-correlated stimulus increased to a level that was higher than its previous one. The phenomenon was labeled *behavioral contrast*. Though data from human subjects on this phenomenon is insufficient, it would be advisable to watch for the possible occurrences of a contrast effect during the use of DRO. For instance, during the times that Leroy's teacher left the room it would be a good idea to measure the rate of his desk-top tapping. A substantial increase over base rate in desk tapping while the teacher was out of the room, coupled with the elimination of the effect during the teacher's presence, would suggest the occurrence of a contrast effect.

Exercise 12.3

Suggest two or three terminal behaviors you think would be best accomplished through the use of a DRO procedure. Defend your selection of the DRO procedure. For one of the terminal goals, outline the steps you would use in the DRO procedure.

Exercise 12.4

DRO is a procedure that is frequently used to demonstrate experimental control in programs involving the *acquisition* of such new behaviors as speech and academic learning, which begin to receive reinforcement from different sources. Can you tell why a DRO-reversal is selected rather than a simple extinction-reversal technique for those behavioral categories? (See Chapter 1 for a description of the reversal technique.)

REINFORCING INCOMPATIBLE BEHAVIORS

The last reductive procedure we will discuss in this chapter will be given the greatest emphasis. The technique of reinforcing a behavior that is *incompatible* with an undesirable behavior has been mentioned several times elsewhere in this text, in the sections on reinforcement, differential reinforcement, stimulus change, extinction, and DRO. But because the procedure is constructive and has much to offer to school personnel, it is being treated separately here.

REINFORCING INCOMPATIBLE BEHAVIORS DEFINED

The technique of reinforcing incompatible behaviors is almost self-explanatory. It simply consists of strengthening a behavior or behaviors that cannot coexist with the undesirable behavior. In utilizing this procedure, the undesirable behavior is first identified and operationalized. Then, potential alternative behaviors that would make the emission of the undesirable behavior impossible are considered. After careful consideration, one or several of the alternative behaviors are selected to be strengthened. For example, Douglas is frequently out of his seat. Being seated is incompatible with being out of his seat. If his in-seat behavior is strengthened, his out-of-seat behavior must decrease. Charlene spends her recess and lunch time quietly isolated in a corner. Turning one end of a jump rope, engaging in conversation, sitting with other students, participating in a game are activities that are incompatible with isolation. Strengthening those behaviors should reduce the frequency of Charlene's moments alone. Vernon gets into frequent trouble with the police. He breaks windows, pilfers objects from stores, sprays paint on walls, and shoots BB's at passers-by. All of this occurs during school hours while Vernon is playing truant. Attending school is incompatible with those behaviors. By strengthening Vernon's school attendance, his lawless behavior should decrease.

REINFORCING INCOMPATIBLE BEHAVIORS IN SCHOOL AND COUNSELING SETTINGS

A great many of the practitioners who have been consulted regarding classroom behavioral problems have elected to use the reinforcement of incompatible behaviors procedure. Allen, Hart, Buell, Harris, and Wolf (1964) worked with a preschooler who seldom played with other children. Rather than punishing or using only extinction on the isolate behavior, they decided to reinforce the youngster with attention when she interacted with other children (incompatible with isolate behavior). Her isolate behavior diminished substantially. A similar approach was used to diminish hyperactivity in a preschooler (Allen, Henke, Harris, Baer, & Reynolds, 1967). Flitting from one activity to another yielded the child no reinforcement. But engaging in one activity for preselected periods of time was socially reinforced. Hyperactivity was reduced as a result.

A similar type of procedure is used to achieve certain specific terminal goals in counseling activities. One of the authors was working with a child who moved her hands in front of her face constantly in a ritualistic fashion. This, among several other autisticlike (repetitive, nonfunctional) behaviors, was selected as a response that should be reduced. It interfered with the child's attending to relevant environmental stimuli and was very distracting in social settings, especially the classroom. The approach selected was to reinforce incompatible behaviors. Therefore, a large group of hand-involved behaviors was shaped and strengthened: playing with sand, placing pieces of puzzles together, piling blocks, painting, and many other instructional and play behaviors. None of those behaviors had been emitted with much frequency in the past. Once they were sufficiently reinforced they began to be emitted much more often. The child was spending most of the counseling session engaged in more normal play and instructional activities. The ritualistic hand movements were never attended to, either positively or aversively. Yet they gradually diminished, since they could not coexist with the more constructive behaviors. A similar approach by the teacher yielded parallel results in the classroom.

Exercise 12.5
a. For the following behaviors, select one or more incompatible behaviors:
    1. rocking back and forth in a chair
    2. frowning
    3. handing in messy papers
    4. thumb sucking
    5. failing to follow directions in general
    6. being tardy
b. Defend your selection of the incompatible behavior(s).

Exercise 12.6
Ask a teacher to tell you which undesirable student behaviors she would like to see eliminated in her classroom. Then observe that teacher's classroom for half an hour. Is the teacher reinforcing behaviors that are incompatible with the undesired behaviors? Describe those and any additional behaviors that would be incompatible with the undesired behavior.

ADVANTAGES OF REINFORCING INCOMPATIBLE BEHAVIORS

Enduring reduction of behavior Once the incompatible behavior is being emitted at a rate that is high and steady enough to interfere with the emission of the undesirable behavior, the latter behavior will have been, at least temporarily, eliminated. But as long as the incompatible behavior is *maintained* at that high, steady rate, the undesirable behavior will not be able to return. Therefore, by utilizing the rules for maintaining high rates of behavior, an enduring reduction of the undesirable behavior can be achieved. For instance, Vernon's school attendance should maintain along with the elimination of stealing and destruction of property. Something like this was actually accomplished by a graduate student as a project for a course assignment. A habitually truant teen-ager whose only apparent interest was sports cars was allowed to earn sports car magazines by working on academic assignments. He was given very simple assignments to complete for which he could earn points. A specific number of points could be used to purchase the magazines. The student's school attendance increased substantially.

Positive approach Extinction, response contingent withdrawal of reinforcement, and punishment all have some negative consequences for the individual. Either reinforcers are withdrawn from him or aversive contingencies are presented. With the reinforcement of incompatible behavior, the individual continues to receive reinforcement. A carefully planned program will yield him regular reinforcement and all the good things that go along with it. If there is any generalized responding to stimuli in the school, it should be positive. The individual is also more likely to remain in a situation when it yields him reinforcement. In the counseling case illustrated above, the autistic child always attended sessions willingly and never made an attempt to leave. Had we scolded, slapped, or withheld our attention for the length of time that the undesired hand movements were present, the situation might have been very aversive to her. She might have tried to leave or, at least, refused to cooperate in the program.

Constructive approach In selecting incompatible behaviors, it is usually possible to find one or more desirable responses whose strengthening would be beneficial to the student. In the illustrative cases cited above, increased social interactions, paying attention to instructional materials, and learning to engage in normal play activities undoubtedly served to help the students progress educationally and socially.

Comfortable approach Many practitioners in educational and counseling settings are very hesitant to use aversive contingencies. They view their job as being one of helping children to develop their fullest possible potentials. They do not want to spend their time scolding, punishing, threatening, or intentionally ignoring children. They do want to help children to learn; to acquire behaviors that are beneficial to them. Reinforcing a productive, desirable behavior that is incompatible with an undesirable behavior is well suited to those ideals.

Exercise 12.7

Talk to the teacher whom you observed for Exercise 12.6. As tactfully as possible ask her (him) why she (he) handled a particular episode by reinforcing incompatible behaviors, if she did use such a procedure, rather than another. What advantages did she note in using the reinforcement of incompatible behaviors? What advantages did you notice?

SELECTING THE INCOMPATIBLE BEHAVIOR

Insuring behavioral incompatibility When selecting the incompatible behavior, or array of behaviors, the practitioner must be careful to ensure that the undesirable and the desirable behaviors cannot be emitted simultaneously. For if such compatibility should inadvertently occur, both behaviors might be strengthened. Suppose Vernon not only got into trouble during school hours while truant but also managed to steal and destroy property while in school. Simply reinforcing school attendance, then, could not assist in the reduction of those behaviors. It might even accidentally strengthen them in school. In that kind of situation it would be necessary to be much more specific in the selection of reinforceable behaviors. Doing schoolwork at his desk, participating in group activities, or engaging in wood working, and art projects might not be compatible with stealing and destruction. One would have to be careful to avoid strengthening such other activities as allowing Vernon to go on errands; to remain alone without supervision; or to have access to free, unstructured time. For there is nothing about those latter behaviors which is incompatible with the undesirable behaviors. He could, conceivably, write on walls while on an errand, go through and remove objects from students' desks while alone in the room, and so on.

Selecting behavior already in response repertoire Given a set of potential incompatible behaviors among which to choose, and all other factors being equal, it is a good idea to select one that is already present in the repertoire of the individual. The goal should be accomplished more quickly if the incompatible behavior is already being emitted at some rate above zero. The time it takes to shape a behavior might involve considerable delay. Given a student who usually engaged in isolate behaviors, one might, for instance, select an incompatible behavior from any of the following: rope jumping, conversing, pushing others on the swing, participating in a debate, and many others. Suppose the child had been observed to play jump rope and swing with other children occasionally. She had never been observed to engage in conversation with others. The former behaviors would probably be much easier to strengthen than the latter. (Then afterwards it would always be possible to begin shaping the latter.)

Selecting behavior likely to be maintained by environment Even though school personnel often spend considerable amounts of time with their students, they cannot remain with them constantly. Again, all things being equal, the incompatible behavior should be one that the remainder of the students' environment will tend to support. Many behaviors, for instance, are incompatible with verbal aggression: polite well-modulated speech, no speech, mimimal speech, whispered words, incomprehensible words, and so on. Some of those behaviors would yield the student little reinforcement in the outside world. Nonspeaking, whispering, and the emission of incomprehensible words would probably undergo extinction. On the other hand, polite, well-modulated speech would be more likely to receive reinforcement from some sources. The point is that the incompatible behavior should be *practical;* practical behaviors have social import and are apt to be maintained through "natural" consequences.

USING REINFORCEMENT OF INCOMPATIBLE BEHAVIORS EFFECTIVELY

Using effective reinforcement procedures The reinforcement of incompatible behaviors is a specific type of reinforcement procedure. And, all the rules for effective reinforcement apply in this situation as well. The reinforcers need to be appropriate for the individual; they should be delivered as soon as possible following the emission of the response, given as often as possible initially, and as the behavior becomes well established, delivered intermittently. (The reader may wish to review some of the material on reinforcement in Chapter 2.)

Combining with other procedures The most obvious procedure that should be used in combination with the reinforcement of incompatible behaviors is extinction. If at all possible, the undesirable behavior should have contingent reinforcement removed. For instance, assume that teacher attention serves as a reinforcer for the isolate child. Along with attending to the youngster as she is playing with other children, teacher attention should be withdrawn at times when the child remains alone. Sometimes this sort of approach is not consonant with an "intuitive" one. It seems that what comes naturally to a parent, teacher, or counselor is not *always* the most effective technique. In this illustration, for instance, the natural tendency might be for the teacher to cajole, urge, or otherwise try to encourage the child to play with the group. Such attention may, despite all good intentions, actually serve to strengthen isolate behavior. Again, this underscores the importance of an empirical approach: *measured* observations should tell what effects a given procedure is having.

It is also possible to use a punishment procedure in conjunction with the reinforcement of incompatible behaviors. Punishment should reduce the undesirable behavior quickly, but punishment has many disadvantages. Its combined use with other procedures should, therefore, be limited as much as possible.

If a selected incompatible behavior is not present in the student's repertoire, differential reinforcement, shaping, or chaining can be used to assist the development of that behavior, as was done in the example of the child with the ritualistic hand movements. Or, if the behavior is under stimulus control, the practitioner might use stimulus change, imitative prompts, verbal directions, and other S^D's to occasion the response so that it is available for strengthening. If, for instance, a hyperactive child responded correctly to the direction "Sit down," it would make sense to give him that instruction so that it would be possible to begin the program of reinforcing increasingly longer periods of in-seat behavior. As always, the teacher would have to be very sensitive to the effect of such instructions. Do they simply occasion sitting behavior or do they reinforce out-of-seat behavior by providing contingent attention? In order to find out, the teacher could try the instructions for a few days and see what effect they had upon frequency or duration of out-of-seat behavior. If the attention were reinforcing, there would be an increase in the behavior. It would, in that case, be preferable to wait for in-seat behavior to be emitted by itself rather than to give the instruction. Then the program of reinforcing in-seat behavior could be started.

Exercise 12.8

Select one of your own undesirable behaviors, such as oversleeping, nail biting, overeating, smoking, and so on. Select a behavior that would be incompatible with that behavior. Find a reinforcer that you are certain will be effective with you. Plan a program in which that reinforcer is delivered contingent upon the emission of a desirable incompatible behavior. If "self-control" is a problem for you, give some one else contingency control over your behavior. After obtaining a stable baseline on your performance, start reinforcing the incompatible behavior according to your planned program. Plot both the frequency of the undesirable behavior and the frequency of the incompatible behavior on a graph. Describe the results. For example, the following graph illustrates such a program for an individual who bites her nails while watching television.

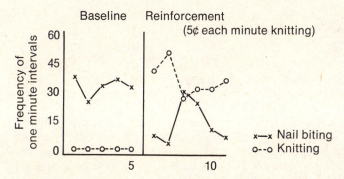

FIGURE 12.1.   One-hour television watching session (fictional data)

Exercise 12.9

Try a program similar to the one for Exercise 12.8 with your pet. For instance, suppose your dog jumps up on people when they come into the house. You might try reinforcing him for sitting on the command "Sit!" Organize your program and data handling the way you did for the previous exercise.

Exercise 12.10

Try a program similar to the one for Exercise 12.8 with a student or a client. Be sure that you select a set of competing behaviors that are easy to measure. Be sure you have a good, solid reinforcer and control of the contingencies. Organize your program and data handling as described in Exercise 12.8.

DISADVANTAGES OF REINFORCING INCOMPATIBLE BEHAVIORS

Slow rate of responding   Just as any reinforcement procedure takes time to achieve its results, reinforcing incompatible behaviors accomplishes its aims fairly slowly. Until the incompatible behavior is being emitted at a fairly high rate, time is still available for the undesirable behavior to be emitted. Until the behavior of interacting with other children occurs frequently, the isolate child still has the opportunity of remaining by herself. Until in-seat behavior is emitted sufficiently often, out-of-seat behavior can remain at high, disturbing levels. By combining this procedure with others, it may be possible to speed up the process to some degree. Using punishment or stimulus change in order to rapidly reduce the undesirable behavior, while the incompatible behavior is being simultaneously reinforced, may serve to reduce the time lag. But, it should be borne in mind that once punishment is introduced, some of the major advantages of reinforcing incompatible behaviors (that it is a positive and comfortable approach) may be lost.

SUMMARY

Satiation is a procedure that harnesses the effects of applying heavy reinforcement in order to achieve a reduction in response rate. It works best when used with responses that require some effort, and should be reserved for behaviors that are not too serious and which can be tolerated for a time. Satiation will show its effects sooner if the individual has not been deprived of the contingent reinforcer for very long and if he has an opportunity to receive the same reinforcers for alternative responses.

Differential reinforcement of other behaviors can be a rapid, effective method for reducing undesirable behaviors, provided that reinforcement is withheld following each emission of the undesirable behavior, and that it is possible, at least initially, to program very frequent reinforcement for other behaviors. The procedure is probably best reserved for use with individuals who emit other undesirable behaviors infrequently.

When a behavior that is incompatible with an undesirable behavior is reinforced, the undesirable behavior should diminish in rate. Reinforcing incompatible behaviors, therefore, brings about behavioral reduction indirectly. A constructive, desirable behavior impedes the emission of an undesirable one. If the desirable incompatible behavior is properly strengthened and maintained, the results of this procedure can be long lasting. Because the approach is positive, teachers and other school personnel can use it with comfort. Appropriate reinforcement techniques, an assurance of incompatibility, and combined use with other procedures, particularly extinction of the undesirable behavior, should accomplish the behavioral reduction with maximal effectiveness. Though slower than some reductive procedures, the reinforcement of incompatible behaviors has many advantages that make it worthy of selection as a regular modification procedure.

REFERENCES

Allen, K. E., Hart, B. M., Buell, J. S., Harris, F. R., & Wolf, M. M. Effects of social reinforcement on isolate behavior of a nursery school child. *Child Development,* 1964, **35**, 511–518.

Allen, K. E., Henke, L. B., Harris, F. R., Baer, D. M., & Reynolds, N. J. Control of hyperactivity by social reinforcement of attending behavior. *Journal of Educational Psychology,* 1967, **58**, 231–237.

Baer, D. M., Peterson, R. F., & Sherman, J. A. The development of imitation by reinforcing behavior of similarity to a model. *Journal of the Experimental Analysis of Behavior,* 1967, **10**, 405–416.

Ferster, C. B., & Perrott, M. C. *Behavior principles.* New York: Appleton-Century-Crofts, 1968.

Holland, J. G., & Skinner, B. F. *The analysis of behavior.* New York: McGraw-Hill, 1961.

Reynolds, G. S. Behavioral contrast. *Journal of the Experimental Analysis of Behavior,* 1961, **4**, 57–71.

PART V

CARRYING OUT
AND EVALUATING
THE PROGRAM

Throughout the previous twelve chapters we have seen many behavior modification procedures described: procedures for increasing the occurrence of behaviors, for teaching new behaviors, for maintaining existing behaviors, and for reducing or eliminating the occurrence of behaviors. Chapters 13 and 14 present material that will assist the reader in selecting the most appropriate procedure(s) for particular school situations. Chapter 13 answers, on a comparative basis, such questions as: How is each procedure used most effectively? How rapid and permanent is the effect of a given procedure? What additional procedural characteristics must be considered before a final selection can be made? Chapter 14 discusses a number of environmental factors, such as personnel characteristics and school and community attitudes, that can influence the results of a behavior modification program. It elaborates on techniques for increasing the likelihood that a given program will be successful and the general limitations and advantages of using behavior modification in the schools.

Chapter 15 is concerned with single-subject research methodology and the need for empirically demonstrating the effectiveness of behavior modification procedures in the school. It discusses the factors that need to be considered when planning and conducting experimental single-student research. It illustrates how such research can be easily conducted in the school setting, and most importantly, it discusses how behavior modification procedures assume the responsibility for holding themselves accountable for behavioral changes by demonstrating the effectiveness of those procedures.

13 SELECTING A PROCEDURE

Objectives

After having completed your study of this chapter, you should be able to:

1. For each behavior modification procedure discussed in the text,
   a. describe its operation through an educational illustration
   b. list and give concrete illustrations of the variables that serve to maximize its efficiency
   c. identify the procedure's temporal characteristics, duration of effect, and other characteristics
   d. describe the relevance of considering each of the factors identified in 1b and 1c to the selection of a procedure
2. Given a specific problem, setting, and several behavioral procedures designed to achieve the same specific goal, select one or more of the procedures and defend your selection over each of the procedures not selected.

In Chapter 1 we outlined some of the factors the behavioral specialist should consider when initiating a program of behavior change in the schools. We emphasized the need to identify the problem and select an objectively measurable goal behavior. Once the goal behavior is identified, it becomes possible to select a procedure designed to achieve it. To *increase a behavior,* for instance, positive or negative reinforcement; removal of interfering conditions; or a stimulus control method, such as generalization training, stimulus change, or the provision of a model can be used. To *teach new behaviors,* response differentiation, shaping, chaining, or fading would be possible procedures. To *maintain behaviors* once they are being emitted at the desired level, one or more of several schedules of intermittent reinforcement would be good choices. Extinction, some form of response contingent withdrawal of reinforcement, punishment, differential reinforcement, stimulus change, or some method that utilizes positive reinforcement can be used to *eliminate or reduce undesirable behaviors.*

Since he can choose from several alternative procedures, each designed to achieve the same goal, the behavioral specialist is free to consider other factors that relate to a particular situation: How is the procedure used most effectively? Is it crucial to achieve the change quickly? What kinds of stimuli are necessary to the effective use of the procedure? How permanent is the effect of a given procedure? What additional factors need to be taken into consideration? This chapter will review each of the behavior change procedures discussed in Parts I through IV in order to assist the behavioral specialist in selecting appropriate procedures for a variety of situations. The reader should be cautioned, however, that although the following comparative descriptions of the behavioral procedures are *usual* characteristics, they should *not* be viewed as universal ones. Furthermore, these characteristics are based on our current embryonic knowledge. Some are likely to be refined and others supplanted through the results of future research endeavors.

INCREASING A BEHAVIOR

The rate at which a behavior is emitted will increase as a function of either positive or negative reinforcement. The rate of behavior can also be increased by removing interfering stimuli or by manipulating stimuli in the environment, as in generalization training or stimulus change. Table 13.1 should prove useful to the practitioner who is concerned with selecting a procedure designed to increase the rate of an emitted behavior.

The behavioral specialist needs to ask himself several questions

TABLE 13.1 Procedures for Increasing a Behavior

PROCEDURE	OPERATION	MAXIMIZING EFFICIENCY	TEMPORAL CHARACTER-ISTICS[a]	DURATION OF EFFECT[a]	OTHER CHARACTERISTICS[a]
Positive Reinforcement	Positive reinforcer presented following response	1. Reinforce immediately 2. Sufficient quantity to maintain behavior without rapid satiation 3. Determine type of reinforcer appropriate for individual 4. Use high frequency behaviors as reinforcers 5. Use a variety of reinforcers and reinforcing situations 6. Try to use reinforcement found in natural environment 7. Provide opportunity for reinforcer sampling 8. Reinforce every response 9. If delay ultimately important, program in a gradually longer delay 10. Combine with modeling and other S^D's	Gradual	Long lasting	1. Positive (possible positive generalization) 2. Constructive 3. May occasion positive self-statements
Negative Reinforcement	Remove aversive stimulus following response	1. Remove aversive stimulus immediately 2. Stimulus sufficiently aversive to individual 3. Apply every time 4. For situation in which no positive alternatives available	Gradual	Long lasting	1. Negative (possible negative generalization) 2. Avoidance, escape, and aggressive behaviors

Procedure				
Remove Interfering Conditions	Remove interfering stimuli	1. Remove stimuli that signal response will be punished 2. Remove stimuli that occasion behaviors incompatible with response	Rapid	Temporary (while stimulus alteration remains in effect)	1. Responding may be restricted to specific stimulus conditions through differential reinforcement
Generalization Training	Present stimuli that were present during original training of response	1. Emphasize common elements 2. Combine with modeling	Gradual	Long lasting	1. Can be made longer lasting if occasioned response reinforced
Stimulus Change	Change discriminative stimulus	1. Determine appropriate discriminative stimuli for each individual 2. Develop discriminative stimuli by pairing presentation with reinforced response	Rapid, when stimuli have control over individual's behavior Gradual, if need to develop S^D's	Temporary (while stimulus alteration remains in effect)	

Providing A Model	Expose individual to model's behavior	1. Reinforce model's behavior
		3. Select model who is
		  a. prestigous
		  b. similar to imitator
		4. Model simple behaviors
		5. Combine with reinforcement and generalization training
		6. Point out similarities and use other S^D's to occasion imitation.
			Gradual, can speed up strengthening process somewhat	Long lasting, when imitative acts reinforced	1. Can be used to facilitate many other procedures

---

[a] Assume procedure used with maximal efficiency.

223

when selecting a procedure designed to increase the occurrence of a behavior:

1. Is it possible, given a specific student problem in a specific setting, to use the procedure effectively? Though immediate continuous reinforcement of correct responding in arithmetic assignments would improve a given individual's performance, will a teacher with thirty other students be able to successfully carry out the procedure? Does she have access, for instance, to programmed texts that would assist her in her task?

2. How quickly does the behavioral increase have to occur? Is the low rate of responding of such a serious nature that the behavior must be increased immediately, or is it possible to take more time and achieve a lasting effect? For example, suppose Helen was scheduled to take a standardized achievement test, and it was very important that she give her optimal performance. In earlier classroom testing situations, among other "anxious" students, she too became "anxious": she fidgeted, had trouble "concentrating," perspired, and emitted other behaviors that interfered with her performance. Yet when she took tests in the teacher's office, away from the other anxious students, Helen's performance was superior. In Helen's case, it might be justifiable to select a removing-the-interfering-conditions procedure and let her take the test in the teacher's office in order to achieve the rapid, though temporary, rate increase. At other times, the slower but more enduring effects of positive reinforcement could be applied to Helen's responses on tests in the normal classroom testing setting.

3. For what duration should the change last? A teacher may be happy to teach in a relaxed atmosphere, allowing students to leave their seats to do research or discuss material with the other students. This teacher may be content if her students remain seated quietly just while guests are present.

Questions of this type need to be answered each time a procedure is to be selected, but they must be answered within the context of the situation. The behavioral specialist needs to be aware not only of the characteristics of each procedure and of the student's behavior but also of his own behavioral characteristics. He needs to know, for instance, how effectively he operates with given stimuli, among specific individuals, and within given situations. And, since he operates within the constraints imposed by the school structure, the community, and society as a whole, his decisions should be guided by practical and ethical considerations. (Issues of this type are considered in Chapter 14.)

Exercise 13.1

The following list contains several behaviors that are being emitted at a low rate. Offer at least two alternative procedures for increasing the rate with which the behavior is being emitted. Discuss the pros and cons for using each procedure. Tell which one you would select. Defend your selection.

a. completing math assignments

b. contributing to group discussions

c. listening quietly

d. saying "Thank you" and You're welcome"

e. complimenting people

f. smiling

TEACHING NEW BEHAVIORS

The kinds of new behaviors that concern school personnel can be taught in any of several ways. They can be refined from more global behaviors, as in response differentiation. This might involve reinforcing only those phrases in an individual's speech that are well modulated or reinforcing the subset of teacher management behaviors that include praise and attention contingent upon desirable student behavior. For another student, the same terminal behaviors might need to be shaped by reinforcing approximations to appropriately modulated speech or approximations to the use of contingent praise with students. Chaining, too, can be used, when phrases of well-modulated works are grouped together into longer sequences or when the teacher learns to chain the sequence: (1) wait for the response, (2) immediately reinforce with praise. Finally, fading can be used to bring behavior that is controlled by supplementary S^D's under the control of fewer and subtler S^D's. For example, the student can be first prompted through gestures and instructions to use the appropriate tone of voice and, as time progresses, those prompts can be gradually eliminated. Or, as in the case reported in one study (Hall et al., 1968), the teacher can be first prompted to use contingent attention. The prompts can then be gradually faded.

Table 13.2 summarizes the various characteristics of each procedure for training a new behavior. In selecting a procedure, each of the characteristics listed in Table 13.2 should be considered. Implied in that list are several important points: (1) the need to provide appropriate consequences; (2) the necessity for "knowing" each individual through close, objective observation; (3) the necessity of deciding upon the direction that the change is to take through a clear specification of the terminal goal; (4) the availability of appropriate stimulus materials. One thesis this text has frequently repeated is that many school-related behaviors change primarily as a function of environmental consequences. Yet, in the discussions of the different procedures, the importance of such stimuli as effectively designed instructional materials and of various forms of prompts and cues, has been emphasized. Given reasonable

TABLE 13.2 Procedures for Teaching a New Behavior

PROCEDURE	OPERATION	MAXIMIZING EFFECTIVENESS	TEMPORAL CHARACTERISTICS[a]	DURATION OF EFFECT[a]	OTHER CHARACTERISTICS[a]
Response Differentiation	Reinforce subset of behavior	1. Clearly define behavioral dimensions, restrictions, and requirements 2. Use effective reinforcement procedures only for relevant subset of behaviors 3. Use effective extinction procedure with irrelevant subsets of behavior	Gradual	Long lasting	Positive, constructive approach
Shaping	Reinforce successive approximations to goal	1. Keep your eye on goal 2. Start with behaviors in individual's repertoire 3. Start with behaviors that most closely resemble goal behavior 4. Select step size that can be easily, but not too easily, achieved 5. Remain at a given step long enough to incorporate within individual's repertoire, no longer 6. Watch for behavioral disintegration; if it appears to be imminent, drop back a step or two	Gradual	Long lasting	Positive, constructive approach, requires careful planning.

	7. Combine with use of imitative and other prompts 8. Use effective reinforcement procedures throughout 9. Strengthen newly acquired behavior			Positive, constructive approach
Chaining	Reinforce as a unit combination of more than one response or link	1. Select links in individual's repertoire 2. Start with final link 3. Occasion response combinations with imitative and other prompts 4. When response components absent from repertoire, first shape component	Gradual; if links already in repertoire, may be faster than shaping Long lasting	
Fading	Gradually remove S_D's	1. Identify prompts that reliably occasion desired response 2. Remove prompts gradually and progressively 3. Prompt minimally, just enough to reliably occasion response	Prompted response emitted rapidly; can speed up effects of other acquisition procedures Long lasting	Minimizes errors; can be used to facilitate both shaping and chaining; helps to overcome overdependence on artificial prompts

a Assume procedure used with maximal effectiveness.

227

tools and response requirements and effectively delivered consequences, the individual will learn. But the use of carefully selected instructional aids can speed up the process and serve to reduce errors.

Exercise 13.2

Offer at least two alternative procedures for teaching each of the terminal goals listed. Tell what factors you would consider in selecting each procedure and discuss the pros and cons of using each.

a. typing the word "mother"
b. drawing an octagon
c. operating a slide projector
d. reciting the *Preamble* to the Constitution
e. constructing a paragraph
f. serving with a volleyball

MAINTAINING BEHAVIORS

Once a new behavior is acquired and strengthened, the concern becomes one of maintaining that behavior. This can be achieved only if the environment produces the appropriate consequences for that behavior, and one of the best procedures to use for accomplishing this goal is to use intermittent reinforcement. To assist the behavioral specialist in selecting from among the various procedures, the characteristics of intermittent reinforcement are reviewed in Table 13.3: effectiveness, efficient use, resistance of the reinforced behavior to extinction, and other attributes. Table 13.3 then presents some of the simple, specific intermittent schedules with reference to the same characteristics.

There are several points that the behavioral specialist should consider in selecting a maintenance schedule: (a) the rate of responding he hopes to maintain, (b) the necessity for regularity or consistency of responding, (c) the opportunity for the individual to engage in competing responses, and other practical issues. The goal for the student who learned to modulate his speech properly may have carried some maintenance specifications. For instance, the student was to continue to use appropriately modulated speech at his current rate all the time or half the time or three times a day or during discussion periods only. (In the latter instances it would not matter if he engaged in competing behavior part of the time.) When the maintenance goals are clearly specified, the selection of a maintenance schedule is made easier because the desired rate and consistency of responding are specified or implied in the goal. In the case of the classroom teacher who had learned to use positive attention contingent upon desirable behavior, it would make sense for the teacher and behavioral specialist to select a maintenance goal that would include

TABLE 13.3 Procedures for Maintaining Behaviors

PROCEDURE	OPERATION	MAXIMIZING EFFICIENCY	RESPONSE CHARACTERISTICS		OTHER CHARACTERISTICS
			REINFORCEMENT IN EFFECT	REINFORCEMENT REMOVED	
Intermittent Reinforcement (in general)	Reinforce some, but not all, emissions of a specific behavior	1. Switch gradually and progressively from continuous to intermittent reinforcement 2. Supplement changeover with S^D's 3. Supplement changeover with other reinforcers, especially those found in natural environment	Maintains performance; topography may be irregular at first	Performance maintains longer than CRF	Delays satiation; efficient, convenient
SCHEDULES Fixed Ratio (FR)	Reinforce every nth emission of the behavior	1. Start with low ratios, increase gradually and progressively 2. Temporarily reduce ratio requirement if responding begins to disintegrate	High response rates; post reinforcement pause following high ratio requirements; otherwise generally consistent pattern of responding	Responding will cease over time, especially with low ratio histories; bursts of responding followed by pauses	Easy to program
Variable Ratio (VR)	Reinforce the response following an average of n responses	1. Start with low ratios, increase gradually and progressively 2. Temporarily reduce ratio requirements if responding begins to disintegrate	High response rates; consistent responding	Longer responding than FR but will ultimately cease; long bursts of responding followed by pauses	More closely approximates contingencies of natural environment

TABLE 13.3 Procedures for Maintaining Behaviors (cont.)

PROCEDURE	OPERATION	MAXIMIZING EFFICIENCY	RESPONSE CHARACTERISTICS		OTHER CHARACTERISTICS
			REINFORCEMENT IN EFFECT	REINFORCEMENT REMOVED	
Fixed Interval (FI)	Reinforce the response after *t* amount of time	1. Start with short intervals, increase gradually and progressively 2. Temporarily shorten interval requirement if responding begins to disintegrate 3. For higher response rate, provide ratio, limited hold, or DRH history	Lower response rates possible, accelerating towards end of interval; post reinforcement pause in some cases	Scallop pattern: gradually accelerating rates, followed by gradually longer pauses; responding ultimately ceases	Much opportunity for competing responses; easy to program
Variable Interval (VI)	Reinforce response following an average of *t* time	1. Start with short intervals, increase gradually and progressively 2. Temporarily shorten interval requirement if responding begins to disintegrate 3. For higher response rate, provide ratio, limited hold, or DRH history	Moderate response rate; consistent responding	Consistent, moderate responding continues; slowly levels off	More closely approximates contingencies of natural environment

Limited Hold	Reinforce responses which are emitted following t time but no later than x time	1. Only reinforce if response emitted within specified time	Rate higher than interval performance	High for a while	
Differential Reinforcement of High Rates (DRH)	Reinforce only bursts of responses emitted with less than t time between each response	1. Increase rate requirement gradually and progressively 2. Lower rate requirement temporarily if rate begins to disintegrate	Very high response rate	High for a while	
Differential Reinforcement of Low Rates (DRL)	Reinforce only responses emitted after t time	1. Reduce t requirement gradually and progressively	Very slow response rate	Slow for a while	Much opportunity for competing responses

a high degree of consistency. For example, when desirable classroom behavior occurs during math class the teacher is to continue throughout the first half of the school year to deliver contingent attention at least four (4) times each math period. To maintain her delivering attention to her students contingent upon their engaging in desirable behaviors, the behavioral specialist could select a variable interval schedule. He could plan daily visits to the teacher's classroom at varying times, when he would comment favorably upon her continued use of the reinforcement procedure. Such a program would tend to assist the teacher to maintain her newly acquired responses, at least until such time as the improved student performances themselves began to take over their naturally reinforcing function.

One more important consideration in the selection of the maintenance schedule is an assessment of the natural environment. Since, sooner or later, artificial reinforcement procedures are usually phased out, it is a good idea to select a schedule toward the end of the program that will begin to approximate the natural one. For instance, teacher A used continuous reinforcement with John. Next term when John was in teacher B's class, the improvements he had made disappeared. Why? The schedule teacher B would most likely have used would have been a variable interval schedule. Perhaps teacher A should have programmed VI reinforcement into the final phase of her program.

Exercise 13.3
a. Select a reinforcement schedule designed to accomplish each of the following:

1. A teacher is to immediately turn away from a student who waves his hand in her face.

2. A student is to continue handing in his history homework each day.

3. A student is to maintain his rate of typing forty words a minute.

4. A student is to continue to form her letters slowly and carefully.

5. Mrs. Burns, the principal, is to visit each teacher's classroom at least once a month.

6. A student is to continue to smile at the others in his class.

b. Tell why you selected each particular reinforcement schedule.

REDUCING BEHAVIORS

The selection of a reductive procedure can be made most intelligently when the behavioral specialist refers back to the original behavioral goal. Careful preplanning should imply which procedural characteristics best suit the particular objective. In doing this, several issues need to be considered: (1) How is the procedure applied most effectively? (2) How quickly is the behavioral reduction achieved? (3) How long will it maintain? (4) Will the behaviors be reduced under most environmental conditions, or will the reduction be limited to only some? (5) Is the procedure positive and constructive, or does it require the use of aversive stimuli and aim toward only removing, but not, substituting behaviors? (6) Are there some side effects that may be expected to accompany the use of the procedure?

Table 13.4 summarizes many of the characteristics of the procedures for reducing behavior. The information found in Table 13.4 may help the behavioral specialist to select his procedure by allowing him to look at the total picture. He can consider not only the rapid achievement of the behavioral reduction but other factors also. One point of caution needs to be inserted here, since so little research has been conducted on the use of these various procedures within the classroom setting: *Just operating on the strength of the characteristics as they are listed here is not enough.* It is also necessary to use systematic, objective observation in order to determine that the procedure is indeed operating in the anticipated direction and to constantly watch for the eruption of undesirable side effects.

Exercise 13.4

Below are listed a few problem situations. Analyze the situation and then specify a goal and select a procedure for dealing with each one. Describe the results you should anticipate. Defend your selection.

a. About three mornings a week Alex comes to his class late. The teacher reports that nothing she has tried will get him to come to class on time. She has scolded him, sent him to the office or out in the hall, and tried ignoring him.

b. Jerry, an otherwise bright student, just cannot seem to get the hang of multiplication. Almost every time the teacher calls on him, he gives an incorrect answer. The teacher usually handles his response by saying something like "Jerry, you're a smart boy; you should know better."

c. Clarence is the school bully. As soon as there are no adults around, he starts to tease and hit the other children. Clarence has been responsible for giving more than one black eye in the school. The situation has been handled in one of several ways: Usually a day or two after the particular fighting episode, Clarence's parents have been asked to come in for conferences; or Clarence has been kept in after school and has, occasionally, been paddled.

d. Mrs. Grouch, the head of the English Department, is making the lives of the teachers in her department miserable. She comes into their rooms unannounced and criticizes them in front of their students.

TABLE 13.4 Procedures for Reducing a Behavior

PROCEDURE	OPERATION	MAXIMIZING EFFECTIVENESS	TEMPORAL CHARACTER- ISTICS[a]	DURATION OF EFFECT[a]	OTHER CHARACTERISTICS
Extinction	Withhold reinforcement following response	1. Identify all reinforcers for particular response and withhold completely 2. Maintain procedure long enough to begin to show effect 3. Provide reinforcement for other behaviors	Gradual	Long lasting	Aversive stimuli not required; temporary increase in response rate; temporary spontaneous recovery; brief period of aggression; sometimes difficult to identify and/or withhold all reinforcers
Timeout	Withdraw reinforcement for t time, contingent upon response	1. Remove all reinforcers for all responses 2. Avoid timeout from aversive situations 3. Apply every time 4. Keep timeout period relatively short 5. Combine with reinforcement of alternative behaviors	Rapid	Long lasting	Negative, stimuli paired with timeout become aversive; non-constructive; may occasion aggression and escape
Response Cost	Withdraw n amount of reinforcers contingent upon response	1. Apply every time 2. Allow for build-up of reinforcement reserve 3. Penalize sparingly 4. Communicate rules 5. Combine with reinforcement of alternative behaviors	Rapid	Long lasting	Convenient; effect depends upon reinforcement history of individual; may occasion aggression and escape

Procedure	Description	Rules	Speed	Duration	Comments
Punishment	Present an aversive stimulus contingent upon a response	1. Prevent escape 2. Apply consistently 3. Apply immediately 4. Maximize intensity of aversive stimulus 5. Combine with extinction 6. Combine with reinforcement of alternative behaviors 7. Communicate the rules of the punishment contingency	Can stop behavior immediately	Long lasting; may be permanent	Facilitates discrimination; instructive to classmates; may occasion negative generalization, avoidance, escape, and aggressive behavior; may occasion the punished response or the act of punishment by observers under other conditions; may occasion negative statements about self
Differential Reinforcement for Stimulus Control	Reinforce response only in the presence of S^D	1. Use effective reinforcement and extinction procedures 2. Minimize frequency of incorrect responses 3. Add additional S^D's 4. Use reductive procedures for responses in presence of $S^\triangle$	Gradual	Long lasting	Enables use of stimulus change
Stimulus Change	Alter discriminative stimuli	1. Use systematic observation to determine effective discriminative stimuli for individual 2. Avoid using as reinforcer for undesirable behavior 3. Combine with reinforcement	Rapid	Temporary	Constructive, preventive; effectiveness depends on learning history of individual
Satiation	Reinforce response	1. Provide large quantities of immediate reinforcement 2. Select responses that require much effort and that can be tolerated 3. Keep deprivation conditions low	Gradual	Temporary	Positive

TABLE 13.4 Procedures for Reducing a Behavior (cont.)

PROCEDURE	OPERATION	MAXIMIZING EFFECTIVENESS	TEMPORAL CHARACTER-ISTICS[a]	DURATION OF EFFECT[a]	OTHER CHARACTERISTICS
Differential Reinforcement of Other Behaviors (DRO)	Reinforce on regular schedule *except* following response	1. Schedule reinforcement carefully 2. Increase ratio or interval requirements gradually and progressively 3. Insure response not reinforced at other times	Rapid	Long lasting	Positive; "other" behavior could be worse; behavioral contrast possible if response allowed to occur at other times
Reinforcing Incompatible Behaviors	Reinforce behavior incompatible with undesirable response	1. Insure behavioral incompatibility 2. Select incompatible behavior from repertoire 3. Select behavior apt to be maintained by environment 4. Use effective reinforcement procedures 5. Combine with other procedures	Gradual	Long lasting	Positive, constructive, comfortable

[a] Assume procedures used with maximal effectiveness.

She ruins her colleagues' lunch by spending the whole hour complaining about the stupid children in the school and how teachers no longer are capable of maintaining discipline. During faculty meetings she objects vociferously to any attempts at innovation. Several of the English faculty are considering leaving their jobs because no one has been able to change Mrs. Grouch's manner.

SUMMARY

This chapter was written to assist the behavioral specialist in selecting the most effective behavior modification procedure(s) for a given situation. In order to make such a selection, several factors need to be considered: (1) There must be a clear specification of the behavioral goal. (2) Each procedure's operation; the variables that serve to maximize its efficiency; the temporal characteristics; the duration of the effect; and other characteristics also need to be identified. A careful consideration of such factors prior to selecting a procedure will lead to improved efficiency in behavior modification programs.

REFERENCES

Hall, R. V., Lund, D., & Jackson, D. Effects of teacher attention on study behavior. *Journal of Applied Behavior Analysis,* 1968, **1,** 1–12.

14 OTHER ISSUES TO CONSIDER
IN DESIGNING THE PROGRAM

Objectives

After having completed your study of this chapter, you should be able to:

1. List four school personnel characteristics and describe how each can influence the success of a behavior modification program.
2. Discuss, with an illustration, how to cope with personal characteristics that might interfere with the success of a behavior modification program.
3. List five practical considerations and describe how each can hinder the success of a behavior modification program.
4. Discuss how *each* practical consideration can contribute to the success of your program; give a concrete illustration for each factor.
5. List the four major limitations of behavior modification in the schools and describe the conditions under which each is a limitation; describe the conditions under which the "limitation" may be an asset.
6. List the three major advantages of behavior modification in the school and discuss why each point listed is an advantage.
7. After having studied Chapters 13 and 14, illustrate with an educational example and identify in learning terminology ten different behavioral procedures that can enhance the effectiveness of the consulting relationship.

Chapter 13 was designed to assist the reader in selecting a behavioral procedure by summarizing each procedure that has been included in the text. In the following material some additional factors are considered which school personnel ought to take into account prior to designing a specific behavior modification program. Some of these considerations relate to the environment in which the program is to take place, such as the characteristics of the personnel involved, the physical properties of the building, and the availability of materials and supplies. Other issues relate to techniques for increasing the likelihood that a given program will be successful, while still others relate to the general limitations and advantages of using behavior modification procedures in the schools.

PERSONNEL CHARACTERISTICS

Just as each school is composed of many individual students, each member of the school's staff has his own individual characteristics. These characteristics should be assessed prior to selecting any set of procedures. The behavioral repertoires of the staff members involved (especially as they relate to the responses necessary to carrying out a given program), the reinforcers and discriminative stimuli that control their behavior, and the motivation of those persons to achieve the behavioral change are all important aspects of such an assessment.

RESPONSES IN REPERTOIRE

For any given behavior modification program to be effective, it is necessary that the appropriate contingencies be applied. Because of their own learning histories, some personnel may be able to apply one set of contingencies more easily than others. For instance, some teachers, counselors, and supervisors will have had years of experience in using positive reinforcement effectively, while others will have learned to apply aversive techniques with sufficient precision to be able to achieve many educational goals. It is usually easier for those with experience in positive reinforcement to use such procedures as shaping, differential reinforcement, DRO, and the reinforcement of incompatible behaviors. Conversely, it is usually easier for those with experience in using aversive techniques to use punishment, response cost, timeout, and negative reinforcement. This does not necessarily mean that it is useless for the individual adept in the application of aversive stimuli to attempt to apply the positive procedures. It does suggest, however, that it may delay the results a little longer.

When the assessment of the response characteristics of the individuals who are going to be involved in a particular program suggests a mutually determined need for modification of those responses, the same procedures for behavior modification that we have been discussing are applicable. The laws of behavior apply to all of us. For example, observation has disclosed that the participating school personnel have the requisite responses in their repertoires for the proposed procedure, but those responses are emitted at an insufficiently high rate. There are many ways to increase that rate; consultants can, for instance, come into the classroom to give instructions and differentially reinforce the teacher's behavior. A similar approach can be taken in counseling and supervisory sessions. Workshops, seminars, and meetings can be used to provide instruction. Even more preferable, since actual individual participation is involved, are opportunities for trying out the procedures on a small scale. One possibility would be for each of the members interested in improving his skills to select and carry out a very simple behavior modification procedure himself, under the supervision of a behavioral specialist. Many of the exercises included in this text could prove helpful in that respect. Other possibilities are role playing, microteaching, and microcounseling. For instance, one section of a workshop could be devoted to having the participants enact the roles of the different individuals involved in a given program: the student, the teacher, the counselor, the principal, and so on. This would allow those individuals to simulate or practice the appropriate responses in the artificial situation prior to attempting them in the real environment. Microteaching (Allen & Ryan, 1969) and microcounseling (Ivey, Normington, Miller, Morrill & Haase, 1968), the isolation, study, and application of specific elements that occur in the teaching or counseling interaction, allow various techniques to be tried, first, in isolation and, then, in combination before a large program is launched. Feedback by means of a video tape recordings can enhance the effectiveness of training by means of microteaching or microcounseling.

School personnel who have sufficient motivation to do so, should be able to train themselves. For instance, suppose a principal decides to assess his own behavior. He begins by counting the statements that he makes to teachers and categorizes them as positive, negative, or neutral. Finding, perhaps, that the negative far outweighed the positive, he could program a change in his own behavior. He could, for example, make his time on the golf course contingent upon a specific increase in the proportion of negative to positive statements. Since many of the readers of this text will have no other persons available to help them to alter their own response repertoires when a given program necessitates such a change it will be essential for them to attempt to apply appropriate behavior modification procedures to their own behavior and, hopefully, reap the contingencies of success.

Exercise 14.3

Interview or spend a day with someone who is functioning as a supervisor or consultant in a school. Ask him to describe the methods he uses to help his staff improve their performance. Evaluate his procedures in terms of his use of effective reinforcement contingencies.

DISCRIMINATIVE STIMULI

School personnel have a tremendous advantage: their training has brought their behavior under the control of many discriminative stimuli. Educators can usually follow written and oral directions. They are able to imitate modeled behavior fairly precisely. They are often responsive to signs, signals, and gestures. For this reason, the whole process of training behavioral specialists can probably be hastened with the use of such aids. (If this were not the case, the authors could hardly justify this text; or any authors, any text.) When the goal is one of teaching personnel to use given behavioral procedures, it makes sense to provide them with the kinds of discriminative stimuli which will facilitate their learning: textbooks, films, video-taped and live demonstrations, lectures, slides, and other instructional materials. Cues, such as those used by motion picture directors; cards; gestures; and other signals can also be used during training sessions and during the operation of the actual program. It is a good idea to determine, through objective observation, which S^D's seem to have the greatest control over a given individual's behavior. These S^D's can then be used to occasion the desired responses so that they can be frequently reinforced.

Exercise 14.4

Plan a workshop in the use of behavior modification procedures in the schools for the personnel in a particular school district. Outline the steps you would follow and describe the instructional materials you would use.

MOTIVATION

In Chapter 1 we discussed the importance of carefully considering the individuals involved in a program of behavior change. We stressed the importance of obtaining the mutual consent of those individuals prior to designing the behavior modification program. Assuming that the willingness of the participants to carry out the program has been determined, all concerned should have some motivation to achieve the change. However, some school personnel will be more motivated to carry out a given program than others. (The amount of motivation is probably determined by a combination of previous learning experiences and current environmental S^D's and contingencies). Individuals who seek out the

Exercise 14.1

Pick a simple behavior of your own, one that you would like to change, such as the amount of time you study, the number of times you compliment a given individual, or the number of minutes you spend exercising. Assess your own behavior to find a preferred activity that you spend a great deal of time doing, such as golfing, fishing, gardening, cooking, and so on. (see the discussion of the Premack principle, in Chapter 2). Using either a stopwatch to count time or a counter, such as a golf counter, to count frequencies, first assess your operant level of the desired behavior for a specified time, over several days. Then specify a number of minutes at your preferred activity to be available as a reinforcing contingency for performing the desired behavior. Then begin strengthening the desired behavior. Continue recording your data for several weeks. To test for the effectiveness of the contingencies, drop them out for a few days. If a substantial drop in your performance becomes evident, reinstate the contingencies. Once you appear to have reached a stable goal, maintain the altered behavior by switching to intermittent reinforcement. Plot your data on a graph.

AVAILABLE REINFORCERS

School personnel, like everyone else, operate under reinforcement contingencies. Some of these reinforcers are pretty obvious, such as salaries, raises, promotions, and evaluations by supervisors. Other reinforcers are perhaps not quite as explicit: the satisfaction of doing an effective job; approval from students, peers, supervisors, parents, and the community; special assignments; being consulted as an expert; and many others. These subtler reinforcers may operate without an individual being aware of their effect. Their effect may even be denied. Also, because professionals in the schools have often experienced long delays in reinforcements during their years of professional training, they are probably able to tolerate similarly long delays in the school settings. For instance, a principal may work hard for eight or ten years before obtaining the reinforcer of a promotion to a higher supervisory position. The coach may exert himself for months or years before his team wins the state championship. The "dedicated teacher" in a poverty area may spend lots of her time individualizing instruction and encouraging her students before one of them rewards her by winning a scholarship to a university. In performing in the face of such delayed contingencies, the potency of those contingencies may be obscured. The behavioral specialist may encounter difficulties in trying to isolate those reinforcers that are effective for a given individual.

Even though some of the reinforcers that are the most relevant for an individual may fail to be identified, there are many that are available in just about any school setting. Salaries, for instance, which are used everywhere, are usually delivered contingent upon the individual's attending his job regularly. Merit raises are one attempt to refine the salary contingency by specifying some additional requirement regarding the quality of the time the individual spends at his job. Promotions, too, are often supposed to depend upon the quality of the individual's performance. Certainly, the evaluations made of teaching performance can serve to reinforce the individual being observed. For instance, a supervisor makes a point of emphasizing as many of the positive aspects of a teacher's classroom performance as possible. Because he is applying effective reinforcement contingencies, the teacher should consequently increase or maintain those particular aspects of her behavior.

Yet, even though educators can tolerate long reinforcement delays, when it comes to attempting to change the behavior of school personnel, one's own included, immediate reinforcement should produce the best results. Because raises and promotions, special assignments, student achievement, and peer and community approval are all often delayed, it may be necessary to identify some other reinforcers. These should be reinforcers that can be delivered immediately and that have been identified as being effective for that particular individual. Among those most likely to fit into this category are immediate verbal approval, smiles, nods, tally marks, results entered on a table or plotted on a graph, and similar forms of feedback. Some illustrations follow.

A teacher had spent several years teaching mathematics on the secondary level. As a part of an experimental program, he was assigned to teach a small group of elementary-school-aged children. When he started that program, he found that he could not control the children. Unlike his former high school students, these new pupils did not simply follow directions and get to work. Not wanting to resort to aversive techniques, he requested the assistance of the school psychologist. Mutually, they decided to use a positive reinforcement approach with the whole group. Desirable and undesirable behaviors were operationalized, and the teacher was instructed to praise and generally attend to the children who were engaging in desirable behaviors. This was difficult for the teacher at first, so he was given frequent immediate feedback. The consultant sat in the room and nodded and smiled when the teacher reinforced his students. At the end of the session, the number of intervals in which reinforcement had been delivered were tallied and graphed. The teacher then had to form a visual feedback regarding his own behavior. Simultaneous with this, the students' behavior was graphed. The teacher was further reinforced by seeing the gradually increasing

percentage of intervals in which the students engaged in deisrable behaviors.

In another case, a teacher was having difficulty with one particular student. Though all of the other students in the class were working hard and behaving appropriately, that one student clowned around and was generally disruptive. By scoring the student's and the teacher's behavior, it was discovered that, for some reason, when this particular student worked quietly he was generally ignored by the teacher while all the others in the class were receiving attention for good behavior. The teacher agreed to try to increase his attention to the student, contingent upon the student's good behavior. Yet even with the teacher's expressing his willingness to cooperate in this endeavor, his rate of contingent praise failed to increase substantially. It was then decided that a tally of the number of times the teacher used contingent praise with the student would be kept. Numbers large enough to be seen from the back of the room were drawn in sequential order on pages of a stenographer's pad. The pad was placed in an upright position and each time the teacher praised the student, a page was flipped over. The teacher was then able to glance over at the pad to see how he was doing. This procedure did seem to work. The number of contingent praise statements increased substantially and the student's behavior showed tremendous improvement.

In both cases described above, it was possible to gradually discontinue the recording and most of the other forms of feedback. The eventual improvement in the students' behavior seemed to provide the necessary reinforcement to maintain the teachers' behavior. Follow-up observations several months later showed that the students' improved behavior had maintained.

To summarize, it is important to program contingencies for school personnel as well as for students. When a given behavior appears to be fairly resistant to change, immediate, continuous use of appropriate reinforcers will achieve the best results.

Exercise 14.2

Whether you are a student, a teacher, an administrator, or some other type of professional, there are reinforcers that operate on your behavior.
a. See how many reinforcers you can list which you believe may effect your behavior at home.
b. Try to find about five reinforcers that effect your behavior at school.
c. What evidence can you offer to support your identification of those stimuli as reinforcers?

assistance of consultants and supervisors and who follow their suggestions, those who volunteer to participate in workshops and other training situations, those who search for new management and instructional methods in books and journals, and those who demonstrate a deep fondness for students and who express a desire to help those students to realize their fullest potential, are probably the kinds of people who would make the greatest effort to help a program succeed. Obviously, it is important to consider the individuals involved when selecting a particular procedure. All things being equal, it is preferable to design a program that will involve the participation of motivated individuals.

Exercise 14.5

Suppose you were either a school psychologist or a guidance counselor who had just been hired to work in a school beset with many classroom management problems. You are expected to spend about one third of your time in consulting activities. Tell how you would decide how and with whom you would begin your consulting functions.

PRACTICAL CONSIDERATIONS

A familiarity with the characteristics of the personnel to be involved in a given program is one major practical factor to consider while designing a behavior modification program. There are, naturally, other issues to consider: (1) Are the goals of the project reasonable? (2) Does the school have adequate control of contingencies? (3) Are all the school personnel as well as the students and parents willing to cooperate? (4) Does the physical environment allow for the application of a particular procedure? (5) Are the necessary materials available? (6) What is the attitude of the school and outside community toward the use of a given procedure? (7) What are some of their concerns? An assessment of these issues should provide some important additional guidelines to designing a program.

REASONABLE GOALS

Although we discussed goal selection in Chapter 1, it deserves repetition. Goal selection is extremely important. No matter how much thought is given to all other aspects of procedural selection, an unreasonable goal will doom the procedure to failure. A fish cannot be taught to play tennis on a clay court and a human being cannot be taught to fly like a bird without the addition of elaborate accessory equipment. Only goals that stand a chance of succeeding should be selected. This requires an assessment of the individual's present behavioral repertoire so that a goal behavior just a few steps beyond, not something out in left field, is attempted at first. A reasonable initial goal for an unusually quiet child might be to double the number of times she participates in class discussion rather than work toward a goal of having her become discussion leader. A reasonable first goal for a student who is failing in math is for him to raise his letter grade from an F to a D, not to aim towards making him an A student right away. A reasonable initial goal for a teacher who never praises her students is for her to praise them at least three times an hour, not for her to use praise once a minute. A practical goal for a moderately retarded child is to teach him to read signs, fill out forms, or to attend his job assignment regularly, not to work toward his acceptance in college. This is not to say that such idealistic goals are out of the question. The point is that the reasonable goal focuses on that which can be accomplished in the near future. Then once that goal is achieved, it is possible to specify a new goal and select the procedure appropriate to its attainment.

Exercise 14.6

Refer back to the problem situations in Exercise 13.4 (p. 233). Offer a goal for each one that you consider reasonable. Tell why you consider the goal to be reasonable.

CONTINGENCY CONTROL

It should be evident to the reader by now that the individual administering the behavior modification program must have control of contingencies. To use reinforcement, shaping, differential reinforcement, satiation, and many other procedures, there must be a strong reinforcer available. To use negative reinforcement and punishment, strong aversive stimuli must be available. Schools do have control of such reinforcing contingencies as grades, promotions, assignments, and many of the other reinforcers previously discussed. But sometimes they do not have control of the contingencies that have the greatest control over a given individual's behavior. Peer approval,[1] a particularly potent source of reinforcement for teen-agers, is frequently difficult for school personnel to control. The influence of members of the family and the community is also frequently outside of the school's realm. In order to utilize, neutralize, or counteract those contingencies that are exerting a strong undesirable effect upon an individual's behavior, school personnel may need to discover a contingency that will exert a greater influence. This

---

[1] The reader may wish to refer back to Chapter 8 for means of controlling peer approval (see p. 145).

requires ingenuity. But, in the event that such a contingency is discovered, there still exists an ethical dilemma: Does the professional have the right to counteract the influence of peers, family members, or the community?

COOPERATION OF INDIVIDUALS INVOLVED IN PROGRAM

The notion of contingency contracting (see Chapter 1, p. 7) provides one answer to the ethical dilemma we have just discussed. If a mutual agreement is reached by all the individuals concerned regarding goals and procedures, it should also be possible to mutually agree on a set of contingencies. Then, even if those contingencies are ordinarily outside of the school's realm, it may be possible to use them.

A simple example may help to clarify this point. A twelve-year-old boy almost never completed his social studies class assignment. Neither grades, praise, threats, nor scolding had any effect upon his performance. His parents were asked to attend a conference regarding his performance. They proved to be equally concerned about it. During the course of the discussions, they mentioned that the boy wanted a new bicycle very badly. Everyone agreed on the use of the bicycle as a long-range reinforcer. Ordinarily, bicycles and other expensive, tangible items are not available to school personnel to use as contingencies. But in this case, the parents were willing to purchase the bike. Student, teacher, and parents mutually agreed that items completed on social studies assignments would be exchangeable for parts to the bike: x number of items completed would "buy" the handlebars, and so on. In that situation, a way was found to obtain control of a strong external contingency.

Exercise 14.7

Many of the social problems involving America's youth today, such as drug abuse, dropping out of school, and mob destruction of property, are probably at least partially maintained by contingencies that are beyond the aegis of the schools. Speculate on what those contingencies might be. Can you think of any ways in which the school and the outside community might be able to cooperate in order to identify and apply different but equally potent reinforcers toward the solution of those problems?

PHYSICAL ENVIRONMENT AND AVAILABLE MATERIALS

Certain procedures require special physical facilities; others require the use of specific materials. In order to use timeout effectively, it is necessary to have an adequate timeout area. In order to use a token system backed up by tangible or edible reinforcers, it is necessary to have such items available. Shaping academic performance by means of small progressive steps may require the availability of particular programmed instruction materials. In selecting a procedure, it is wise to consider such requirements. If they are essential but are not available in the particular setting, either they must be obtained or alternative procedures need to be selected.

SCHOOL AND OUTSIDE COMMUNITY ATTITUDES

Different school systems and communities often reflect varying attitudes toward classroom management procedures. Some school systems use punishment procedures, such as paddling, freely. Others would be horrified at the use of such a method. In still other systems, the use of such forms of physical punishment is illegal. In some communities reinforcement procedures such as token systems are regarded as immoral since they "breed a materialistic attitude" in the students. Others are all for it because token systems "are a microcosm of the national economic system." Still others are delighted with token systems because they work better than anything else with a specific population of children; they know that once the altered behavior of the students reaches and maintains at a particular level, it is possible to begin to shift over to other reinforcing contingencies, such as grades, praise, and other forms of attention. Some communities believe that the schools coddle the students. In others, the schools are seen as being overly punitive.

When the time comes to plan a behavior modification program it is always advisable to consider such attitudes. Selecting a procedure that the school or outside community is violently opposed to can cause more trouble than it is worth. How, then, can such attitudes be assessed? Certainly meeting for the purpose of arriving at a behavioral contract is one way to get an idea of the attitudes of the individuals whose involvement is most significant. But there are other sources of such information as well. The application of procedures that involve major deviations from traditional methods should be preceded by discussions with members of the community. Teachers and other school personnel can discuss their ideas informally with their colleagues and the parents. The plan can be proposed to the whole faculty or to the Parent Teachers Association, and their reactions can be assessed. Since school board members are representatives of the community, their attitudes can also be assessed.

If it is found that there is considerable opposition to a given procedure, there are a few alternatives available: the plan can be abandoned; it can be pursued over the objections of the community; an attempt can be made to change community attitudes; a mutually agreeable alternative procedure could be substituted. For instance, parents may be very upset at the idea of their children being given candy reinforcers. Yet they may have no objection to their children working toward incentives such as gold stars or special activities. A substitution of the latter contingencies would make sense. Proceeding over intense objections such as those we mentioned previously, is inviting failure. The community and the school each polarize at opposite ends, and the children are caught in the middle. When there are no alternative procedures that would accomplish the same purpose (it is difficult to believe that no alternatives would exist, given all the potential procedures and the possible variations we have described in this text) it would seem best to abandon the given procedure, unless one was able to change the community's attitudes.

Attempting to change community attitudes can prove to be an effective approach. Sometimes a strong objection is the result of not knowing all the facts, and a simple explanation can solve the problem. A teacher proposed a procedure in which she would give James his favorite chocolate candy each time he scored over 90 percent on his spelling test. When the other teachers in the school and the parents of the other children heard about her plan they became very upset. They did not mind James receiving the candy, but they felt it would be unfair to the rest of the children. When the teacher explained that she planned to give candy to the other children during milk break while James was earning his for improved spelling performance, they were satisfied.

Sometimes misunderstandings occur because very technical language is used to explain a proposed procedure. Many school personnel are unfamiliar with the definitions of technical terms, such as many of those included in this text. Words, selected here because they are precise as well as because they are used in scientific writing, often conjure up mechanistic associations. People, then, rebel against the fact that children are being treated like "laboratory specimens" or little "robots." Terms like "conditioning," "reinforcement," "discriminative stimuli," "aversive control," and even the more general term of "behavior modification" are examples of words which occasionally generate a negative emotional response. It is frequently better, with an audience unsophisticated in the use of that kind of language, to substitute more palatable terms: "teaching" or "instruction," for *conditioning* and *shaping;* "prompts," "hints," "cues," or "directions" for S^D's; "privileges," "incentives," or "rewards" for *reinforcers;* "penalties" or "costs" for *aversive stimuli;* and "learning," "developmental programs," or "precision teaching" for *behavior modification.*

However, using more acceptable terms is insufficient. The behavioral specialist must take the responsibility of demonstrating how the procedure is likely to benefit the child and, when applicable, the communities involved. If he is not able to marshal his arguments with honest statements to support his plan, he ought not to propose the program in the first place.

Exercise 14.8

Go to your local school board office and ask to see the policy on classroom management or discipline. Which of the procedures included in this text would conform most closely to the application of those policies?

LIMITATIONS OF BEHAVIOR MODIFICATION IN THE SCHOOLS

Behavior modification has adopted the principles derived from the scientific analysis of behavior and has applied them to problems in the real world. Though behavior modification has much to offer in certain areas, in others its application is not relevant. In addressing oneself to a given school-related problem, a precise formulation of the issue is essential since behavior modification is better suited to some types of issues than to others. It is particularly relevant to questions related to motivation and the organization and presentation of instruction, but it is not relevant to the instructional content. It is helpful with decisions for individuals, but it may not be the best approach for certain types of group decisions. Behavior modification, therefore, does have limitations in its scope. But, besides scope limitations, the approach has some others. The person directing a behavior modification program needs specialized training to perform his task properly, and such training takes a substantial time investment. But the greatest limitation of the *behavioral analysis* approach, is its relative infancy, particularly with regard to its applications in the schools. We will discuss these factors in this section.

INDIVIDUALIZED APPROACH

The philosophy of educating children as individuals, individualizing instruction as well as motivational and management techniques, is a prevalent attitude among today's educators. Behavioral analysis and its applied extension, behavior modification, is ideally suited to individual prediction and control. Once the functional relationships which exist between an individual's behavior and the variables controlling that behavior are discovered, one can predict that the individual will probably behave similarly in the future, given the same conditions, and that behavioral control is likely or possible. There are times, however, when it is more practical to make *group* predictions and decisions. Textbooks are usually bought in large quantities, and purchasers want to know which book will best suit their group. Schools have to be constructed to best meet the needs of groups of students. Testing programs are often designed to evaluate how well a group of students in a given school or district compares to other groups or to national group norms. Instructional specialists are hired in relationship to the requirements of a school district as a whole. For group instruction, it is often helpful to predict which of several methods will have the best results with a particular *population* of students. Behavior modification, because it tends to be individually oriented, is not usually the most practical system for handling many of those issues. It would often make sense to use statistical procedures to arrive at such predictions and decisions.

The fact that behavior modification is generally oriented to the individual, however, does not mean that its procedures cannot be used for such purposes as group motivation and group management. Many studies have demonstrated that contingencies, such as those described in this text, can be used in group situations as well as with individuals. For example, one of the authors was involved in a program in which points were given to nursery school children contingent upon their lying down quietly during rest period (Taylor & Sulzer, 1971). Following a baseline, those individual children who rested quietly for specific periods received points that could be exchanged for extra minutes of recess. The points increased their rest behavior substantially. Following a return to baseline conditions, a point system was put into effect in which the entire group had to rest quietly in order for the group to earn the points. Rest behavior during that condition was equal to, or better than, that under the individual contingency condition.

The previous example demonstrates how a specific contingency, points exchangeable for extra minutes of recess, proved effective for the whole group. In cases in which it can be demonstrated that specific variables control the behavior of each of the individuals in a group, it is possible to use a group approach. These authors have found, for instance, that most of the students with whom they have worked respond well to group reinforcement: group token reinforcement; giving bonus points to each student because the whole class worked hard; group attention, such as visits by other members of the staff; and verbal priase such as, "You are all working so nicely." Such generalized reinforcers appear to be particularly appropriate for group contingency application.

Stimulus control principles can also be applied to groups of individuals. Once it is determined that some individuals perform better with one kind of instructional method, for example, programmed texts, and other individuals perform better with a different type of instructional method, for instance lectures and discussions, the individuals can be organized for effective group instructional methods. Although an assessment of the most effective S^D for each individual would probably take more time and effort than using group sampling techniques, the payoff should be greater.

When each of the individuals is assigned to a group based on his assessed performance, error of the type found in group statistical designs does not play as great a part. This by no means intends to imply that individual analysis of behavior is capable of making perfect predictions. Far from it. There are an infinite number of unidentified and uncontrolled variables that can effect an individual's performance — his physical state, deprivation level, competing stimuli (some of these variables are discussed in Chapter 15). It simply contends that when decisions such as those regarding the selection of instructional materials are based on the individual's own behavior, they should prove more effective than those that are extrapolated from a group norm and applied to that individual.

In deciding whether a group or an individualized approach is the best choice, therefore, several factors need to be considered: does the problem concern an individual or a group, what kind of time is available, and what are the other practical concerns. In cases in which decisions for large numbers of students need to be made without expending considerable time and effort, and where extrapolation to the individual is not essential, an individualized approach would be inefficient.

METHOD, NOT CONTENT

Behavior modification consists of sets of principles and their application as procedures. It provides guidelines for all sorts of instructional techniques. But behavioral specialists are not experts in other subject matter areas. They can serve as advisors for deciding *how* particular information may best be presented in a given situation, but they are not the ones to decide *what* that information should consist of. Experts in the particular subject matter need to provide that type of information. For example, a behavioral specialist can give a biology teacher advice about how the teacher might shape students to follow the steps required to dissect a frog and to identify parts of the frog's anatomy. But the behavioral specialist is neither the person to justify *why* frog dissections are important nor to have information available regarding frog anatomy or dissection techniques. A subject matter specialist (in this case, the biology teacher) would have to provide that information. Then the behavioral specialist could help the teacher to program the steps required to dissect a frog. Each step could be broken down into small components in which the student would be given an instruction or asked a question and then be provided with feedback about the appropriateness or accuracy of his response. The biology teacher would provide the content; the behavioral specialist, the method.

Such cooperation between the subject matter expert and the behavioral specialist suggests some very exciting possibilities. As the content specialist learns from the behavioral specialist how to organize and present his material more effectively, he will not be required to spend as much time in remediation. He will then be able to use this time to further develop his expertise and to continue to develop new and better instructional materials.

TRAINED PERSONNEL REQUIRED

In order to function as a behavioral specialist in the schools, the individual must be familiar with the basic principles of behavior. He must also be able to conduct effective programs. This requires that he have both conceptual and applied training which, hopefully, was conducted under supervision. But fortunately, not all of those persons who participate in the application of such programs have to be experts in the field. For example, one study (Andrews, 1969) reports that teachers are able to successfully implement many aspects of behavior modification after attending four to five in-service training sessions. Also, many of the functions necessary to an adequately designed behavior modification program can be delegated to others. Often persons with less sophisticated training can be taught to perform their specific task quite easily. Teachers, other members of the school staff, parents, and even students themselves have been trained to become reliable data recorders. Other individuals can be similarly trained to conduct other functions too. For instance parents, teacher's aids, or older students can be trained to administer specific instructional programs. In the Juniper Gardens Children's Project in Kansas City, parents from that economically deprived section of the city were trained to administer short instructional programs to preschoolers.[1] Other people can also be taught to deliver social reinforcement, to help administer token systems, to graph data, to organize materials, and to perform many other duties. As long as their tasks are specified clearly and they are given supervised practice, such persons can be trained to perform their functions extremely well. The few days or weeks it might take the behavioral specialist to teach a nonprofessional to perform a delegated task are usually more than compensated for by the amount of time the specialist saves later on. If instead of having to sit in a class daily collecting data, he need stop in only occasionally to perform a reliability check to compare his observations with the observer's, he will have more time for consulting, training others, and designing other programs. While behavior modification requires the participation of trained personnel in conducting its programs, it is not necessarily a serious limitation to have only one professionally trained behavioral specialist, as long as he, in turn, can train others.

---

[1] The film *Spearhead at Juniper Gardens* (University of Kansas Film Library, Lawrence, Kansas) shows parents being trained to teach preschool children.

LIMITED BEHAVIORAL PRINCIPLES

Some of the basic principles that behavioral psychology has discovered have been examined in this text. The authors tried to show how these principles can be applied to the school setting. Other principles, such as those relating to respondent or classical conditioning, avoidance behavior, complex schedules of reinforcement, and many others, have been omitted because they were judged to be either less relevant to the school setting or too complex for the purposes of this text. Much is known about behavior. The many volumes of literature, the text books, journals, and edited works, many of which are cited in the reference lists of this text, give evidence to that fact. But the full-fledged *scientific* study of behavior only dates back to the last century and is, therefore, a relatively young science. Principles and laws, particularly as they relate to the subtleties of human behavior, are limited. Human behavior is extremely complex and what is known about it is infinitely small in comparison to what is not known. Fortunately, however, new findings are being reported in the literature all the time. Some of those relate to school problems and can be found in the *Journal of Applied Behavioral Analysis* and the other journals cited in the references. Other findings involve populations other than those of the schools, and the educator finds that he often must take those findings and extrapolate from them those aspects that might apply to his own school population. One of the basic goals of this text has been to prepare the reader to be able to read such technical literature. This is one reason why procedures were given their technical names and why they were so carefully defined. Armed with those technical terms and definitions, it is hoped that the reader who plans to use behavior modification procedures in the school will keep abreast of the literature that relates to the programs he is conducting. This is one way that he can profit by the experience of others. It is also hoped that as the reader conducts his own behavioral programs, he will communicate the results to others by submitting them to journals or reporting them at meetings. Through such efforts, the rate with which the mysteries of human behavior can become unravelled should be accelerated.

Exercise 14.10

Interview a school superintendent or building principal. Ask him to list three problems that he feels are most crucial. Which of the problems that he describes do you feel could be treated with a behavior modification approach? Which would be best handled by another approach? Support your conclusions.

ADVANTAGES OF BEHAVIOR MODIFICATION IN THE SCHOOLS

Now that we have discussed some of the limitations of the behavior modification approach we will shift our attention to the advantages of applying behavior modification procedures in the schools. Familiarity with the major advantages may serve to guide individuals who are designing programs for dealing with particular school-related problems. Since many of the positive aspects of the behavior modification approach should be obvious to the reader by now, we will limit this discussion to summarizing three of the most significant advantages: (1) its effectiveness in dealing with motivational and instructional problems; (2) its pragmatic, problem-oriented approach; (3) its own built-in evaluation system. Therefore, if the issue under consideration involves motivational or instructional problems, if practical consequences are important, or if an evaluation of the program is desirable or necessary, behavior modification is appropriate.

EFFECTIVENESS

Applied behavioral analysis has been given considerable attention within the past few years. There is one simple explanation for its increasing popularity: it has a high rate of success with motivational and instructional problems. It has demonstrated that effectiveness with many kinds of populations in many different settings: institutionalized psychiatric populations (Ayllon & Azrin, 1968; Schaefer & Martin, 1969); behaviorally disordered children (Tharp & Wetzel, 1969); juvenile delinquents (Cohen, Goldiamond, Filipczak, & Pooley, 1968); persons with language problems (Sloane & MacAuley, 1968); in counseling situations (Krumboltz & Thoreson, 1969); and in the schools (Karraker, & King, 1969). Cases of the successful application of behavior modification procedures to various behavior problems have been compiled in many different volumes (Ulrich, Stachnik, & Mabry, 1966; Krasner & Ullman, 1965; Ullman & Krasner, 1965; Franks, 1964, 1969) and reported in several journals (*Journal of Applied Behavioral Analysis, Behavior Research and Therapy, Journal of the Experimental Analysis of Behavior, Journal of Experimental Child Psychology,* and others).

Particularly in school settings, such procedures have been successfully used to motivate individuals to increase their rates of emitting certain behaviors, such as studying (Hall, Lund, & Jackson, 1968; Bushell, Wrobel, & Michaeles, 1968); task completion (Birnbrauer, Wolf, Kidder, & Tague, 1965; Wolf, Giles, & Hall, 1968; Karraker, 1968; Campbell & Sulzer, 1971); achievement by college students (McMichael &

Corey, 1969); and many others. Disruptive classroom behavior has been brought under control in several instances (Madsen, Becker, & Thomas, 1968; Thomas, Becker, & Armstrong, 1968; Hall et al., 1968; Zimmerman & Zimmerman, 1962; Becker, Madsen, Arnold, & Thomas, 1967); and the journals continue to publish reports of the achievement of all sorts of behavioral goals in the classroom.

The principles which relate to reinforcement, shaping, and stimulus control have been applied to the design of programmed instruction (Skinner, 1961). In many cases such programs have done an effective job of teaching (Gallenter, 1959). However, one study (Lindvall & Bolvin, 1967) concludes that programmed instruction ". . . has largely failed to make its potential impact upon the schools because they have tended to adopt programmed materials instead of the principles of programmed instruction [p. 217]." So called programs that fail to meet all of the requirements for the effective application of behavioral procedures should not have significantly more success than conventional forms of instruction. The necessary requirements, such as those outlined by Skinner in the *Technology of Teaching* (1968) need to be adhered to if the potential impact is to be realized.

Exercise 14.11

Go to the library and look at a book or journal that includes reports on current research in behavior modification. Try to find an article that relates to your own professional field of interest. Summarize the article and tell how you could apply the findings in your job.

PRAGMATIC, PROBLEM-ORIENTED APPROACH

Many educators have embraced with enthusiasm the idea of applying behavioral procedures. Educators, like behavior modifiers, are often pragmatists; they are concerned with the *practical consequences* of a given procedure, rather than its theoretical implications. They are more commonly concerned with the *hows* than with the *whys*. Teachers want to know how to be able to change behavior: to teach new motor skills, conceptual problem-solving skills, and others; to increase precision of responding; to eliminate unwanted behaviors; and to find ways to keep their students responding. Principals, guidance counselors, and others who perform consulting roles have similar concerns. All of them, along with the behavior modifier, want to find practical solutions to specific problems. Applied behavioral analysis, with its pragmatic, problem-solving approach, allows them to work toward accomplishing those goals.

BUILT-IN PROCEDURAL EVALUATION

Continuous behavioral observation and recording plays an integral role in the system used by applied behavior analysis. This has two major advantages. It not only provides a means for evaluating whether a completed procedure has effectively changed the behavior of the individual but it also provides information about the direction in which a particular procedure is headed during the progress of the program. Educators who are concerned with the selection of educational procedures should find the latter aspect particularly relevant because it allows for a more flexible system. Traditionally, when educators have a particular problem, for instance, planning an instructional program or instituting a given discipline policy, they go to the literature to see which methods have worked best for others. Typically such methods have been evaluated by using pre- and posttest measures. First, the subjects in the experimental and control groups are tested or evaluated by some measure(s). The experimental group is then exposed to a change or "treatment" of some type while conditions are kept constant for the control group. At the end of the treatment, the same or equivalent measures that were first used on both groups are reapplied. If the experimental group is shown to measure significantly higher than the control group at the end of the treatment, it is concluded that the treatment was an effective one for those subjects. If the measures of the performance of the control and experimental groups are similar or if the control group performs better, then the experimental treatment is regarded as either no different than control conditions or as a failure, as assessed in the particular study. In the latter situation, there is often no way of discovering where things went wrong. Perhaps performance improved before it deteriorated; perhaps the direction of the effect was opposite from that expected from the very beginning. Unless measurement is consistently applied throughout the course of the program, valuable information of that type is lost. Because behavior modification requires consistent measurement throughout the entire program, it is possible to determine how the procedure is working from day to day. The direction and rate of change are available for examination. So, if no change is occurring or if the change is working in a direction opposite to the anticipated one or if the procedure is clearly effective for some subjects and not others, it is then possible to alter the procedure before too much time and effort has been invested. In Chapter 15 we will discuss the methods that applied behavioral analysis uses in order to evaluate the effectiveness of a given behavioral procedure.

One of the major thrusts in educational research today is the issue of accountability. Evidence to support that a given program is, or has been, successful is being demanded. This is a healthy sign for education. It implies that faith alone is no longer adequate to support the selection of a set of procedures and that presentation of more empirical evidence is required. For as such evidence continues to accumulate, educational methods will become increasingly precise and effective. Applied behavioral analysis is eminently suited to that requirement.

SUMMARY

While the most important issue to consider in designing a behavior modification program is the suitability of a given procedure for the achievement of a specified behavioral goal, other issues need to be considered as well. Personnel differ from school to school along several dimensions: their behavioral repertoires, the reinforcers available to them, their responsiveness to instruction, and their motivation to alter their own behavior. Those characteristics can effect the outcome of a given program. Practical considerations, such as the appropriateness of the goal, the necessity for contingency control, the school's physical environment, the materials that are available, and school and outside community attitudes should be taken into account since they, too, can influence the success of a program.

Some questions and problems are not best suited to a behavioral modification approach. Some types of group decisions and the selection and development of academic course content are best handled by other approaches and fields. In some cases, procedures that would effectively alter a particular problem behavior have not been discovered. Behavior modification, because of its infancy, has not yet begun to realize its potential. Therefore, some programs will have to be discovery oriented rather than handled as replications of the work done by others. Fortunately, behavioral analysis offers guidelines for attempting such discoveries.

Certain types of problems are particularly well suited to a behavior modification approach. The approach has much to offer when the problem is related to motivation, classroom management procedures, or instructional programming; if practical consequences of a program are of prime importance; or when accountability is an important factor.

REFERENCES

Allen, D., & Ryan, K. *Microteaching.* Reading, Mass.: Addison-Wesley, 1969.

Andrews, J. K. The results of a pilot program to train teachers in the class-room application of behavior modification techniques. Title III ESEA. ED. 031754, ERIC, 1969.

Ayllon, T., & Azrin. N. H. *The token economy: A motivational system for therapy and rehabilitation.* New York: Appleton-Century-Crofts, 1968.

Becker, W. C., Madsen, D. H., Arnold, C. R., & Thomas, D. R. The contingent use of teacher attention and praise in reducing classroom behavior problems. *Journal of Special Education*, 1967, **1,** 287–307.

Birnbrauer, J. S., Wolf, M. M., Kidder, J. D., & Tague, C. Classroom behavior of retarded pupils with token reinforcement. *Journal of Experimental Child Psychology*, 1965, **2,** 219–235.

Bushell, D. Jr., Wrobel, P. A., & Michaeles, M. L. Applying "group" contingencies to the classroom study behavior of preschool children. *Journal of Applied Behavior Analysis,* 1968, **1,** 55–62.

Campbell, A., & Sulzer, B. Naturally available reinforcers as motivators towards reading and spelling achievement by educable mentally handicapped students. Paper presented at the American Educational Research Association Meetings, New York, February, 1971.

Cohen, H. L., Goldiamond, I., Filipczak, J., & Pooley, R. *Training professionals on procedures for the establishment of educational environments.* Silver Springs, Maryland: Educational Facility Press, Institute for Behavioral Research, 1968.

Franks, C. M. *Conditioning techniques in clinical practice and research.* New York: Springer, 1964.

Franks, C. M. *Behavior therapy: Appraisal and status.* New York: McGraw-Hill 1969.

Gallenter, E. *Automatic teaching: The state of the art.* New York: Wiley, 1959.

Hall, R. V., Lund, D., & Jackson, D. Effects of teacher attention on study behaviors. *Journal of Applied Behavioral Analysis,* 1968, **1,** 1–12.

Ivey, A. E., Normington, C. J. Miller, C. D., Morrill, W. H., & Haase, R. F. Micro-counseling and attending behavior: An approach to prepracticum counselor training. *Journal of Counseling Psychology Monograph Supplement,* 1968, **15** (1–12, pt. 2).

Karraker, R. J., & King, N. B. *Readings in classroom management.* New York: MSS Educational Publishing Co., 1969.

Karraker, R. J. Token reinforcement systems in regular public school classrooms. Paper presented at the annual meeting of the American Educational Research Association, Chicago, February, 1968.

Krasner, L., & Ullmann, L. P. *Research in behavior modification: New developments and implications.* New York: Holt, Rinehart and Winston, 1965.

Krumboltz, J. D., & Thoresen, C. E. *Behavioral counseling: Cases and techniques.* New York: Holt, Rinehart and Winston, 1969.

Lindvall, C. M., & Bolven, J. O. Programmed instruction in the schools: An application of programming principles in "individually prescribed instruction."

In NSSE Yearbook, *Programmed Instruction,* Phil C. Lange (Ed.). Chicago: University of Chicago Press, 1967.

Madsen, C. H., Becker, W. C., & Thomas, D. R. Rules, praise, and ignoring: Elements of elementary classroom control. *Journal of Applied Behavior Analysis,* 1968, **1** (1), 139–150.

McMichael, J. S., & Corey, J. R. Contingency management in an introductory psychology course produces better learning. *Journal of Applied Behavior Analysis,* 1969, **2** (2), 79–84.

Schaefer, H. H., & Martin, P. L. *Behavioral Therapy.* New York: McGraw-Hill, 1969.

Skinner, B. F. Why we need teaching machines. *Harvard Educational Review,* 1961, **31,** 377–398.

Skinner, B. F. *Technology of teaching.* New York: Appleton-Century-Crofts, 1968.

Sloane, H. N., Jr., & MacAuley, B. D. *Operant procedures in remedial speech and language training.* Boston: Houghton Mifflin, 1968.

Taylor, L. K., & Sulzer, B. The effects of group and individual contingencies on testing behavior. Unpublished paper, Southern Illinois University, 1971.

Tharp, R. G., & Wetzel, R. J. *Behavior modification in the natural environment.* New York: Academic Press, 1969.

Thomas, D. R., Becker, W. C., & Armstrong, M. Production and elimination of disruptive classroom behavior by systematically varying teacher's behavior. *Journal of Applied Behavior Analysis,* 1968, **1,** 35–45.

Ullmann, L. P., & Krasner, L. *Case studies in behavior modification.* New York: Holt, Rinehart and Winston, 1965.

Ulrich, R., Stachnik, T., & Mabry, J. *Control of human behavior.* Glenview, III.: Scott, Foresmen, 1966.

Wolf, M. M., Giles, D. K., & Hall, R. V. Experiments with token reinforcement in remedial classroom. *Behavior Research and Therapy,* 1968, **6** (1), 51-64.

Zimmerman, E. H. and Zimmerman, J. The alteration of behavior in a special classroom situation. *Journal of the Experimental Analysis of Behavior,* 1962, **5,** 59–60.

15

EVALUATING THE EFFECTIVENESS OF THE BEHAVIOR MODIFICATION PROGRAM

Objectives

After having completed your study of this chapter, you should be able to

1. Define and offer illustrations for each of the following terms:
   a. event sampling
   b. time sampling
   c. reliability
      (1) obtaining reliability data
      (2) calculating reliability
   d. confounding variables
      (1) environmental
      (2) task
      (3) subject
   e. applied research
   f. single-subject experimental designs
      (1) reversal
      (2) multiple baseline
   g. functional relationships
2. Describe a situation for which time sampling would be the most appropriate observational method to use. Justify your answer. Do the same for event sampling.
3. List and describe the factors that can lower a reliability score. Also, specify how one could control for, or minimize, each factor listed.
4. Justify the need for applied research.
5. List and describe the possible limitations of single-subject designs.
6. Specify the strengths of single-subject designs.
7. Specify two reasons why "follow-up" is a necessary activity.
8. Conduct a single-subject research experiment.

The last chapter of this text is designed to help the reader successfully complete the final requirements for conducting a behavior modification program: evaluation, maintainance of behavioral changes, and communication of findings. We have previously discussed methods for defining the problem and selecting the goals. Various behavioral procedures and methods for using them effectively, plus some guidelines for selecting and applying them in a school setting, were our major concern. Here we will emphasize measurement and experimental design, the two essentials of the model (the complete model is presented in Chapter 1) that allow behavior modification to qualify as a data-based scientific approach rather than as an approach founded on faith. The major advantage of such an approach is that of *accountability.* By scoring its data objectively and analyzing the effects of its procedures scientifically, each behavior modification program holds itself accountable for its results; a self-evaluation system is an integral part of its structure.

This accountability feature has probably served as one of the major bases for the enthusiastic reception that behavior modification has been given by so much of the public as well as by practitioners in fields concerned with behavioral change. Many people are no longer content to accept methods that are used simply because the practitioner is trained to use them, because he has a strong intuitive feeling that they will work, or because the student, client, or an informal observer reports that they work. The public wants and deserves evidence that given methods are working for *their* children. The professional also demands such evidence. Hopefully this will contribute to the current trend toward increased accountability in educational, as well as in other applied social and behavioral disciplines.

MEASURING BEHAVIOR

In order to determine if a particular diet helps an individual to lose weight, he is weighed before, then after, the diet is put into effect. The measure, pounds, provides the objective evidence that a change has occurred. In a similar manner, inches are used as units to measure changes in height; pulses per minute, changes in rate of heartbeat, and so forth. Behavior modification also uses standard units to measure changes of behavior, thereby adhering to one of the two critical foundations of science:

> . . . underlying every science is observation and measurement, providing a description of events and a way of quantifying them so that experimental manipulation may be achieved. It might be said that the two critical foundations of science are observation and

experiment and that measurement provides a meaningful way in which events and their manipulation may be ordered. The ultimate goal in science is, of course, an ordering of facts into general, consistent laws from which predictions may be made, but it inevitably starts with observation [Bachrach, 1962, pp. 30, 31].

Throughout this text, we have stressed the need to describe what an individual does through objective observation and measurement.

Some behaviors produce an enduring change and are therefore easier to measure than others. Correctly completed arithmetic problems are enduring because they are written on paper and can be preserved. Assuming that the sizes and levels of difficulty of the problems are kept relatively constant, numbers of correctly completed arithmetic problems can be counted and changes in rate of output can be compared. Number of paragraphs written, reports turned in, cakes baked, dresses sewn, wood-working projects completed, and graphs drawn are all products of behaviors which produce enduring changes in the environment. Such productions can be easily measured and compared to productions under different conditions.

Other behaviors, however, do not produce enduring environmental changes, and their measurement is consequently more difficult. Sitting quietly and attending to a task, contributing to a group discussion, smiling, praising students, fighting, coming late, and many other behaviors are transitory. They cannot be assessed accurately after the fact. In order to measure such behaviors, it is necessary to record observations while the behavior is ongoing or to find some method for preserving the transitory event. Recording behavior as it occurs requires the presence of a live observer or some form of instrumentation. Fortunately, when a program necessitates the presence of a live observer, it is not, as we have already mentioned, always essential that he be a professional. Nonprofessionals such as parents, aides, community volunteers, and even high school and grade school children, can be trained to observe and record data reliably. In the subsequent discussion we will deal with several methods of recording and tabulating data. We will also consider some alternative recording systems for preserving normally transitory behavioral events.

EVENT SAMPLING

Event sampling is one observational method for measuring ongoing behavior. It is a procedure in which the frequency or duration of a specific behavior is recorded over a specific period. The specific interval may, for instance, be a classroom period or a day.

Event sampling is particularly appropriate for measuring responses that are *discrete;* that is, those that have *clearly definable beginnings and ends.* The number of pages completed, days present, answers correct, times tardy, paper airplanes thrown, times leaving the room, and experiments or projects successfully completed are all illustrations of responses that are discrete events. These events can be tabulated with either a pencil and paper or some sort of counter, such as a hand counter (like those used to count the number of people who enter museums or those designed to calculate grocery price totals) or even electromechanical counters, which are available from electronics instrument suppliers.

If the duration of an event is of particular concern, that too, can be accomplished with relative ease with the aid of a wall clock, a stopwatch, or a time clock. Suppose a teacher is interested in reducing the time it takes a student to begin his work. She could start a stopwatch at the moment she announced "work time" and stop it when the student picked up his pencil or book. The elapsed time could then be recorded. One study (Campbell & Sulzer, 1971) wanted to measure how long students had their workbooks available so that the rate with which they worked on specific assignments could be calculated. They had the students punch cards in a time clock just as they were about to start an assignment and punch out when they stopped.

Provided that measurements are only being taken on a few subjects, it is possible that the classroom teacher herself can record events. In fact, when the dependent behavior occurs infrequently, it is probably not economical, except for reliability purposes, to require the presence of another data recorder. For instance, it would be silly to have an observer in the room in order to count the number of book reports turned in by a particular student each month or the number of times a given student was tardy each week.

TIME SAMPLING

Many school-related behaviors are not clearly discrete. It is difficult to tell when some responses begin and end. With such behaviors, time sampling provides the clearest data. For instance, suppose a student makes lots of loud, disruptive noises, such as shouting across the room, hitting his desk with hard objects, and moving his chair around. It would be difficult to either count the number of times such responses occurred or to measure their duration. When does one episode of chair moving end and another begin? It is, however, possible *to score the presence or absence of such responses within a short time interval.* This is what is involved in a time-sampling procedure: *recording the presence or absence of the behavior within short, uniform time intervals.*

We will use a recent study (Whitley & Sulzer, 1970) to illustrate. A student was observed Monday, Wednesday, and Friday during a seventy-minute reading class. An observer watched the student for ten seconds in order to determine if he was out of his seat or talked out. If either of those behaviors were emitted at any time during the ten-second interval, the entire interval was scored minus. If neither occurred, the interval was scored plus. For five seconds following each ten-second observation period, the observer recorded the scores. A similar system was used to score time intervals during which the teacher "paid attention" to the student. For that behavior, the observer scored the interval with a check. Here is an example of the type of recording sheet that was used in that study:

Sometimes it is necessary to sample several behaviors simultaneously. A coded behavioral sample sheet can be used for this purpose. Letter codes for each behavior of concern are designated. The presence or absence of each of the behaviors is then scored by making a slash mark through the letter that stands for the behavior being emitted during the interval that the subject is being observed. It is possible to use such a system to make repeated measurements on one subject or to measure different individuals in a group several times. Here is an example of how such a behavioral sample sheet[1] was used in a recent study (Sulzer, Hunt, Ashby, Koniarski, & Krams, 1971). Several problem behaviors in a fifth grade class had been identified. These were operationalized, then listed and coded (operational definitions are not included):

O = no problem behavior being emitted
S = out of seat
H = hitting others
Y = yelling, talking out, or making noises
T = throwing objects

Teacher behaviors were also coded in a similar manner:

O = no response
V = verbal praise
N = near student
C = physical contact
P = punishment

By referring to the operational definitions of each of those categories,

---

[1] Designed by Lawrence Payne.

observers recorded the emission of various behaviors. Figure 15.1 shows one of the sheets scored by an observer.

Each ten seconds one student's behavior was scored, along with the teacher's behavior in relation to that student at that time. For instance, if, at the moment the scoring was taking place, the student was hitting

		10	20	30	40	50	60
1	Student	OSHYT	OSHYT	OSHYT	OSHYT	OSHYT	OSHYT
	Teacher	OVNCP	OVNCP	OVNCP	OVNCP	OVNCP	OVNCP
2	Student	OSHYT	OSHYT	OSHYT	OSHYT	OSHYT	OSHYT
	Teacher	OVNCP	OVNCP	OVNCP	OVNCP	OVNCP	OVNCP
3	Student	OSHYT	OSHYT	OSHYT	OSHYT	OSHYT	OSHYT
	Teacher	OVNCP	OVNCP	OVNCP	OVNCP	OVNCP	OVNCP
4	Student	OSHYT	OSHYT	OSHYT	OSHYT	OSHYT	OSHYT
	Teacher	OVNCP	OVNCP	OVNCP	OVNCP	OVNCP	OVNCP
5	Student	OSHYT	OSHYT	OSHYT	OSHYT	OSHYT	OSHYT
	Teacher	OVNCP	OVNCP	OVNCP	OVNCP	OVNCP	OVNCP
6	Student	OSHYT	OSHYT	OSHYT	OSHYT	OSHYT	OSHYT
	Teacher	OVNCP	OVNCP	OVNCP	OVNCP	OVNCP	OVNCP
7	Student	OSHYT	OSHYT	OSHYT	OSHYT	OSHYT	OSHYT
	Teacher	OVNCP	OVNCP	OVNCP	OVNCP	OVNCP	OVNCP
8	Student	OSHYT	OSHYT	OSHYT	OSHYT	OSHYT	OSHYT
	Teacher	OVNCP	OVNCP	OVNCP	OVNCP	OVNCP	OVNCP
9	Student	OSHYT	OSHYT	OSHYT	OSHYT	OSHYT	OSHYT
	Teacher	OVNCP	OVNCP	OVNCP	OVNCP	OVNCP	OVNCP
10	Student	OSHYT	OSHYT	OSHYT	OSHYT	OSHYT	OSHYT
	Teacher	OVNCP	OVNCP	OVNCP	OVNCP	OVNCP	OVNCP
11	Student	OSHYT	OSHYT	OSHYT	OSHYT	OSHYT	OSHYT
	Teacher	OVNCP	OVNCP	OVNCP	OVNCP	OVNCP	OVNCP
12	Student	OSHYT	OSHYT	OSHYT	OSHYT	OSHYT	OSHYT
	Teacher	OVNCP	OVNCP	OVNCP	OVNCP	OVNCP	OVNCP
13	Student	OSHYT	OSHYT	OSHYT	OSHYT	OSHYT	OSHYT
	Teacher	OVNCP	OVNCP	OVNCP	OVNCP	OVNCP	OVNCP
14	Student	OSHYT	OSHYT	OSHYT	OSHYT	OSHYT	OSHYT
	Teacher	OVNCP	OVNCP	OVNCP	OVNCP	OVNCP	OVNCP
15	Student	OSHYT	OSHYT	OSHYT	OSHYT	OSHYT	OSHYT
	Teacher	OVNCP	OVNCP	OVNCP	OVNCP	OVNCP	OVNCP
16	Student	OSHYT	OSHYT	OSHYT	OSHYT	OSHYT	OSHYT
	Teacher	OVNCP	OVNCP	OVNCP	OVNCP	OVNCP	OVNCP

FIGURE 15.1   Sample of a coded behavioral sheet

another child, a slash mark would be made through the H. If the teacher was simultaneously scolding the student for hitting, a slash mark would be made through the P. Ten seconds later, another student was scored, and so on until each student in the class was observed. This sequence was followed ten times, yielding ten behavioral samples for each student.

The duration of intervals selected can vary. If there is a need to show very subtle changes, intervals even shorter than ten seconds may be selected. But, in the experience of these authors, as the interval becomes shorter, agreement between observers begins to diminish. It is also possible to lengthen intervals, depending upon the characteristics of the response. Care must be taken, however, that such an interval does not distort the validity of the data. For instance, suppose a thirty-second interval had been selected, and a student stamped on the floor once loudly. Though this response may have lasted only a second, the data would show thirty seconds worth of disruptive behavior. However, a thirty-second interval could be very appropriate for a behavior of longer duration such as sitting or pencil sharpening. Thus, the selection of the interval length must depend upon the specific response and environmental factors. Consequently, selection of interval length will undoubtedly vary somewhat from program to program.

It is also possible to vary the interval of time reserved for recording. Some behavioral observations can be recorded very quickly; others take time. The problem with a long recording interval is that the behaviors that occur during that interval cannot be scored. The longer the recording interval, the less the data reflect the real ongoing behavior.

One limitation of time sampling is that it is not practical for studying some important, yet infrequently occurring, behaviors. Fights between two particular students, for example, may occur no more than once a week. Since, with time sampling, observations are not continuous, it is possible that those infrequent events would fail to be recorded. However, if such behavior occurred in class as often as once a week, it would probably be necessary to do something about it. Thus, as a general rule of thumb, Arrington (1943) suggests that if the dependent behavior occurs on the average of less than once in fifteen minutes, an observational procedure other than time sampling should be selected. For most situations of that type, event sampling provides a good alternative.

INSTRUMENTATION

There are times when it is neither practical nor convenient to have a live observer present to record ongoing behavior. Transitory behavioral events can be preserved, however, through the use of instrumentation that is relatively easily accessible to school personnel. Audio tapes can preserve verbal behavior for measurement at a later time. Films and video tapes recorded through one-way mirrors, from wall-mounted cameras, or even by nonprofessional operators directly in the setting can also be analyzed at a later time. Films and video tapes have the advantage of preserving both motor as well as verbal behaviors and they can be replayed if the scoring of a behavioral event is questionable. It is not always necessary to have live observers score behavior continuously to achieve reliable data. Tape recorders and cameras can also be used to sample behaviors by preselecting the times when the recorder or camera will be started or stopped. One study, (Sanders, Hopkins, & Walker, 1969) used a time-lapse still camera mounted in a classroom to obtain permanent photographic records of behavioral samples by automatically exposing the film according to a preselected schedule. They found that their system had several advantages: it saved observer time; the equipment was easily obtained; the records could be easily stored. The method was inexpensive, and the percent of interscorer agreement was very high. The continued development of instrumentation designed to preserve transitory behavioral events should result in more efficient and reliable recording systems.

Exercise 15.1

Go to a classroom or a library or any location where you will be free to measure behavior for at least an hour and select two behaviors to measure. One should be a frequently occurring discrete behavior with a clearly definable beginning and end. The other should be a behavior that is not clearly discrete; that is, a behavior that cannot be easily counted. Measure both behaviors and plot them on a graph.

OBSERVATIONAL RELIABILITY

A lady known to us has a set of scales which varies as much as five pounds from one weighing to the next. If she weighs herself once and the scales read 150 pounds she gets off and immediately steps on again. This is repeated until the scales read 145 pounds. At that point she walks away smiling. "The diet is working." Of course her conclusion is erroneous. The scales are not reliable, and she really has no way of knowing if the diet is working or not. A reliable set of scales, consistent in their measurement, would provide her with appropriate evidence. Behavioral measurement requires the same sort of consistency. Before formal data can be collected, it is necessary to insure that observations can be reliably scored.

One way of determining whether behavioral measures are reliable is through simultaneous recording by independent observers. There must be close agreement between the two, demonstrating that the behavior under observation is being measured similarly. If a high percentage of agreement is not obtained, any recorded change in the observed behavior by a single observer may be due to a change in his observing and recording responses rather than in the observed behavior (Baer, Wolf, & Risley, 1968). One source of error, for instance, might be brought about by an observer's expectancies. An observer may tend to err, without being aware of doing so, by recording results in the anticipated direction. Thus, if one was aware that a reinforcer was being applied, he might be more likely to record an increase in behavior. If he knew that the reinforcer had been withdrawn, his tendency might be to record a decrease in the behavior. Obviously, whenever possible, reliability observers should not be informed of the experimental manipulation being made during that particular phase in order to avoid such an occurrence. They need only be informed of the behaviors to be observed.

Reliability in behavior modification experiments is usually calculated by comparing how well two or more independent observers agree among themselves and is frequently reported in percentages. The percentage is obtained by dividing the number of agreements by the number of agreements plus disagreements and multiplying by 100. For instance, two independent observers observed the out-of-seat behavior of a math class for ten seconds and recorded for five. Six minutes of their thirty-minute time-sample record might look like this:

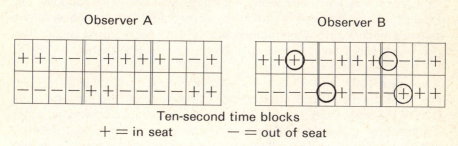

Observer A   Observer B

Ten-second time blocks

$+$ = in seat $-$ = out of seat

A comparison between the two records shows that there were four instances in which the observers failed to record identical scores. These are circled on observer B's record. There were twenty instances in which they did agree. The calculation of the reliability score, or *reliability coefficient,* therefore would look like this:

$$\frac{\text{no. of agreements}}{\text{no. of agreements} + \text{no. of disagreements}} = \frac{20}{24} = 0.833 \times 100 = 83\frac{1}{3} \text{ percent}$$

Reliability checks should be made *prior* to any formal data collection as well as *during* each of the different phases of the program. An effort needs to be made to ensure that the observers do not cue one another;

269

that they are indeed observing only the dependent response rather than each other's scores. Then, a high percentage of agreement, about 90 percent, suggests that scoring techniques are acceptably reliable (Wright, 1960). If the reliability score falls far below that, for instance, less than 80 percent, some changes need to be instituted before the program is allowed to proceed.

Most frequently, poor interobserver agreement is the result of a failure to give an adequate operational definition to the response. For instance, with the illustrative example discussed above, there may have been an inadequate definition of out-of-seat behavior. One observer may have scored the subject as being in his seat when just one knee was touching the seat. The other may have scored the same student as being out-of-seat. A clarification of the definition, such as "out-of-seat" means that no part of the subject's body touches the seat, would rectify the situation. Subsequent reliability scores would likely be higher, and the investigators would be justified in going ahead with their program.

In order to assume that the sampled behavior truly represents the behavior, interobserver reliability should be assessed over several full-length sessions. As with obtaining a baseline measure, one brief sample of behavior is insufficient. It is subject to too much error. Suppose the situation with the student's knee on the chair had not occurred until the second or third session. This problem would only have been identified if there were at least that many reliability sessions. Or, suppose the dependent behavior were emitted very infrequently. Several observation sessions under various conditions would then be required before the definitions and other observational methods could be tested.

Exercise 15.2

Return with a friend or classmate to the location you used for your observation for Exercise 15.1. Both of you should score the same subject for a half hour. Give your friend your measurement criteria. Seat yourselves in such a way that you cannot inadvertently cue one another. Calculate a reliability coefficient. Evaluate your reliability.

Exercise 15.3

Plan a program to change a specific behavior of a student, colleague, friend, relative, or yourself.
a. Specify your observational method and justify its selection.
b. Have a second observer assist you with collecting data.
c. Measure the behavior for a specified period of time for several days.
d. Have each observer graph his data separately. The horizontal line could be labeled "days"; the vertical line should be labeled with the measure of the dependent behavior (see Figure 1.2).

e. Are the baseline measurements on each separate graph about the same from one day to the next? Are the two graphs similar to one another?

f. Calculate your reliability.

EXPERIMENTAL CONTROL

Once the behavioral specialist has selected his measures and been able to demonstrate that they are reliable, he plans a method for evaluating the effectiveness of the procedures he is to apply. At first glance, this evaluation may appear to be deceptively simple: First measure the typical behavior of the individual, then put the procedures into effect and measure again. Suppose a classroom teacher had a difficult time motivating her new class to work hard on their reading assignments. She selects a token system, backed up by items from the dime store, as the procedure to produce the desired behavior. Her plan is to first count the number of workbook items correctly completed by each child each day for a week. Then she plans to put the token system into effect for the rest of the semester. If the children's average work output increases, she reasons, she can conclude that the token system was effective.

Unfortunately things are not quite that simple. Let's take a closer look at the situation. Would a substantial increase in workbook items completed necessarily indicate that the token system was responsible? Not in this case. It is possible that simultaneous with the institution of the token system other factors arose that could have affected the outcome of the program. Such factors are called *confounding variables* and are often divided into three classes: subject, task, and environmental (Underwood, 1957).

Subject confounding variables include the entire domain of student characteristics, his demographic background, previous learning history, and present behaviors. A partial list of potential subject confounding variables would include the specific behavioral problem and its frequency and time of onset and the student's stated expectancies, reinforcement history, sex, age, and behavioral repertoire. The behavioral repertoire is dependent, of course, upon the student's previous learning experiences and genetic endowment. Thus, in the situation in which a token system was used to bring about an increase in workbook items completed, such an increase might have been brought about by an increase in age (maturation) or some other confounding variable rather than by the token system.

Task confounding variables come "from aspects of the experimental task (apparatus or stimulus) on which the experimenter is not focusing, aspects other than his arbitrarily defined independent variable, [that is, the selected behavior modification approach] [Kiesler, 1966, p. 132]." For example, teachers or behavioral specialists may inadvertently emit noncontrolled verbal or nonverbal behaviors that confound the effects of the independent variable or treatment. If teacher attention or approval was associated with the delivery of tokens (using the previously mentioned illustration), the effect of the token reinforcement procedure is confounded. It would be impossible to determine whether it was the tokens or the teacher attention or approval, or some combination of those variables, which brought about the increase in workbook items completed. Thus, though a functional relationship has apparently been demonstrated, the results might actually be due to a task confounding variable, such as the experimenter's approval or tone of voice or some nonverbal cue, rather than the independent variable itself (such as the use of tokens).

Environmental confounding variables are ones that change concurrently with the experimental variable and yet are not subject or task variables. Examples of these within the experimental setting include variations in the time of day or in seating arrangements. For example, baseline data on a student might have been consistently recorded just before lunch when the student was in seat A. Treatment may have been instituted after lunch when he was in seat B. Any stimulus changes that occur concurrently with the experimental variable can confound the effects of the experimental variable, thus making the conclusions reached ambiguous. The well-known Hawthorne effect, in which behavior increased when lighting intensity changed (Cook, 1962) could also be an environmental confounding variable, or uncontrolled stimulus change. Environmental confounding variables can also occur outside the experimental setting, such as the death of a subject's friend or relative or a change in his employment.

How, then, does behavior modification answer such a challenge? First it ensures that each experimental phase is of a sufficient length that the confounding effects of outside environmental variables are substantially reduced. For instance, if a subject were known to have started a paper route part way through a given experimental phase, it would be necessary to extend that phase long enough so that the effects of his having a paper route would become manifest and could be accounted for. Introducing a new experimental change simultaneous with the subject's new job would undoubtedly introduce ambiguity into the data interpretation.

Next, it provides some kind of experimental analysis, or *experimental design,* in which the possible influences of confounding variables are screened out. Such a screening process enables the experimenter to evaluate the effects of the treatment (independent variable) less ambiguously. To accomplish this screening process, the subject is used as his own control in order to avoid subject confounding variables and *all conditions are maintained as constants throughout all phases of the program.* In the token system illustration, for example, it would be necessary to maintain the following conditions before, during, and following the procedural changes: the presence of observers, recordkeeping methods, classroom discipline techniques, teacher planning, and all other possible environmental confounding variables (Kiesler, 1966); plus the general length and levels of difficulty of the responses required of the students and all other task confounding variables. (Naturally when classroom experiments require collection of academic performance data over prolonged periods of time, the length of assignments will vary somewhat from day to day and the levels of difficulty will gradually increase. But, because none of the changes are abrupt and because they are not introduced simultaneous with the introduction of a new experimental phase but are distributed evenly throughout all phases, they are treated as if they are constants.) Then it becomes possible to ". . . manipulate an individual subject's behavior in a precise and reliable fashion . . . to turn some quantitatively consistent aspect of behavior on and off by the manipulation of specific variables . . . [Sidman, 1960, p. 342]." Experimental control is thus demonstrated. If it were possible to increase or decrease the number of correctly completed problems of equivalent length and difficulty by presenting or withholding the token system, the effectiveness of the system would be demonstrated. If some condition other than the token system were responsible for the improvement, no decline in performance would accompany its removal nor would a subsequent increase accompany its reintroduction. By demonstrating experimental control, factors such as passage of time and other environmental and task variables can no longer be held accountable for the behavioral changes.

Because experimental controls are a necessary aspect of the behavior modification method, each time a behavioral specialist conducts a program he is, in a sense, conducting an experiment and acting as an applied researcher. Like the basic laboratory researcher, the behavioral specialist is concerned with discovering factors that control behavior. But his primary concern is with improving the effectiveness of socially important behaviors (Baer et al., 1968). As we have already seen, however, the average school setting seldom provides an ideal setting for research. Therefore, it becomes very important to structure the situation very carefully, that is, to use adequate experimental controls. "The analysis of socially important behavior becomes experimental only with difficulty [Baer et al., p. 92]." For this reason, we will now discuss some single-subject experimental designs that have been found to be particularly useful in conducting behavior modification programs in school settings.

SINGLE-SUBJECT EXPERIMENTAL DESIGN

Does praising Mike, contingent upon his completion of arithmetic problems result in an increase in his arithmetic output? Does the word "no" from Jane's teacher result in an immediate and long-lasting cessation of Jane's marking on the desk? A valid conclusion regarding the effectiveness of such environmental changes could only be made if data were collected under controlled conditions. Single-subject experimental designs provide one excellent structure for such a data collection system. Single-subject experimental designs can demonstrate the existence of functional relationships between the dependent behaviors, such as completion of arithmetic problems or desk marking, and the selected behavior modification procedure, or independent variable, such as praising or saying "no."

Single-subject research yields a principle or law of behavior applicable to a particular individual (Bijou & Baer, 1960). For example, Mike's completion of arithmetic problems was demonstrated, under conditions experimentally controlled by a single-subject design, to have increased as a function of his being praised by his parents, teachers, the guidance counselor and others. Praise was found to be a general reinforcer for him, and a valuable principle of Mike's behavior was discovered.

Sometimes principles that relate to a single individual are found to be equally applicable to a number of individuals. When the same results are found to repeat over and over again with a great many subjects, the finding is said to be a general *principle* or *law.* This principle should then apply to groups of students with characteristics similar to those of the single individuals in each of the original studies. When results fail to replicate, "the changes in experimental technique that the experimenter must use in order to replicate [the results] in other children may often give a meaningful clue to the nature of each child's past history [Bijou & Baer, 1960, p. 151]." Such clues may also lead to the identification of confounding variables that must eventually be controlled if optimal behavioral control is to be achieved.

A particularly significant advantage of the single-subject design is that it avoids one of the strongest confounding factors in behavioral research, *individual subject differences.* The single-subject design allows comparisons to be made between an individual under one condition and the same individual under other conditions. For example, a basic reversal design (to be described in the following discussion) was used to help answer the question, "Does praising Mike, contingent upon his completion of arithmetic problems, result in an increase in his arithmetic output?" Mike's own performance was compared during the baseline period (no praise), treatment period (praise), and reversal period (no praise). Mike was not compared to Joe, Susie, or Jim, only to himself. And, therefore, differences between individual subjects could not effect the outcome of the analysis.

Although the single-subject design does eliminate, or least substantially reduce, the problem of subject confounding variables, additional provision must be made, as mentioned before, to insure that other forms of uncontrolled variables, such as task and environmental variables, do not inadvertently enter the situation and effect the outcome of the program. Therefore, to repeat, in every single-subject experimental design, it is a requirement that *all conditions, other than the systematic changes in the independent variable* (in the behavior modification field, usually the procedure), *be kept constant throughout the entire program.* With the confidence that other variables are being prevented from effecting the outcome, it then becomes possible to test for the effect that the manipulation of the procedure has upon the behavior.

Two single-subject designs are particularly well suited to the maintenance of control conditions: *reversal* and *multiple baseline* designs. Variations of these designs have frequently appeared in the *Journal of Applied Behavior Analysis* and other journals. Additional variations and designs are likely to appear as the behavior modification field continues to develop. Our discussion will be limited to the more commonly used designs.

Reversal designs The term "functional relationship" indicates that a change in the independent variable produces systematic changes in the dependent variable (Holland & Skinner, 1961). If a particular independent variable (here the presentation of praise) is functionally related to the behavior of a particular individual (here the individual's rate of answering questions), the contingent presentation of the praise should systematically effect the individual's rate of answering questions. If the praise is a reinforcer, the rate of emission of answering questions should increase. If the praise is an aversive stimulus, the rate of behavior should decrease. If the praise is indeed a reinforcer and is withheld, this should also have a systematic effect. Under such an extinction procedure, the rate of emission should begin to decrease. When such systematic changes in the dependent variable (rate of asking questions) are manifested as a function of the contingent presentation and withdrawal of an independent variable, it provides evidence for the existence of a lawful functional relationship. One then becomes confident that it is indeed the

275

procedure that has accounted for the changes in behavior, rather than some uncontrolled confounding variables. This is the logic upon which reversal designs are based.

Reversal designs have a characteristic form. First baseline performance is measured. Next the independent variable is introduced. Then the independent variable is removed. Usually the independent variable is again introduced. The first baseline conditions are frequently identified as the A phase; the experimental conditions, when the independent variable is introduced, as the B phase. The return to baseline conditions, when the independent variable is temporarily removed, is frequently referred to as the *reversal,* or the *probe;* because the conditions are identical with the baseline conditions, the phase is also labeled A. The reintroduction of the independent variable is again labeled B. Hence a reversal design is often referred to as an ABAB design. Figure 15.2 illustrates these phases in a class room program on disruptive student behavior. This particular study (Whitley & Sulzer, 1970) also included a follow-up case, subsequent to the termination of the formal program.

There are some variations in the basic ABAB design that can be used when particular problems present themselves. In one variation, the reinforcer is presented in all phases of the study, but during baseline conditions, there is no systematic connection between the dependent variable (that is, the response) and the reinforcer. For instance, one study (Sulzer, Hunt, & Loving, 1970) conducted a tutoring program with 10 nine- and ten-year-old volunteers. The reinforcers were points backed up by access to preferred activities, such as games, crafts projects, films, trips, and so on. The dependent variable was the student's performance (number and percent correct) on academic assignments such as those in reading and arithmetic workbooks. It was reasoned that if the baseline conditions consisted of the task assignment and *no* reinforcement, the students would not attend the voluntary sessions. Therefore, reinforcing activities were made available to the students noncontingently during baseline. They were allowed to participate in the activities regardless of their performance on academic work. Then, once the experimental phase was put into effect, the students were required to earn access to the activities. Though the difference in performance between the A condition and the B condition was not as dramatic as it probably would have been if there had been a total lack of reinforcement in the baseline phase, and increase in performance was manifested. Of more practical importance is the fact that all but one of the students continued to voluntarily attend the sessions regularly.

A second variation of the ABAB design is the omission of the traditional baseline phase. This BAB design is used most frequently when repeated baseline measurements would be patently absurd: either the

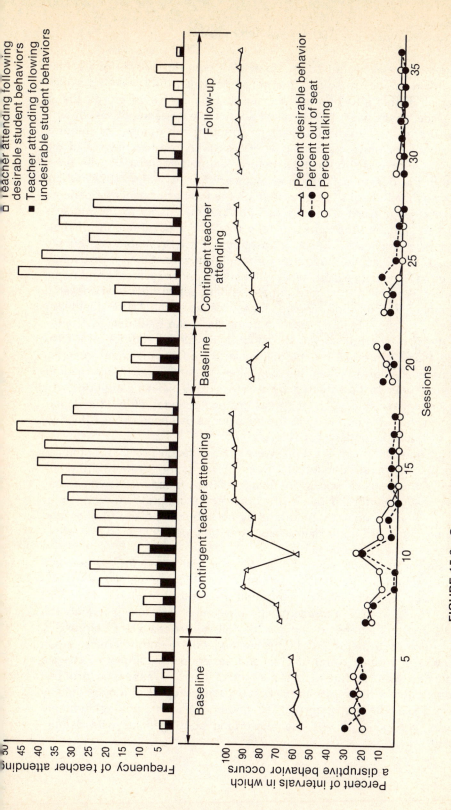

FIGURE 15.2 Occurrences of various pupil behaviors in relation to teacher attending

Reprinted by permission from D. A. Whitley and B. Sulzer, Reducing disruptive behavior through consultation. *The Personnel and Guidance Journal*, 1970, **48**, fig. 1. Copyright 1970 by the American Personnel and Guidance Association, Inc.

individual has never emitted the dependent behavior or the frequencies of such emissions are so rare that measurement would make no sense. Examples of this situation are measuring the number of words that a first grader reads when he has never shown any evidence of responding to word presentations in the past or counting the number of minutes a person spends on a particular work task when he has never had the opportunity to perform the task before. The latter situation was illustrated in the design used by one study (Ayllon & Azrin, 1968) which assessed the effect of a token system on the job performance of patients in a psychiatric ward. The jobs had not been available to the patients before so it made little sense to take repeated measurements of their typical performance. However, a baseline point is available and should be used. In the above illustration, it would be zero. Since it is usually difficult to anticipate exactly what will happen under reversal conditions, it does make sense to record initial baseline performance whenever it is feasible either through repeated measures, as in the ABAB design, or by recording the "obvious" starting point, as in the BAB design.

A third variation of the ABAB design involves the addition of a DRO phase, (see Chapter 12 for the discussion of differential reinforcement of other behaviors). When the dependent behavior, such as reading behavior, fails to be effected by a return to baseline conditions, the independent variable, such as praise, can be applied to all *but* the dependent behavior. A sharp drop in the behavior is evidence of the effectiveness of the independent variable.

Brigham and Sherman (1968) were able to teach preschool children to accurately imitate English and Russian words by reinforcing the imitation of the English words. By using a DRO procedure in which they differentially reinforced behaviors other than imitation of English or Russian words, accurate imitations by all subjects on the English and Russian word promptly decreased. And that demonstrated the effectiveness of the reinforcement.

A similar approach was used by Wheeler and Sulzer (1970) in a language training program. The percent with which sentences were correctly used by a speech-deficient child are plotted in Figure 15.3. The label "Train. form I" represents an experimental phase in which the child's approximations to the use of full sentences were reinforced. The return to baseline conditions yielded only a minor effect. When DRO was instituted (train. form II) and the child's incomplete sentence production was reinforced, his percent of correct responses dropped substantially. With a return to the first experimental condition, he quickly returned to a high rate of correct responding. The functional relationship between the behavior and the reinforcing contingencies was demonstrated.

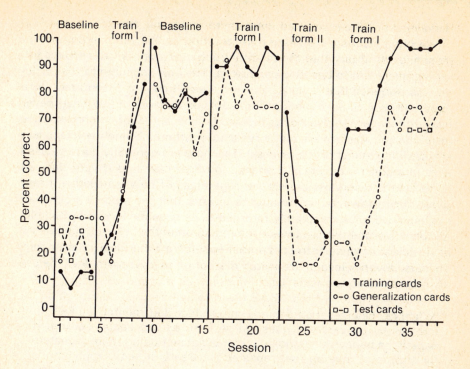

FIGURE 15.3 Percent of form 1 responding for six experimental conditions
Reprinted by permission from A. J. Wheeler and B. Sulzer, Operant training and generalization of a sympathetic response form in speech deficient children. *Journal of Applied Behavior Analysis,* 1970, **3**, fig. 1. Copyright 1970 by the Society of the Experimental Analysis of Behavior, Inc.

Advantages and disadvantages of reversal The major advantage to using a reversal procedure is, of course, that it shows the functional relationship between the dependent behavior and the procedure. It provides for accountability in the program. But in addition to the accountability factor, the reversal design can be used by the educational consultant as a teaching tool. The reversal can demonstrate to the classroom teacher just how effective her new procedures are. The design also provides her with a basis for contrasting the effects of her typical (baseline) approach with the one that has demonstrated its effectiveness. Because a reversal design can involve alternating reinforcement and extinction conditions it may also facilitate the subject's transfer from continuous to intermittent schedules.

There are a few disadvantages in using a reversal design. First of all, establishing and measuring baseline conditions takes time and the conditions themselves do not contribute to the actual behavioral change.

However, we have discussed many more important aspects of baseline conditions that justify their use. In addition to the time issue, school personnel often fear that the modified behavior may fail to recover following the return to baseline conditions. The only recourse to that argument is evidence that once a behavior is acquired it is reacquired more rapidly (Keller & Schoenfeld, 1950). In our experience we have never failed to recover the desirable modified behavior, though in one instance (see Chapter 14) recovery did prove a little difficult. Sometimes teachers are unwilling to institute a reversal. Teachers are generally quite pleased when a student's behavior changes, and they may find it very difficult to accept the reversal requirement, regardless of how instructive it may prove to be. However, informing the teacher that the student's behavior may not need to be completely returned to its baseline level may be helpful. Usually a one-third to two-thirds reduction in the behavioral measure is sufficient to demonstrate the existence of a functional relationship. There is, nevertheless, a temporary disruption in a program with the use of reversal designs. However,

> Whether they [reversal designs] are in fact detrimental is likely to remain an unexamined question so long as the social setting in which the behavior is studied dictates against using them repeatedly. Indeed, it may be that repeated reversals in some applications have a positive effect on the subject, possibly contributing to the discrimination of relevant stimuli involved in the problem [Baer, Wolf, & Risley, 1968, p. 94].

Multiple baseline design The multiple baseline design is one possible alternative to the reversal design. It is usually employed when the target behavior appears to be irreversible or in situations in which reversal designs are highly undesirable. The following is a description of the design:

> In the multiple-baseline technique, a number of responses are identified and measured over time to provide baselines against which changes can be evaluated. With these baselines established, the experimenter then applies an experimental variable to one of the behaviors, produces a change in it, and perhaps notes little or no change in the other baselines. If so, rather than reversing the just produced change, he instead applies the experimental variable to one of the other, as yet unchanged, responses. If it changes at that point, evidence is accruing that the experimental variable is indeed effective, and that the prior change was not simply a matter of coincidence. The variable then may be applied to still another response, and so on. The experimenter is attempting to show that he has a reliable experimental variable, in that each behavior changes maximally only when the experimental variable is applied to it [Baer et al., 1968, p. 94].

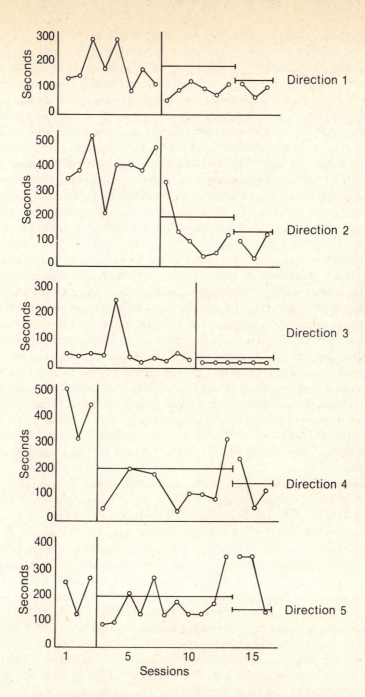

FIGURE 15.4 Number of seconds elapsed between presentation and compliance with several different verbal directions. Vertical line
indicates introduction of tokens for that response. Horizontal
line indicates maximal amount of time allowed for eligibility
for reinforcement.

Adapted from Fjellstedt and Sulzer (1971).

The multiple baseline is illustrated in a study with a child who was assigned to a special education class for emotionally distrubed children because he "failed to follow instructions" (Fjellstedt & Sulzer, 1971). The dependent variable in the study consisted of a number of seconds that elapsed following the presentation of an instruction and the child's compliance with the instruction *(latency).* A token system backed up with play periods and toys served as the independent variable. Figure 15.4 depicts the child's *latency of responding* to several sets of instructions. The vertical line indicated the session during which token delivery was instituted for a given direction. The horizontal line indicated the maximum latency allowed for eligibility for reinforcement. Though the experimental procedure, token delivery, was instituted at various times for different instructions, the effect of the procedure quickly manifested itself within a session or two. The multiple baseline provided support that the independent variable was functionally related to the dependent variable; that tokens could reduce latency of following directions.

Another study, (McAllister, Stachowiak, Baer, & Conderman, 1969) also used a multiple baseline research design to demonstrate the effect of teacher praise and disapproval upon two high school classroom target behaviors. Following baseline assessments, contingencies were first placed upon inappropriate talking, while baseline conditions were maintained on inappropriate turning around. Inappropriate talking diminished during that phase, while turning around remained relatively stable. Next, the contingencies were applied to turning around. A rapid decrease in that behavior was achieved. The effectiveness of the contingency was demonstrated.

Other considerations with single-subject designs   A few other issues related to single-subject design are worthy of consideration. First, it is never certain how many reversals or baselines are needed to show the unquestionable effect of the experimental variable. However, when a statistical analysis is employed, as in group designs, the suitability of the chosen inferential statistic must also be judged. Thus, in either single-subject or group designs "the judgments required are highly qualitative, and rules cannot always be stated profitably [Baer et al., 1968, p. 95]." The question remains an open one.

There are no hard and fast rules regarding the length of time initial baseline conditions should be preserved. The guideline is to look for stability; that the behavioral measure varies only within a certain well-defined range. It may take just a few days in order to make a judgment that such stability has been identified or it may take many days. In Figure 15.2, baseline performance was very stable, varying no more than 10 percentage points over a five-day period. Baseline performance in Figure 15.4 varied quite a bit more, over 20 percent on the first set of behaviors and about 50 percent in the second sets. There was a subjective judgment that the typical performance range had been identified. When baseline performance does vary considerably, it seems most advisable to be cautious and maintain baseline conditions for a few additional days.

It is possible that subjective judgment can influence the decision about what constitutes a change in behavior. What may be said to be an obvious increase or decrease in a behavior by one person may not be considered as such by another. However, the influence caused by the subjectivity that can enter into a design can be considerably reduced by prior selection of "acceptable" behavioral levels.

One essential criterion for determining whether a significant behavioral change has occurred or not is (according to Baer et al., 1968) its practical importance. If the behavior has been altered enough to satisfy relevant school personnel, parents, and the student, that criterion has been met. Such a criterion should be determined *prior* to the administration of the procedure in order to reduce any subsequent indecision or bias in reporting the results.[2]

Another consideration is one that was discussed previously; the single-subject design is *not* necessarily the most practical way to make normative group decisions. Group experimental research designs are more appropriate for making such decisions. For example, suppose a decision had to be made about whether to adopt a new set of programmed reading materials developed to help teach elementary school students to read. A group design that would compare the average reading scores of a sample of students who had been randomly selected to use the materials with the scores of a control group, a sample of students who did not use the materials, could provide valuable information for making such an administrative decision. However, if the behavioral specialist, teacher, or parent want to know if the new materials will help John, a single-subject design would be in order.

Exercise 15.4

Go to the library and look through some recently published journals that contain reports of behavior modification experiments. Select three articles that use a single-subject experimental design. For each article list:

a. the dependent variable(s)
b. the independent variable
c. the procedure for demonstrating experimental control

---

[2] For those who have studied group statistics you will note that this is analogous to the use of group designs, since the criteria for significance (the alpha level) should, of course, be selected prior to conducting the experiment.

Exercise 15.5

a. Refer back to your plan for Exercise 15.3. Describe in words the steps you would take in order to demonstrate that the behavioral change was a function of your procedures.

b. Carry out the program and present your results on a graph.

MAINTAINING AND FOLLOWING UP THE BEHAVIOR CHANGE

Once the effectiveness of a procedure has been demonstrated, it is, naturally, reintroduced and maintained until the behavioral goal is met. It is also important to follow up the behavior change in order to assure its maintenance and generality. Just because a behavior change has occurred does not, of course, mean that the change will persist nor generalize to other responses or situations. The environment must be structured so as to maintain the behavior change or cause it to generalize. An appropriate maintenance procedure should be selected and used (see Part III) along with procedures designed to enhance generalizations (see Part I). If the environment is not structured to maintain the behavior change, and if generality is not programmed, the behavior change will neither persist nor generalize. Thus it is of utmost importance that this follow-up course be planned in advance. Whenever possible a terminal behavior should be selected that will have social import so that it will maintain and generalize through natural consequences.

Periodic contacts with the persons who effect the individual's behavior, such as his teacher and parents, are advisable. Such contacts can provide an opportunity for reinforcing the use of the appropriate procedures by these individuals, thereby further assuring the maintenance of the modified behavior. However, it is important not only for the environment to be structured to maintain the dependent behavior, but also for observational data on the student's behavior to be periodically collected so that it can be *known* for certain if the behavior is being maintained. When necessary, alterations in the maintenance procedure should be instituted in order to assure continued maintenance of the behavior following the termination of the behavioral program.

COMMUNICATING THE RESULTS OF THE PROGRAM

The behavioral specialist's responsibility does not end with evaluation and follow-up. He has an additional obligation to communicate what he has discovered about an individual or group of individuals. The principle of a student's behavior should be reported to the other school personnel who interact with him, so that they can help him more effectively. The same is true of principles that apply to groups of individuals. Those principles can then be effectively applied to other groups which possess the *same characteristics.* (Be sure to clearly specify your subject's characteristics in your report so that the findings can be generalized to other individuals with similar characteristics.)

When novel procedures are found to be repeatedly effective, those procedures should be shared with the rest of the educational community through publications in journals and reports at meetings, workshops, and conventions. If each behavioral specialist shares discoveries, a body of increasingly effective procedures will accumulate, and the field of education and all of society will benefit.

SUMMARY

The emphasis of this chapter has been upon evaluation. The requirement that behavior modification hold itself accountable for the procedures it applies was discussed. To accomplish this, it was suggested that the behavioral specialist use scientific methodology: that he use standard and reliable measures and experimental controls. Several measurement techniques which have been found to be useful in the educational setting, such as event and time sampling, as well as methods for preserving transitory events. A number of techniques for evaluating the effects of behavioral procedures were offered. A consideration of several categories of confounding variables emphasized the need for using experimental controls in evaluation. Single-subject designs, particularly the reversal and multiple baseline designs, were described and illustrated. Some attention was also given to the need for follow-up, maintenance, and generalization procedures, since modified behavior will persist and generalize only if the environment is supportive of the altered behavior. Lastly, the responsibility of the behavioral specialist to communicate his discoveries to the educational community was discussed. Students, educators, and society as a whole stands to profit from an accumulation of principles of school-related behavior.

REFERENCES

Arrington, R. E. Time-sampling in studies of social behavior: A critical review of techniques and results with research suggestions. *Psychological Bulletin*, 1943, **40,** 81–124.

Ayllon, T., & Azrin, N. H. *The token economy: A motivational system for therapy and rehabilitation.* New York: Appleton-Century-Crofts, 1968.

Bachrach, A. J. (Ed.) *Experimental foundations of clinical psychology*. New York: Basic Books, 1962.

Baer, D. M., Wolf, M. M., & Risley, T. R. Some current dimensions of applied behavior analysis. *Journal of Applied Behavior Analysis*, 1968, **1,** 91–97.

Bijou, S. W., & Baer, D. M. The laboratory-experimental study of child behavior. In P. H. Mussen (Ed.), *Handbook of research methods in child development*. New York: Wiley, 1960.

Brigham, T. A., & Sherman, J. A. An experimental analysis of verbal limitation in preschool children. *Journal of Applied Behavior Analysis*, 1968, **1,** 151–158.

Campbell, A., & Sulzer, B. Motivating educable mentally handicapped students toward reading and spelling achievement using naturally available reinforcers in the classroom setting. Paper presented at the meetings of the American Educational Research Association, New York, February 1971.

Cook, D. L. The Hawthorne effect in educational research. *Phi Delta Kappan*, 1962, **44,** 116–122.

Fjellstedt, N., & Sulzer, B. Reducing latency of responding to adult instructions by means of a token system. Unpublished paper, 1971.

Holland, J. G., & Skinner, B. F. *The analysis of behavior*. New York: McGraw-Hill, 1961.

Keller, F. S., & Schoenfeld, W. N. *Principles of psychology*. New York: Appleton-Century-Crofts, 1950.

Kiesler, D. J. Some myths of psychotherapy research and the search for a paradigm. *Psychological Bulletin*, 1966, **65,** 110–136.

McAllister, L. W., Stachowiak, J. G., Baer, D. M., & Conderman, L. The application of operant conditioning techinques in a secondary school classroom. *Journal of Applied Behavior Analysis*, 1969, **2,** 277–285.

Sanders, R. M., Hopkins, B. L., & Walker, M. B. An inexpensive method for making data records of complex behaviors. *Journal of Applied Behavior Analysis*, 1969, 221.

Sidman, M. *Tactics of scientific research*. New York: Basic Books, 1960.

Sulzer, B., Hunt, S., Ashby, E., Koniarski, C., & Krams, M. Increasing rate and percentage correct in reading and spelling in a fifth grade public school class of slow readers by means of a token system. Paper presented at the University of Kansas Symposium on Behavior Analysis in the Classroom, Lawrence, Kansas, May, 1971.

Sulzer, B., Hunt, S., & Loving, A. The contingent use of reinforcers usually available in the classroom. Unpublished manuscript, Southern Illinois University, 1970.

Underwood, B. J. *Psychological research,* New York: Appleton-Century-Crofts, 1957.

Wheeler, A. J., & Sulzer, B. Operant training and generalization of a syntactic response form in a speech deficient child. *Journal of Applied Behavior Analysis*, 1970, **3,** 139–147.

Whitley, D. A., & Sulzer, B. Assisting a fourth grade teacher to reduce a student's disruptive classroom behaviors through behavioral consulting. *The Personnel and Guidance Journal,* 1970, **48,** 836–841.

Wright, H. F. Observational child study. In P. H. Mussen (Ed.), *Handbook of research methods in child development*. New York: Wiley, 1960. P. 71–139.

GLOSSARY

Abscissa: The horizontal axis on a graph. In behavior modification the abscissa usually is labeled with a scale that depicts the passage of time in minutes, days, or trials.

Accountability: Providing an objective demonstration of the effectiveness of given programs.

Adaptation: The gradual reduction of responses that are emitted temporarily as the individual adjusts to the introduction of new stimuli into the environment.[1]

Adaptation period: The phase in a behavior modification program during which the subject adjusts to any novel stimuli that have been introduced into the environment.

Aggression: "The occurrence of responses that may inflict injury on other organisms."[2]

Applied research: Research that is directed toward an analysis of the variables that can be effective in improving the behavior under study.[3] Applied research is often conducted in a natural setting.

Aversive stimulus: A stimulus that has the effect of decreasing a behavior when it is presented as a consequence of (contingent upon) that behavior. A stimulus that the individual will actively work to avoid. A stimulus, the contingent removal of which results in an increase in the rate of the dependent behavior.

Back-up reinforcer: An object or event that has already demonstrated its reinforcing effect on an individual. It is received in exchange for a specific number of tokens, points, or other generalized reinforcers.

Backward chaining procedure: Effecting the development of a behavioral chain by training the last element or link in the chain first; the next to last, next; and so on until the entire chain is emitted as a single complex behavior.

Baseline: "A stable and, usually, recoverable performance upon which the effects of experimental variables can be assessed."[4] Used in this text interchangeably with "base rate" and "operant level." *See also* Operant level.

Base rate: *See* **Operant level; Baseline.**

Basic research: Research that is directed toward the discovery of the relationships between any variables. Basic research is usually conducted in a laboratory setting.

---

[1] Reese, E. P. The analysis of human operant behavior. In J. Vernon (Ed.) *Introduction to general psychology: A self-selection textbook.* Dubuque: Brown, 1966.

[2] Catania, A. C. *Contemporary research in operant behavior.* Glenview, Ill.: Scott, Foresman, 1969.

[3] Baer, D. M., Wolf, M. M., & Risley, T. R. Some current dimensions of applied behavioral analysis. *Journal of Applied Behavioral Analysis,* 1968, **1,** 91–97.

[4] Catania, 1968.

Behavior: Any observable and measurable external or internal act of an organism. A response. *See also* Response.

Behavior modification: Changing behavior through the systematic application of the methods and experimental findings of behavioral science.

Behavioral approach: An approach in which concepts, in order to be considered, are operationally defined into directly observable and measurable behaviors. Thus, a behavioral approach deals only with directly observable and measurable behaviors.

Behavioral chain: A sequence of behaviors that occurs semiautomatically in a determinate order.

Behavioral contract: The specification of the goals and procedures of a behavior modification program, reached through agreement between the behavior modifier and client or subject and modifiable by joint agreement.[5]

Behavioral contrast: A phenomenon that may occur if a behavior is placed on one reinforcement schedule under one stimulus condition and on another schedule under a different stimulus condition. In such a situation a decrease in the rate of the behavior under one stimulus-correlated condition may be accompanied by an increase in the rate under the other stimulus-correlated condition.

Behavioral dimensions: Measurable descriptive characteristics of a behavior such as frequency, intensity, duration, and topography.

Behavioral goal: The specification of the set of responses to be emitted by the subject at the completion of a given behavior modification program. Usually the criteria for achievement of the goals and conditions under which the responses are to be emitted are also specified. When limited to academic instruction, this is often referred to as the instructional objective. *See also* Target behavior; Terminal behavior.

Behavioral repertoire: See **Repertoire, behavioral.**

Behavioral specialist: A behavior modification consultant who is specially trained to advise and assist individuals to conduct programs in behavior change.

Chain: Two or more performances combined into a more complex behavioral sequence, occurring in a determinate order.

Complex behavior: A behavior consisting of two or more subsets of responses. (Almost all of the behaviors that behavior modifiers are concerned about are complex behaviors.)

Conditioned aversive stimulus: A stimulus, initially having no aversive properties, that acquires the properties of a negative reinforcer or punishing stimulus as a result of its being presented repeatedly just prior to or accompanying (1) the absence or withdrawal of reinforcement or (2) the delivery of primary or other conditioned aversive stimuli.

Conditioned reinforcer: A stimulus, initially having no reinforcing properties, that has been repeatedly paired with the delivery of primary or strong conditioned reinforcers so that it acquires the property of being able to strengthen or maintain a behavior.

---

[5] Sulzer, E. Reinforcement and the therapeutic contact. *Journal of Counseling Psychology,* 1962, **9,** 271–276.

Confounding variables: Variables that introduce ambiguity into an experimental study. Such variables make it impossible to precisely evaluate the effects of the independent variable. *See also* Environmental confounding variables; Subject confounding variables; Task confounding variables.

Contingencies: The relationships between a given response and its environmental consequences. Contingencies may have the effect of strengthening, maintaining, weakening, or eliminating a behavior.

Contingency control: The ability to manipulate the environmental consequences of a given behavior in order to achieve a specific behavioral goal.

Continuous reinforcement (CRF): A schedule of reinforcement in which each occurrence of a response is reinforced.

Continuous response: A response that does not have a clearly discriminable beginning or end. Pouting, smiling, orienting toward, and other behaviors are often treated as continuous responses because it is difficult to determine when the emission of the behavior begins and terminates.

Criterion: A specification of an acceptable level of performance that the subject is to achieve. Criteria are used to evaluate the success of a given behavior modification program.

Dependent behavior: The behavior being modified.

Dependent variable: Anything that varies as a reaction to a change in another variable (the independent variable). In behavior modification the dependent variable is usually the behavior that is modified or measured. *See also* Independent variable.

Deprivation: "The reduction in the availability of a reinforcer that increases the reinforcer's effectiveness."[6]

Differential reinforcement for stimulus control: The reinforcement of a response or responses under one stimulus condition but not under another stimulus condition. Or, when the response(s) is reinforced under one stimulus condition while *other* responses are reinforced under different stimulus conditions.

Differential reinforcement of high rates (DRH): A schedule that involves the selective contingent reinforcement of a grouping of responses which occur in rapid succession. High rates are differentially reinforced while low rates are not.

Differential reinforcement of low rates (DRL): A schedule in which responses that are spaced relatively far apart in time are selectively reinforced. Low rates are differentially reinforced while high rates are not.

Differential Reinforcement of Other Behaviors (DRO): A procedure in which a reinforcer follows any response an individual makes, except for one particular response. Thus, the individual receives scheduled reinforcement *except* when he engages in a particular specified behavior. This procedure results in a decrease of the specified behavior.

Direct observation: A method of obtaining behavioral data which records the behavior as it occurs. Event and time sampling are both methods of direct observation.

Discrete response: A response that has a clearly discriminable beginning and end. Lever presses, sneezes, written answers to addition problems, are examples of discrete responses.

---

[6] Catania, 1968.

Discriminate: Respond differently in the presence of different stimuli.

Discrimination: An event that has occurred when a discriminative stimulus (S^D or $S^\triangle$) controls the frequency of a behavior.

Discrimative stimuli: S^D—A stimulus in the presence of which a given response is reinforced. $S^\triangle$—A stimulus in the presence of which a given response is not reinforced. Discriminative stimuli are said to be established when, after several pairings with the occurrence or nonoccurrence of reinforcement, their presence or absence is accompanied by reliable changes in the rate of response.

DRH: See **Differential reinforcement of high rates.**

DRL: See **Differential reinforcement of low rates.**

DRO: See **Differential reinforcement of other behaviors.**

Emission: "The occurrence of a response without a specific eliciting stimulus."[7]

Empirical: Founded upon experimentation.

Environmental confounding variables: Environmental confounding variables do not include subject characteristics, apparatus, or other treatment variables. They are uncontrolled environmental variables that change concurrently with the independent variable. An example might be a change in seating during each phase of a reversal experimental design. Under such conditions, it is difficult to unambiguously evaluate the effects of the independent variable.

Errorless discrimination procedure: Teaching the acquisition of a discrimination by carefully arranging a sequence of discriminative stimuli so that only correct responses are occasioned.

Event sampling: An observational procedure in which the frequency or duration of a specific discrete behavior, such as times tardy or number of pages completed, is recorded over a specific extended period of time. The specific time interval may be, for instance, a classroom period or day.

Experimental analysis of behavior: A scientific analysis designed to demonstrate functional relationships between behavioral procedures (*independent variables*) and dependent behaviors (*dependent variables*).

Experimental design: An aspect of an experiment that is directed toward the elimination of confounding variables (experimental control). Single-subject (individual organism) experiments are designed to demonstrate the existence of a functional relationship between the dependent variable (*the dependent behavior*) and the independent variable (*the procedure*).

Extinction: A procedure in which the reinforcement for a previously reinforced behavior is discontinued.

Extinction induced aggression: The aggressive responses that accompany the early phases of an extinction program.

Fading: The gradual removal of discriminative stimuli, such as cues and prompts.

FI: Fixed interval: *See also* Interval schedules of reinforcement.

Fixed interval (FI) schedule: *See* **Interval schedules of reinforcement.**

Fixed ratio (FR) schedule: *See* **Ratio schedules of reinforcement.**

FR: Fixed ratio: *See also* Ratio schedules of reinforcement.

Functional relationship: A lawful relationship between two variables. In behavior

---

[7] Catania, 1968.

modification, a dependent behavior and a given procedure are *functionally related* if the behavior systematically varies as a function of the application of the procedure.

Generalization, stimulus: "The spread of the effects of reinforcement (or of other operations . . .) in the presence of one stimulus to other stimuli that differ from the original stimulus along one or more dimensions."[8]

Generalization, response: (*Induction.*) The spread of effects of reinforcement to responses outside of a specific response being trained.[9] For instance, reinforcement of a particular writing response may be accompanied by other writing responses that are similar but not identical to the reinforced response.

Generalization training: A procedure designed to facilitate the occurrence of generalization.

Generalized reinforcer: A conditioned reinforcer that is effective over a wide range of deprivation conditions as a result of having been paired with a variety of previously established reinforcers.

Imitation: Matching the behavior of a model.

Imitative prompt: A behavior by a model designed to occasion a matching response by the imitator.

Incompatible behavior: A behavior that cannot be emitted simultaneously with another behavior. A behavior that interferes with the emission of another behavior. *See also* Reinforcing incompatible behavior.

Independent variable: The variable that is manipulated. In behavior modification the independent variable is often a behavioral procedure. *See also* Dependent variable.

Indirect observation: A method of obtaining behavioral data that relies on "memory" or on reports of what occurred, such as interviews and questionnaires. The behavior is not recorded as it occurs.

Intensity of response: The physical force of a response.

Intermittent reinforcement: A schedule of reinforcement in which some, but not all, of the occurrences of a response are reinforced.

Interval schedules of reinforcement: A schedule in which reinforcement is made contingent upon the passage of *time* before the response is reinforced. (a) *Fixed interval (FI) schedule*—When a particular response is scheduled for reinforcement following the passage of a specific amount of time, and that time is held constant. For example, an FI 3 indicates that reinforcement follows the first occurrence of the *primed response* after three minutes have passed. (b) *Variable interval (VI) schedule*—When a variable time interval must occur prior to the reinforced response. The time interval usually varies within a specified average. For example, a VI 6 indicates that an average of six minutes passes before the *primed response* receives contingent reinforcement. *See also* Primed response.

Learning history: The sum of an individual's behaviors that have been conditioned or modified as a result of environmental events.

Limited hold: A restriction placed on a schedule which requires that the response

---

[8] Catania, 1968.
[9] Catania, 1968.

eligible to receive reinforcement must be emitted within a particular time limitation or reinforcement will not be made available.

Link: The response, or performance, that is combined with others in the development of a behavioral chain.

Masochism: The apparent "enjoyment" of punishment. In this case, the apparent punishing stimulus is not actually playing a punishing role but a reinforcing role.

Multiple baseline design: A single-subject experimental design that involves: (1) Obtaining base rates of several dependent behaviors; (2) applying the independent variable to *one* of the dependent behaviors until it is substantially changed while the other dependent behaviors changed little if any; (3) applying the independent variable to a second dependent variable as in 2 above.

This procedure is continued until it is demonstrated that each behavior systematically changes when the independent variable is applied to it.

Negative reinforcement: The removal of a negative reinforcer or aversive stimulus as a consequence of the response.

Negative reinforcer: A stimulus that, when removed or reduced as a consequence of a response, results in an increase or maintenance of that response. (*See* Aversive stimulus, which is used in this text in place of the term "negative reinforcer.")

Occasion: To increase the likelihood of the emission of a response by arranging prior stimulus conditions.

Operant behavior: Behavior that is controlled by its consequences.

Operant level: "The unconditioned level of an operant [response], or the rate at which responses occur before they have been reinforced."[10] Used in this text interchangeably with *baseline* and *base rate. See also* Baseline.

Operation definition: The product of breaking down a broad concept, such as "aggressive," into its observable and measurable component behaviors (hitting other students, biting the teacher, and so on).

Ordinate: The vertical axis on a graph. In behavior modification, the ordinate is usually labeled with a scale that measures the dependent behavior, for example *frequency* of responses.

Positive reinforcement: The delivery of a positive reinforcer contingent upon a response.

Positive reinforcer: A stimulus that, when presented as a consequence of a response, results in an increase or maintenance of that response.

Pragmatic: Practical, functional.

Premack principle: A principle that states that contingent access to high frequency behaviors serve as reinforcers for the performance of low frequency behaviors.

Primary aversive stimulus: A stimulus, such as a strong electric shock or a severe spanking, that is aversive in the absence of any prior learning history.

Primary reinforcer: Reinforcing stimuli that have the effect of maintaining or perpetuating life, such as food, water, sex, and warmth.

---

[10] Catania, 1968.

Primed response: A term associated with interval schedules of reinforcement to designate the first response that is eligible for reinforcement following the termination of the required interval. *See also* Interval schedules of reinforcement.

Probe: A phase in a behavior modification experiment designed to test the effect of a given procedure. A *reversal* is a probe since it removes the behavioral procedure for a brief period of time to test the procedures' effects. *See also* Reversal procedure.

Programmed instruction: The selection and arrangement of educational content based upon principles of human learning.[11]

Prompt: An auxiliary discriminative stimulus that is applied to help occasion a given response. Prompts are usually faded before the terminal goal is judged as having been achieved.

Punishing stimulus: A contingent stimulus that, when presented, results in a reduction in the occurrence of the dependent behavior. In this text the term *aversive stimulus* is used interchangeably with *punishing stimulus*. *See also* Aversive stimulus; Negative reinforcer.

Punishment: A procedure in which the contingent presentation of a stimulus reduces the rate of the occurrence of the dependent behavior.

Ratio schedules of reinforcement: A schedule in which reinforcement is made contingent upon the emission of a *number* of responses before one response is reinforced. (a) *Fixed ratio (FR) schedule*—When a specific number of responses must occur prior to the reinforced response. For example, an FR 3 schedule indicates that each third response is contingently reinforced. (b) *Variable ratio (VR) schedule*—When a variable number of responses must occur prior to the reinforced response. The number of responses usually varies about a specified average. For example, a VR 6 means that six performances *on the average* are required prior to each reinforcement.

Reinforcement: A procedure that has occurred when the contingent use of a stimulus results in an increase or maintenance of a dependent behavior.

Reinforcement density: Frequency or rate with which responses are reinforced. The lower the ratio or shorter the interval required by a given reinforcement schedule, the *denser,* the reinforcement.

Reinforcement history: See **Learning history.**

Reinforcement of incompatible behavior: *See* **Reinforcing incompatible behavior.**

Reinforcement reserve: The unconsumed quantity of reinforcers held by an individual. Frequently refers to a number of *tokens* or other generalized reinforcers. *See also* Token reinforcer.

Reinforcement schedule: *See* Schedule of reinforcement.

Reinforcer: A stimulus, the contingent use of which results in the increase or maintenance of the dependent behavior, abbreviated S^+ in this text. (It is often abbreviated S^R, primary reinforcer, and S^r, secondary or conditioned reinforcer.)

Reinforcer sampling: A procedure that enables the subject to come in contact

---

[11] Taber, J. K., Glaser, R., & Schaefer, H. *Learning and programmed instruction.* Reading, Mass.: Addison-Wesley, 1965.

with a reinforcer in order that he may experience the positive characteristics of the stimulus. The procedure is useful in developing new reinforcing consequences for a given individual.

Reinforcing incompatible behavior: A behavioral procedure that increases the occurrence of a behavior or behaviors that cannot coexist with another, usually "undesired," behavior.

Reliability: A term used to refer to consistency of measurement. It is usually calculated in single-subject studies by comparing how well two or more independent observers agree among themselves. It is often calculated and reported in percentages by dividing the number of agreements by the number of agreements plus disagreements, and then multiplying the fraction by one hundred. Reliability measures should be reported for each phase of a single-subject design when feasible.

Repertoire, behavioral: "The behavior that a particular organism, at a particular time, is capable of emitting, in the sense that the behavior exists at a nonzero operant level, has been shaped, or, if it has been extinguished, may be rapidly reconditioned."[12]

Replicate: To repeat an experimental procedure or finding.

Respondent behavior: Behavior that is elicited or controlled by its antecedents. Reflex behavior.

Response: An observable and measurable behavior. Used interchangeably with *behavior. See also* Behavior.

Response cost: A procedure in which there is contingent withdrawal of specified amounts of available reinforcers.

Response differentiation: A procedure that involves reinforcing a behavioral *subset* that conforms to clearly specified behavioral dimensions.

Reversal procedure: A probe technique that involves the removal of the procedure in order to test the effectiveness of the procedure. For instance one frequently utilized single-subject experimental design involves: (1) obtaining a base rate of the dependent variable; (2) applying the independent variable until a substantial change in the dependent variable is recorded; (3) the reversal, a discontinuation of the independent variable and a reintroduction of the conditions in effect during the baseline period, until a substantial reversal in the value of the dependent variable is obtained; and, (4) a reapplication of the independent variable to reinstate the change. Such a procedure is used to demonstrate a *functional relationship* between the *independent* and *dependent* variables. (Often abbreviated, ABAB design.)

Satiation: The reduction in performance or reinforcer effectiveness that occurs after a large amount of reinforcement has been delivered.

Scallop: A pattern on a cumulative response record that is generated by a sequence of positively accelerating curves:

Schedule of reinforcement: "The rule followed by the environment . . . in deter-

---

[12] Catania, 1968.

mining which among the many occurrences of a response will be reinforced."[13]

School personnel: Any individual employed in an educational setting. Teachers, principals, special teachers, school nurses, school social workers, teacher aides, and others are all school personnel.

S^D: See **Discriminative stimulus.**

S-Delta ($S^\triangle$): See **Discriminative stimulus.**

Shaping: A procedure through which new behaviors are developed: the systematic reinforcement of *successive approximations* toward the behavioral goal.

Single-subject experimental designs: Research designs developed for unambiguously evaluating the effects of the independent variable on the behavior of a single organism. *See also* Experimental design; Reversal procedure; Multiple baseline design.

Social reinforcer: A conditioned reinforcing stimulus mediated by another individual within a social context.

Spontaneous recovery: The reappearance of a response that has been eliminated by means of an extinction procedure following a time interval without any intervening reinforced responses.

Step size: The number of new responses in the *subset* required for a particular *successive approximation* in a shaping procedure.

Stimulus: A physical object or event that *may* have an effect upon the behavior of an organism. Stimuli frequently manipulated in behavior modification programs include *reinforcing stimuli, aversive stimuli,* and *discriminative stimuli.*

Stimulus change: A behavioral procedure that employs discriminative stimuli, or stimuli that occasion (S^D's) or inhibit ($S^\triangle$'s) specific behaviors.

Stimulus control: Stimulus control is demonstrated when the stimuli that were present during the modification of an emitted response begin to control the emission of that response. Thus, under stimulus control conditions, the response form or frequency is different under one stimulus, or set of stimuli, than another. These stimuli are referred to as *discriminative stimuli. See also* Discriminative stimulus.

Subject confounding variables: Subject characteristics (demographic, previous learning history, and present behaviors) that have not been controlled in an experiment but may effect changes in the occurrence of the dependent variable. Single-subject designs control for subject confounding variables by comparing the subject's performance under one condition with his performance under other conditions.

Subset of behavior: The group of simpler response components that compose a more complex behavior.

Successive approximations: Behavioral elements or subsets each of which more and more closely resemble the specified terminal behavior.

Supplementary reinforcers: Reinforcers used in addition to the major contingent reinforcer.

---

[13] Reynolds, *A primer of operant conditioning.* Glenview, Ill.: Scott, Foresman, 1968.

Target behavior: A behavioral goal. *See also* Behavioral goal; Terminal behavior.

Task confounding variables: Stimuli associated with the behavioral procedure or treatment which, because they have not been controlled, may effect changes in the dependent variable. For instance tokens delivered by a teacher *confounding* teacher attention with the token delivery.

Terminal behavior: The behavior that is achieved at the end of a behavior modification program. The terminal behavior is described according to all its relevant behavioral dimensions and is usually assigned a criterion by which an acceptable level of performance is to be judged. See also Behavioral goal; Target behavior.

Timeout: A procedure in which access to the sources of various forms of reinforcement are removed for a particular period contingent upon the emission of a response. The opportunity to receive reinforcement is contingently removed for a specified time. Either the behaving individual is contingently removed from the reinforcing environment or the reinforcing environment is contingently removed from him for some stipulated duration.

Timeout room, timeout booth: A facility that is arranged in such a manner that the individual placed therein has little likelihood of receiving reinforcement from the environment.

Time sampling: A direct observational procedure in which the observer records the presence or absence of the behaviors to be changed, within short uniform time intervals. For example, an observer may observe for 10 seconds and record during the following 5 seconds the occurrence or nonoccurrence of the dependent behavior. This procedure may continue for a specified 30 minutes each day.

Token reinforcer: An object that can be exchanged at a later time for another reinforcing item or activity. The extent to which tokens are reinforcing or take on the properties of a generalized reinforcer is dependent on the individual's experience and on what back-up items are available.

Topography of response: The shape, configuration, or form of a response.

Variable interval (VI) schedule: *See* **Interval schedules of reinforcement.**

Variable ratio (VR) schedule: *See* **Ratio schedules of reinforcement.**

VI: Variable interval. *See also* Interval schedules of reinforcement.

VR: Variable ratio. *See also* Ratio schedules of reinforcement.